Where to

*S*O

*S*PECIAL

England 1995

English
Tourist Board

Where to Stay in England 1995 *'Somewhere Special'*
1/94

Published by: **Jarrold Publishing,** Whitefriars, Norwich NR3 1TR, *in association with* **English Tourist Board,** Thames Tower, Black's Road, Hammersmith, London W6 9EL *and* **Celsius**.

Manager Editor, ETB: Jane Collinson
Design, Compilation and Production: Celsius, Winchester
Editorial Contributor: Tessa Chavallier
Colour Photography (excluding line entries and where stated otherwise):
Nigel Corrie (front cover); Celsius, and Britain on View
Cartography: Colin Earl Cartography, Alton
Typesetting: Celsius
Colour Origination: Spectrum LithoScan
Printing: Cambus Litho Ltd
Binding: Crawford Bros (N/c) Ltd

Display Advertisement Sales: Madison Bell Ltd, 3 St. Peter's Street, Islington Green, London N1 8JD. Telephone: (0171) 359 7737.

ISBN 0 7117 0689 1

Important:
The information contained in this guide has been published in good faith on the basis of information submitted to the English Tourist Board by the proprietors of the premises listed, who have paid for their entries to appear. Jarrold Publishing, the English Tourist Board and Celsius cannot guarantee the accuracy of the information in this guide and accept no responsibility for any error or misrepresentation. All liability for loss, disappointment, negligence or other damage caused by reliance in this guide, or in the event of bankruptcy, or liquidation, or cessation of trade of any company, individual or firm mentioned, is hereby excluded. Please check carefully all prices and other details before confirming a reservation.

The English Tourist Board
The Board is a statutory body created by the Development of Tourism Act 1969 to develop and market England's tourism. Its main objectives are to provide a welcome for people visiting England to take their holidays there; to encourage the provision of tourist amenities and facilities in England. The Board has a statutory duty to advise the Government on tourism matters relating to England and, with Government approval and support, administers the national classification and grading schemes for tourist accommodation in England.

Cover photograph: Laurel Cottage Guest House (entry 326)
Title page photograph: Gilbert's (entry 195)

TO BEGIN

All you need to know about the guide and how to use it

An introduction to each of England's regions, with a full-colour map cross-referenced to each perfect place to stay

Contents

*W*elcome to the guide

'SOMEWHERE SPECIAL' IS A NEW GUIDE FOR THE DISCERNING TRAVELLER, FEATURING SOME FOUR HUNDRED HOTELS, GUESTHOUSES, B&BS AND INNS ALL OFFERING THEIR GUESTS THAT LITTLE BIT EXTRA. THE FORMAT IS EASY TO USE, WITH ATTRACTIVE, DETAILED ENTRIES CROSS REFERENCED TO FULL-COLOUR MAPS, PLUS ARTICLES AND FEATURES AS WELL AS HELPFUL HINTS. WHATEVER YOUR BUDGET, AND WHETHER YOU WANT A SHORT GET-AWAY OR A LONGER BREAK, 'SOMEWHERE SPECIAL' OFFERS A CHOICE OF ACCOMMODATION THAT PROMISES A WARM WELCOME AND A STAY THAT'S SPECIAL.

YOUR SURE SIGN OF WHERE TO STAY

As in other English Tourist Board *Where to Stay* accommodation guides, all accommodation included in this invaluable new title has been classified under the Board's national Crown rating scheme (see page 6). In *Somewhere Special*, however, you are promised something extra, for every single entry has a top quality grading of HIGHLY COMMENDED or DE LUXE (see page 8). This means that whatever range of facilities are on offer, they are presented with exceptional care, individuality and quality of service.

QUALITY FIRST

Whether you're looking for no-holds-barred luxury on a grand scale, a short break in a small hotel with character or an intimate bed and breakfast that gives personal attention to perhaps only three or four guests, you're looking in the right guide. The criterion for inclusion in *Somewhere Special* is excellence rather than the range of facilities available – though of course you'll be able to see at a glance exactly what's on offer.

HOW TO CHOOSE

To help you choose somewhere to stay, each entry is illustrated by both a colour photograph and a detailed description. Also displayed are its Crown rating with quality grading and estimated 1995 prices. Facilities are indicated by clear, at-a-glance symbols – see the back flap for a key. You'll also find those important details such as meal times, number of bedrooms, parking spaces and which credit/debit cards are accepted, together with address, telephone and fax numbers.

REGIONAL DIVISIONS

To make finding somewhere special even easier, the guide is divided into four regions, each with its own map: England's North Country, England's Heartland, England's West Country and South and South East England. At the start of each section is a regional introduction followed by a detailed map, cross-referenced to the geographical list of accommodation. Features on topics as varied as cheese-rolling in Gloucestershire and Berwick-upon-Tweed's 'Sixty Years War' with Russia are interspersed throughout the entries to make perusal even more absorbing.

HIGHLY COMMENDED AND DE LUXE

Those establishments awarded a HIGHLY COMMENDED or DE LUXE grading represent only a small percentage of all Tourist Board quality-graded accommodation, so whether you're looking for somewhere large or small, you can expect to find accommodation of the very highest standard, accompanied by those personal touches which can transform a guesthouse, B&B, inn or hotel into *somewhere really special*.

*C*rown ratings and quality gradings

THE ENGLISH TOURIST BOARD'S ACCOMMODATION RATING SCHEME HAS BECOME RECOGNISED AS THE MOST AUTHORITATIVE INDICATOR OF THE LEVEL OF SERVICE YOU CAN EXPECT TO FIND AT YOUR SELECTED GUESTHOUSE, B&B, INN OR HOTEL. OUR TEAM OF INSPECTORS HAS VISITED OVER 11,000 ESTABLISHMENTS THROUGHQUT ENGLAND TO CARRY OUT OBJECTIVE ASSESSMENTS OF THE FACILITIES AND STANDARDS ON OFFER.

THE CROWN SYSTEM EXPLAINED

A system of Crown ratings may be applied to any type of establishment offering 'serviced' accommodation – hotels, guesthouses, inns, B&Bs and farmhouses – and guarantees that it meets the exacting standards expected by the Tourist Board. The number of Crowns is an indication of the range of facilities and services on offer – quite simply, the more crowns, the greater the choice of facilities available. There are six classifications starting at **LISTED**, and then increasing in line with the facilities from **ONE** to **FIVE CROWN**. The Tourist Board lays down strict rules about how these Crown ratings are applied, stipulating, for example, that every classified establishment meets standards for the size of bed, type of bed linen and even the extent of illumination in each room. Acceptance for higher levels of classification include the provision of tourist information, the number – and location – of colour televisions, the use of 13-amp power outlets, the availability of room service and much, much more.

Every establishment classified by the Board must, of course, meet and maintain high standards of courtesy and cleanliness, of catering, and of service appropriate to the type of establishment. But you can expect these high standards to be exceeded by all the entries in *Somewhere Special*.

CROWN RATINGS — A QUICK GUIDE

Listed   You can be sure that the accommodation will be clean and comfortable, but the range of facilities and services may be limited.

You will find additional facilities, including washbasin and chair in your bedroom and you will have use of a telephone.

There will be a colour TV in your bedroom (or in a lounge) and you can enjoy morning tea/coffee in your bedroom. At least some of the bedrooms will have a private bath (or shower) and WC.

At least half of the bedrooms will have private bath (or shower) en-suite. You will also be able to order a hot evening meal.

Your bedroom will have a colour TV, radio and telephone, there will be lounge service until midnight and evening meals can be ordered up to 2030 hours. At least 90% of the bedrooms will have private bath and/or shower and WC en-suite.

Every bedroom will have a private bath, fixed shower and WC en-suite. The restaurant will be open for breakfast, lunch and dinner (or you can take meals in your room from breakfast until midnight) and you will benefit from an all-night lounge service. A night porter will also be on duty.

QUALITY GRADINGS

If a particular place to stay is of a sufficient standard to qualify for a Crown rating (see page 6), the proprietor may also apply for a quality grading. In order to determine which of the four quality grades (APPROVED, COMMENDED, HIGHLY COMMENDED and DE LUXE) should be awarded, a highly-trained Tourist Board inspector assesses every aspect of the establishment. Those establishments awarded a **HIGHLY COMMENDED** or **DE LUXE** grading represent only a small percentage of all Tourist Board quality-graded accommodation.

The rigorous and objective annual English Tourist Board inspection takes into account such factors as warmth of welcome, atmosphere, efficiency, as well as the quality of furnishings and equipment, and the standard of meals and their presentation. Consideration is also given to the style and nature of the accommodation. This means that all types of establishment, whatever their Crown rating, can achieve a high quality grade if the facilities and services they provide, even if limited in scope, are to a very high standard. You will therefore find that *Somewhere Special* features accommodation, from LISTED to FIVE CROWN, that have all been awarded a top quality grading of HIGHLY COMMENDED or DE LUXE. Since only a small percentage are awarded these top two gradings, you know that if your chosen accommodation is in this guide, it is clearly somewhere very special indeed.

AN INSPECTOR CALLS

Before a quality grading is ever awarded, the proprietor arranges for one of 45 Tourist Board inspectors to visit the guesthouse, B&B, farmhouse, inn or hotel for an assessment. The inspector books in advance, but does not reveal his or her identity on arrival. Sadly for those idly contemplating a career move, the inspector does not have a lazy time; he or she is busy noting the standard of decor, the state of the grounds, the quality of the food and the courtesy of the staff. Once the bill has been paid the following morning, the inspector announces his or her identity to the management and tours the building. At the end of the tour, they discuss the conclusions, with the inspector making suggestions where helpful. Only after the visit does the inspector arrive at his conclusion for the quality grade – so the assessment is 100 per cent independent and reliable.

ACCESSIBILITY

It's all very well deciding exactly where you'd like to stay, but if you find difficulty in walking or are a wheelchair user, then you also need to know how accessible a particular establishment is. If you book your accommodation at an establishment displaying the Accessible symbol, there's no longer any guesswork involved. The National Accessibility Scheme forms part of the *Tourism for All* campaign that is being promoted by all three National Tourist Boards. The Tourist Boards recognise three categories of accessibility, based upon what are considered to be the practical needs of wheelchair users:

CATEGORY 1: accessible to all wheelchair users including those travelling independently

CATEGORY 2: accessible to a wheelchair user with assistance

CATEGORY 3: accessible to a wheelchair user able to walk short distances and up at least three steps

Additional help and guidance for those with special needs can be obtained from: Holiday Care Service, 2 Old Bank Chambers, Station Road, Horley, Surrey RH6 9HW. Telephone (01293) 774535, Fax (01293) 784647, Minicom (01293) 776943.

$\mathscr{H}$ow to use this guide

'SOMEWHERE SPECIAL' WILL ENABLE YOU TO FIND THAT SPECIAL PLACE TO STAY IN WHICHEVER REGION YOU ARE PLANNING TO VISIT. EVEN IF YOU ONLY HAVE A ROUGH IDEA OF WHERE YOU WISH TO GO, YOU CAN EASILY USE THIS GUIDE TO LOCATE A REALLY HIGH QUALITY PLACE TO STAY.

T HE GUIDE IS DIVIDED into four regions: England's North Country, England's Heartland, England's West Country and South and South East England. On page 12 you will find a comprehensive break-down of which county is in which region with an accompanying 'England-at-a-Glance' map. At the start of each section is a full-colour regional map which clearly plots by number the location of all the *Somewhere Special* entries, together with the positions of major roads, towns, stations and airports. If you know the area you want to visit, first locate the possible establishments on the regional map and then turn to the appropriate pages in the regional section. The entries are listed by their geographical position, so you'll find that the places you're interested in are usually close to each other in the listing.

Each entry provides detailed information on the nature of the establishment together with the facilities provided and a colour photograph so that you can easily determine whether the place meets the criteria you have in mind. It also lists 1995 estimated prices, so you immediately know whether the entry falls within your price range.

THE ENTRIES IN MORE DETAIL

The entries are designed to convey as much information as possible in a clear, attractive and easy-to-read format. The first line contains the name of the inn, hotel, guesthouse or B&B, together with its Crown rating and quality grading. In *Somewhere Special,* of course, every entry will be either HIGHLY COMMENDED or DE LUXE. Below these come the full address and telephone number of the establishment and, where applicable, its fax number. Entries show the new STD dialling codes which work in parallel with the old ones up until April 1995, when the new codes come into full effect.

Each entry features a full-colour photograph of the establishment and a short description of its main attractions. These details have been supplied by the proprietors themselves – although we do check for accuracy, we advise you to confirm the information at the time of booking. At the foot of each entry comes the all-important practical information:

- The 1995 prices for bed & breakfast and for half board, for both single and double rooms. Prices are correct at the time of going to press, but please check when making a booking.

- Mealtimes for both lunch and evening meal, when available.

- The numbers of bedrooms and bathrooms, and whether the latter are en-suite, private or shared.

- The number of parking spaces.

- The range of any credit and charge cards accepted.

In the bottom right-hand corner of the entry is a list of symbols representing in more detail the range of facilities and services offered. The key explaining what these mean is conveniently placed on the back of the cover flap, which can be kept open while you're browsing through the entries. The symbols cover everything from the provision of private shooting rights to whether or not there's a sauna for guests' use. Most importantly they allow you to see at a glance whether any special requirements you may have can be met.

OTHER FEATURES OF THE GUIDE

As well as the entries – some 400 in all – you'll find many features on a wide variety of subjects scattered throughout the book. The four informative introductions to the regions appear on pages 13, 71, 117 and 159. At the back of the book (pages 193–197) is more detailed information about booking accommodation. You are recommended to read this before committing yourself to any firm arrangements, bearing in mind that all details have been supplied by proprietors themselves.

IN THIS GUIDE, ENGLAND IS
DIVIDED INTO FOUR MAIN
REGIONS. A MAP OF THE
REGION, SHOWING EACH ENTRY
AND ITS NEAREST TOWN OR
CITY AND MAJOR ROAD OR
MOTORWAY, CAN BE FOUND
AFTER THE REGIONAL
INTRODUCTION.

England at a glance

ENGLAND'S NORTH COUNTRY

Cumbria, Cleveland, County Durham,
Northumberland, Tyne & Wear,
Cheshire, Greater Manchester,
Lancashire, Merseyside, Yorkshire
and Humberside.

ENGLAND'S HEARTLAND

Gloucestershire, Hereford & Worcester,
Shropshire, Staffordshire, Warwickshire,
West Midlands, Derbyshire,
Leicestershire, Lincolnshire,
Northamptonshire, Nottinghamshire,
Bedfordshire, Cambridgeshire, Essex,
Hertfordshire, Norfolk and Suffolk.

ENGLAND'S WEST COUNTRY

Avon, Cornwall, Devon, Somerset,
Western Dorset, Wiltshire and the
Isles of Scilly.

SOUTH AND SOUTH EAST ENGLAND

London, Berkshire, Buckinghamshire,
Eastern Dorset, Hampshire, Isle of
Wight, Oxfordshire, East & West
Sussex, Kent and Surrey.

*England's
North Country*

*England's
Heartland*

*England's
West Country*

*South
and
South East
England*

E N G L A N D

*E*ngland's
North Country

Crummock Water

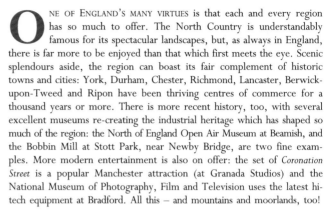

 NE OF ENGLAND'S MANY VIRTUES is that each and every region has so much to offer. The North Country is understandably famous for its spectacular landscapes, but, as always in England, there is far more to be enjoyed than that which first meets the eye. Scenic splendours aside, the region can boast its fair complement of historic towns and cities: York, Durham, Chester, Richmond, Lancaster, Berwick-upon-Tweed and Ripon have been thriving centres of commerce for a thousand years or more. There is more recent history, too, with several excellent museums re-creating the industrial heritage which has shaped so much of the region: the North of England Open Air Museum at Beamish, and the Bobbin Mill at Stott Park, near Newby Bridge, are two fine examples. More modern entertainment is also on offer: the set of *Coronation Street* is a popular Manchester attraction (at Granada Studios) and the National Museum of Photography, Film and Television uses the latest hi-tech equipment at Bradford. All this – and mountains and moorlands, too!

For centuries Yorkshire was subdivided into ridings (or thirds) and was by far England's largest county. That honour is now enjoyed by the biggest of its three offspring, North Yorkshire. Not surprisingly, then, this county contains a remarkable sweep of landscapes, from the fossil-rich cliffs of the North York Moors coast to the flat fertile plain of the Vale of York, and the limestone massifs of the Three Peaks in the Dales to the long-established resorts of Filey, Whitby and Scarborough. Two national parks – the Yorkshire Dales and the North York Moors – give testimony to the scenic splendours of this remarkable area. The former boasts a huge range of geological features (sink holes, clints, grikes, dry riverbeds and waterfalls, for example), while the latter offers a spectacular coastline, made perfect by beautiful villages such as Staithes, Runswick Bay and Robin Hood's Bay. The administrative heart of the county is York: magnificent medieval buildings and stout city walls, together with a handsome collection of museums and excellent shopping, make this city ideal for short breaks.

In its north-western corner the Yorkshire Dales National Park spills over into Cumbria, England's second-largest county – synonymous for many with its own national park, the Lake District. The Lakes' attractions need little elucidation – on a scale unmatched within England is an

Hadrian's Wall

unbeatable combination of soaring peaks, shimmering lakes and stone-built farmhouses. Add small towns as picturesque as Kendal, prehistoric remains of the importance of Castlerigg Stone Circle and associations with literary figures such as Wordsworth and Beatrix Potter, and it soon becomes clear that there is more here than spectacular walking terrain. A coastline of great beauty (highlights include rocky St Bees Head and grassy Silloth) and bleak north Pennine moorland of stark magnificence give proof that there's more than the obvious to discover.

Northumberland, Cumbria's neighbour to the north-east, again has much to offer. The coastline here is wonderful. England's only east-coast islands, Lindisfarne and the Farne

Lake Windermere

Islands look west at sandy beaches stretching for miles, often dominated by imposing castles, as at Bamburgh and Dunstanburgh. Heading inland the terrain climbs steadily towards the Cheviots, forming not only a natural but also the actual border with Scotland. The northern Pennines, much of which fall within the Northumberland National Park, are as wild and remote a corner of the nation as can be found. Small wonder that Hadrian chose to build his defensive wall south of such an imposing wilderness.

Blackpool

Heading south takes the traveller to a largely urban area encompassing both the great and proud city of Newcastle and the Sunderland conurbation. County Durham has many stretches of moorland, their grandeur set off by attractive villages (tiny and unspoilt Blanchland is a fine example) and the historic city of Durham. Further south the bustling port of Hull is the main focus of Humberside, although don't miss the fine medieval and Georgian town of Beverley.

Newcastle upon Tyne

South and West Yorkshire represent the meeting of industry and the Pennines, and thoroughly reward investigation. The mill towns of the Calder, Colne and Aire valleys are often visited for their remarkable 19th-century architecture. Holmfirth in West Yorkshire, the setting for television's *The Last of the Summer Wine*, typifies the fine gritstone architecture of the area. The uplands persist, with Haworth and its Brontë associations, an obvious and attractive draw for visitors and walkers.

Mill towns cling to valleys on both sides of the Pennines. Lancashire, on the western side, used to lay claim to towns built on the once-mighty cotton industry – names such as Accrington, Bolton and Rochdale, all now part of Greater Manchester. Discover too the little-known Forest of Bowland, south and east of Lancaster. The steep fells, cleft by valleys that are wooded and lush, make this area an intriguing corner of upland England. More than any other northern county, however, Lancashire lives through its coastline, for here are Blackpool and Fleetwood, Morecambe and Lytham St Anne's.

North of England Open Air Museum, Beamish

Merseyside is a low-lying coastal county with the conurbation of Liverpool and Birkenhead taking up much of its area. The rejuvenated dockland, imposing Victorian architecture and some fine statuary make Liverpool a thoroughly rewarding city to visit. Chester, with its near-intact city walls, elegant medieval two-tiered shopping malls (the Rows) and Britain's largest Roman amphitheatre is a high point of Cheshire's western side, while its eastern edge slopes up from the Cheshire Plain to the Peak District, where there are some fine walks to be had.

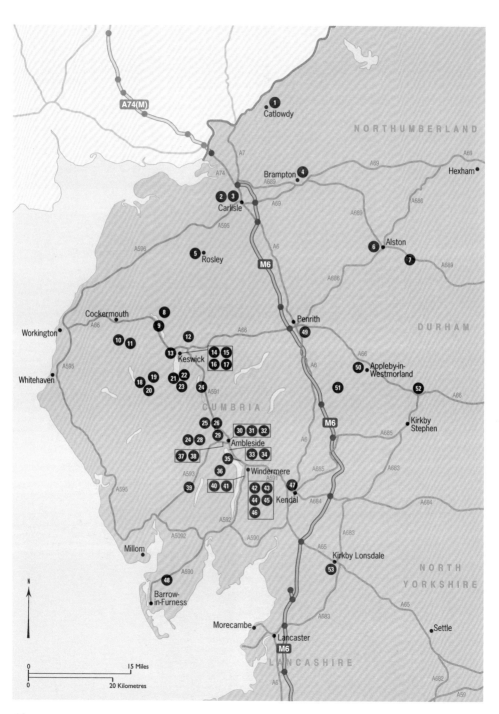

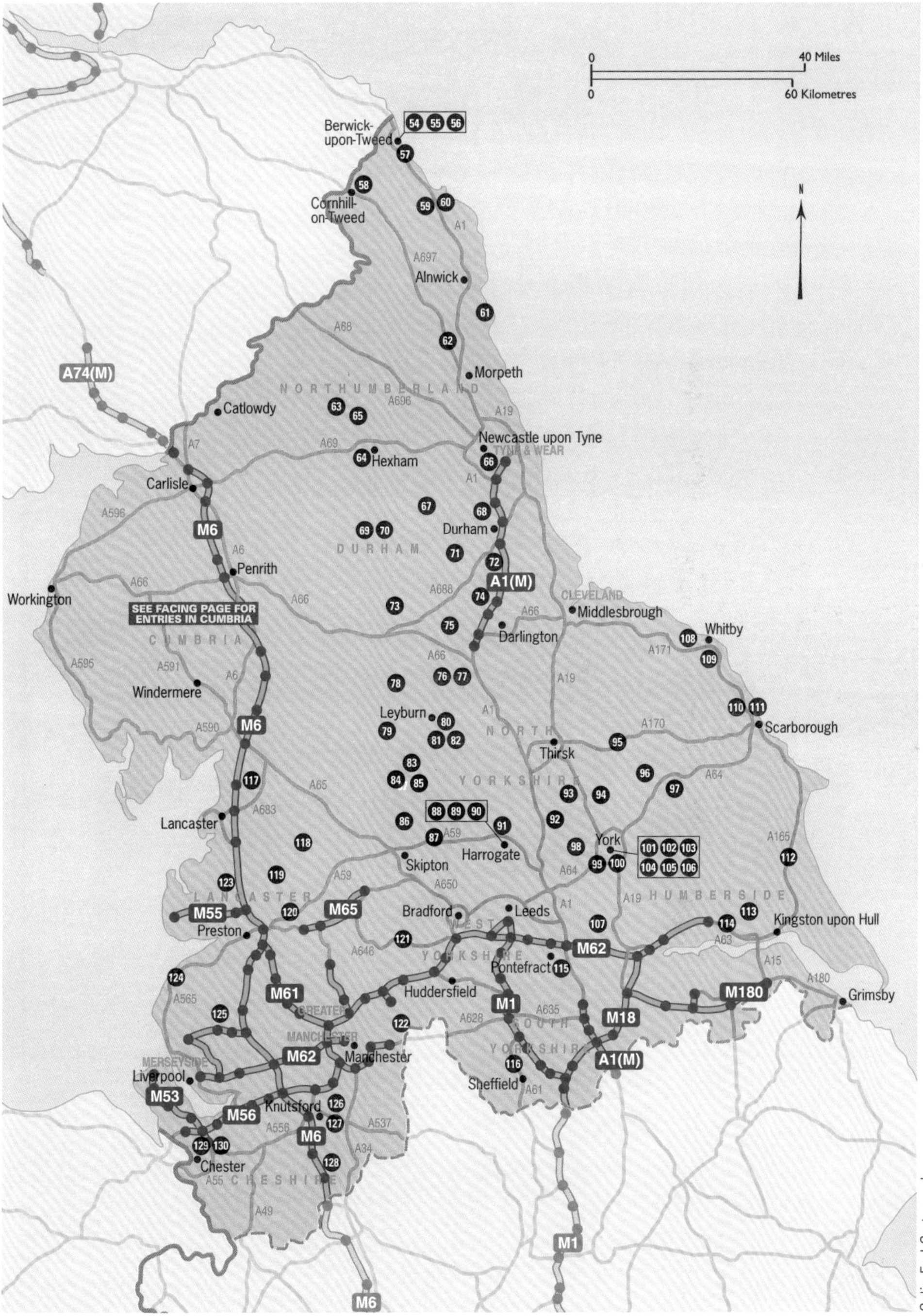
0
40 Miles
0
60 Kilometres
N
Berwick-upon-Tweed
54 55 56
57
58
Cornhill-on-Tweed
59 60
A1
A697
Alnwick
61
62
A68
Morpeth
A74(M)
NORTHUMBERLAND
A696
Catlowdy
63
65
A19
Newcastle upon Tyne
TYNE & WEAR
A7
A69
64
Hexham
66
A1
Carlisle
A596
67
68
69 70
Durham
M6
A6
DURHAM
71
72
Penrith
A1(M)
Workington
A66
A66
73
A688
74
CLEVELAND
Middlesbrough
SEE FACING PAGE FOR ENTRIES IN CUMBRIA
A66
75
Darlington
108
Whitby
CUMBRIA
A171
109
A595
A591
A66
A19
Windermere
A6
76 77
78
110 111
Leyburn
80
A1
Scarborough
A590
M6
79
81 82
NORTH
A170
95
Thirsk
83
117
84
85
YORKSHIRE
96
A64
A65
93
94
97
88 89 90
92
Lancaster
A683
86
91
A59
87
York
A165
118
Harrogate
98
101 102 103
Skipton
99 100
104 105 106
112
123
119
A59
A650
A64
LANCASTER
HUMBERSIDE
A19
M55
120
M65
Bradford
Leeds
113
A1
WEST
107
114
Kingston upon Hull
Preston
121
A63
A646
YORKSHIRE
M62
Pontefract
115
A15
124
A180
M61
Huddersfield
M1
M180
Grimsby
A565
GREATER
A635
125
M18
122
A628
SOUTH
MANCHESTER
YORKSHIRE
M62
Manchester
A1(M)
MERSEYSIDE
116
Liverpool
Sheffield
A61
M53
Knutsford
126
M56
127
A556
A537
M6
129 130
A34
128
Chester
A55
CHESHIRE
A49
M1
M6
Colin Earl Cartography

ETB 4 Crown Highly Commended

AA Red Rosette   RAC Restaurant Award

Award for Excellence

Lakeside Hotel
Lake Thirlmere, Keswick, Cumbria CA12 4TN
Tel: 017687 72478

See entry number 24

Settle–Carlisle Railway

BY ANY SENSIBLE reckoning this railway-line should never have been built. Its very existence is due to a combination of a row between two rival railway companies and Victorian over-confidence.

In the 1850s and 1860s, keen to pocket a share of the lucrative traffic bound for Scotland, the Midland Railway hoped to purchase, from its great rival, the London and North-Western Railway, the right to use the Lancaster–Carlisle stretch. The two companies couldn't agree and in 1866 Parliament passed a bill allowing the construction of a new line involving, among other things, surmounting Ais Gill summit (1,169ft high). It was estimated to cost £2.2 million – an astronomical sum. Closer inspection by the Midland's surveyors soon brought home the folly of their plans, and in 1868 the two companies belatedly agreed terms for co-operation. Parliament, however, demanded that the railway be built.

From that day on the problems seemed endless: bedrock on which to secure viaduct arches lay far deeper than anticipated; cuttings became tunnels; embankments became viaducts; one bog, near Ais Gill, swallowed up 'fill' for 12 months without the embanment proceeding a single yard; floods drowned men in the tunnels.

Railway-building in the Victorian age was a labour-intensive business. Up to 6,500 navvies worked for six-and-a-half years for good wages (10 shillings a day) to compensate for appalling conditions. The graveyards at both Chapel-le-Dale and Cowgill had to enlarge their plots, with, on average, one navvy dying each week. The human cost is unknown, but the financial cost mounted to over £3.5 million.

In 1876 the line opened and, despite regular gloomy predictions, it continues to be open, affording passengers views of enormous beauty. Progress along this line, however, is not rapid – ageing structures such as Ribblehead Viaduct cannot withstand speeding rolling-stock. Not such a bad thing, really, as passengers have more time to marvel at the lunatic nature of this civil engineering miracle.

Friends of the Settle–Carlisle Railway run guided walks designed to coincide with the regular timetable – details appear in the Regional Railways' Leeds–Settle–Carlisle timetable. Information on the frequent steam excursions is available from FSS Rail Tours on 01543 419472.

1 BESSIESTOWN FARM

〰〰〰 HIGHLY COMMENDED

Catlowdy, Longtown, Carlisle, Cumbria CA6 5QP Tel (01228) 577219

One of the nicest bed & breakfasts, warm and welcoming, peaceful and quiet with pretty en-suite bedrooms and delicious home cooking. The indoor heated swimming pool is open mid-May to mid-September. An ideal year-round touring base or break on long journeys, the farm is easily accessible from the M6: take the A7 to Longtown, then the road at Bush Hotel (signed Penton Netherby) for six-and-a-half miles, and at the T-junction turn right for one-and-a-half miles to Catlowdy – Bessiestown is the first on the left.

Bed & Breakfast per night: single occupancy from £24.00–£27.00; double room from £38.00–£44.00
Half board per person: £29.00–£32.00 daily; £180.00–£190.00 weekly
Evening meal 1900 (last bookings 1600)

Bedrooms: 2 double, 1 twin, 1 triple
Bathrooms: 4 en-suite
Parking for 10
Cards accepted: Access, Visa, Amex

---

2 AVONDALE

〰〰 HIGHLY COMMENDED

3 St. Aidan's Road, Carlisle, Cumbria CA1 1LT Tel (01228) 23012

Situated in a quiet position within easy walking distance of the centre of Carlisle, yet only one-and-a-half miles from the M6, our Edwardian house offers elegant and attractive rooms with a wealth of original features. A warm welcome and attentive service await you from the owners, Michael and Angela Hayes, whose wish is that their guests should feel at home and enjoy their stay.

Half board per person: £25.00–£27.00 daily
Evening meal 1830 (last bookings 1200)
Bedrooms: 1 double, 2 twin

Bathrooms: 1 en-suite, 1 private
Parking for 3

---

3 HOWARD HOUSE

〰〰〰 HIGHLY COMMENDED

27 Howard Place, Carlisle, Cumbria CA1 1HR Tel (01228) 29159 or (01228) 512550

Lawrence and Sandra Fisher welcome you to their spacious Victorian townhouse in the city centre's conservation area with four-poster bedrooms, en-suite and family rooms all with colour television and a welcome tray. Let us arrange your birthday, anniversary or wedding party and guided tours of the city, Hadrian's Wall and Lake District. We are in a quiet residential road near the river and golf course yet in the heart of the city. Family historians welcome. Come, let us spoil you!

Bed & Breakfast per night: single occupancy from £13.00–£16.00; double room from £26.00–£34.00
Half board per person: £20.00–£24.00 daily; £133.00–£160.00 weekly

Evening meal 1800 (last bookings 1000)
Bedrooms: 1 double, 1 twin, 2 family rooms
Bathrooms: 2 en-suite, 2 public

4 KIRBY MOOR COUNTRY HOUSE HOTEL   HIGHLY COMMENDED
Longtown Road, Brampton, Cumbria CA8 2AB Tel (01697) 73893 Fax (01697) 741847

Situated on the outskirts of the delightful village of Brampton, the hotel is Victorian in style and was built in 1866. Set in two-and-a-half acres of grounds, it is ideally situated for Hadrian's Wall and the Scottish borders. The conservatory dining room offers the best of English and French cuisine, using fresh produce, and the views are truly outstanding!

Bed & Breakfast per night: single occupancy from £36.50;
double room from £46.00–£48.00
Half board per person: £36.00 daily; £240.00 weekly
Lunch available: 1200–1400
Evening meal 1900 (last orders 2130)

Bedrooms: 3 double, 1 twin, 1 triple
Bathrooms: 5 private, 1 private shower
Parking for 30
Cards accepted: Access, Visa, Amex

5 CAUSA GRANGE   DE LUXE
Rosley, Wigton, Cumbria CA7 8DD Tel (016973) 45358

For guests seeking a quiet base to tour the scenic beauty of the Lake District, our charming Victorian home with spacious gardens is set in the heart of the countryside, yet only fifteen minutes from the M6 motorway. The Scottish borders are within easy reach and historic Carlisle is just eight miles away. To those who enjoy relaxing in comfortable, elegant surroundings with log fires and traditional English cooking, we offer a warm and friendly welcome. We are a non-smoking establishment.

Bed & Breakfast per night: single occupancy from
£22.00–£25.00; double room from £40.00–£48.00
Half board per person: £31.00–£40.00 daily;
£190.00–£260.00 weekly

Evening meal by arrangement 1900
Bedrooms: 1 double, 1 twin
Bathrooms: 1 private, 1 en-suite shower
Parking for 9

6 LOVELADY SHIELD COUNTRY HOUSE HOTEL   HIGHLY COMMENDED
Nenthead Road, Alston, Cumbria CA9 3LF Tel (01434) 381203 Fax (01434) 381515

Relax in this Georgian-style country house standing in a peaceful scenic position and excellent walking country. The Lakes, Hadrian's Wall, Lowlands, Teesdale and other places are all within easy reach, with golf, riding and fishing nearby. Bedrooms are comfortable and well-equipped and the cosy lounges and cocktail bar have log fires. Our cuisine is widely acclaimed and matched by an impressive wine list. We aim to give our guests complete satisfaction, enjoyment and value for money.

Bed & Breakfast per night: single room from
£47.50–£67.50; double room from £95.00–£119.00
Half board per person: £72.50–£84.50 daily;
£415.00–£485.00 weekly
Evening meal 1930 (last orders 2030)

Bedrooms: 1 single, 7 double, 3 twin
Bathrooms: 11 private
Parking for 25
Open: February–December
Cards accepted: Access, Visa, Diners, Amex

7 NENT HALL COUNTRY HOUSE HOTEL 🌊🌊🌊🌊 HIGHLY COMMENDED
Nenthall, Alston, Cumbria CA9 3LQ Tel (01434) 381584 Fax (01434) 382668

The peace and tranquillity of the north Pennines offer a superb setting for Nent Hall. Escape from the world and let us care for you with consideration and that personal touch. We offer elegant dining with freshly-prepared cuisine and a range of specially selected wines for the discerning guest. From this beautiful central location, visit such historic sites as Hadrian's Wall and Durham Cathedral, or enjoy the landscape of the North Lakes and Scottish Borders. 🌊

Bed & Breakfast per night: single occupancy from £50.00–£70.00; double room from £65.00–£85.00
Half board per person: £103.00–£123.00 daily; £610.00–£735.00 weekly
Lunch available: 1200–1400

Evening meal 1900 (last orders 2100)
Bedrooms: 12 double, 4 twin, 2 triple
Bathrooms: 18 en-suite
Parking for 40
Cards accepted: Access, Visa, Amex

8 RAVENSTONE LODGE 🌊🌊🌊 HIGHLY COMMENDED
Bassenthwaite, Keswick, Cumbria CA12 4QG Tel (017687) 76629 or (017687) 76638 Fax (017687) 76629

A warm and friendly welcome awaits you at Ravenstone Lodge, our 19th-century stone-built property nestling at the foot of Ullock Pike, just four miles north of Keswick on the A591. The lodge is set in five acres of spectacular countryside with a private terrace, a large walled garden and ample off-the-road parking space. Enjoy the relaxed atmosphere of our stable dining room, bar and large Victorian-style conservatory.

Bed & Breakfast per night: single room from £26.50–£28.50; double room from £48.00–£53.00
Half board per person: £40.00–£42.00 daily; £261.50–£274.50 weekly

Evening meal 1900 (last bookings 1800)
Bedrooms: 6 double, 2 twin, 1 family room
Bathrooms: 9 en-suite
Parking for 12

9 PHEASANT INN 🌊 HIGHLY COMMENDED
Bassenthwaite Lake, Cockermouth, Cumbria CA13 9YE Tel (01768) 776234 Fax (01768) 776002

A tranquil, traditional, north Lake District inn, adjacent to Bassenthwaite Lake, and surrounded by gardens and woodland providing a wealth of wildlife. Three lounges feature antiques, beams, open fires and fresh flowers. Commended by major guides for high quality English food and service, Pheasant Inn also has twenty individually decorated bedrooms with private facilities. Dogs welcome – kennels available. 🌊

Bed & Breakfast per night: single room from £53.00–£55.00; double room from £64.00–£94.00
Half board per person: £73.00–£75.00 daily; £370.00–£450.00 weekly
Lunch available: 1230–1400

Evening meal 1900 (last orders 2030)
Bedrooms: 5 single, 8 double, 7 twin
Bathrooms: 20 private
Parking for 80
Cards accepted: Access, Visa

10 LOW HALL COUNTRY GUESTHOUSE   🍲🍲🍲 HIGHLY COMMENDED
Brandlingill, Cockermouth, Cumbria CA13 0RE Tel (01900) 826654

A warm welcome, tea by the fire, birthday bouquets and celebration champagne combine to give a glimpse of paradise in your busy world. A friendly atmosphere fills every room in this 17th-century farmhouse commanding uninterrupted views of lake, stream and fell. The cosy oak-beamed dining room sets the scene for your evening, and Enid produces the very best of country cooking using quality seasonal produce. A rural retreat offering excellent value for money. No smoking.

Bed & Breakfast per night: single occupancy from £20.00–£35.00; double room from £40.00–£70.00
Half board per person: £37.00–£52.00 daily; £259.00–£325.00 weekly
Bedrooms: 4 double, 1 twin

Bathrooms: 5 en-suite
Parking for 10
Open: March–October
Cards accepted: Access, Visa

11 NEW HOUSE FARM   🍲🍲🍲 HIGHLY COMMENDED
Lorton, Cockermouth, Cumbria CA13 9UU Tel (01900) 85404

A spectacular fell and valley setting surrounds this carefully restored 17th-century lakeland-stone house that has fine views from each of its en-suite rooms. This is the real Lake District without crowds and it remains quiet even throughout the summer months. New House has fifteen acres with open fields, streams, ponds and woods through which guests may wander. Comfortable accommodation and a cosy dining room with fine traditional cooking complete the picture of this very special country guesthouse. This is a non-smoking establishment.

Bed & Breakfast per night: single occupancy from £30.00–£40.00; double room from £50.00–£60.00
Half board per person: £45.00–£50.00 daily
Evening meal 1930 (last bookings 1900)

Bedrooms: 3 double
Bathrooms: 3 en-suite
Parking for 20

12 LYZZICK HALL HOTEL   🍲🍲🍲🍲 HIGHLY COMMENDED
Underskiddaw, Keswick, Cumbria CA12 4PY Tel (01768) 772277 Fax (01768) 772278

Lyzzick Hall is an enchanting country hotel situated in an idyllic position in the glorious unspoilt northern lakeland. We have stupendous mountain views, together with the opportunity to really get off the beaten track and leave the crowds behind. Being family-run, the high standards are zealously guarded and the atmosphere is genial and relaxed. We have rambling gardens, an outdoor pool for the summer and log fires for cool evenings. How sorry we are when you leave!

Bed & Breakfast per night: single room from £34.00–£36.00; double room from £68.00–£72.00
Half board per person: £44.00–£46.00 daily
Lunch available: 1200–1400
Evening meal 1900 (last orders 2130)

Bedrooms: 3 single, 12 double, 6 twin, 3 family rooms
Bathrooms: 24 en-suite
Parking for 30
Open: January, March–December
Cards accepted: Access, Visa, Diners, Amex

13 DERWENT COTTAGE

🍽🍽🍽 HIGHLY COMMENDED

Portinscale, Keswick, Cumbria CA12 5RF Tel (017687) 74838

Gleaming silver, cut-glass, five spacious en-suite bedrooms and elegant furnishings are all to be found at Derwent Cottage. This lakeland house, dating from the 18th century, stands in an acre of secluded gardens in the quiet village of Portinscale, one mile from Keswick. A four-course candle-light table d'hôte is served at 1900 each evening with classical music in the background. A residential licence is held and drinks and wine are available throughout the evening. We are a totally non-smoking establishment.

Bed & Breakfast per night: double room from £48.00–£62.00
Half board per person: £34.00–£44.00 daily; £224.00–£252.00 weekly
Evening meal 1900 (last orders 1900)

Bedrooms: 5 double
Bathrooms: 5 en-suite
Parking for 10
Open: March–November
Cards accepted: Access, Visa

14 ACORN HOUSE HOTEL

🍽🍽 HIGHLY COMMENDED

Ambleside Road, Keswick, Cumbria CA12 4DL Tel (01768) 772553

Superior detached Georgian house set in lovely colourful garden. Bedrooms with traditional furniture and some with four-poster beds. Acorn House offers excellent accommodation at affordable prices and our generous breakfasts will set you up for the day. Only a few minutes walk into the town centre or to the lake. Private parking. No smoking in bedrooms.

Bed & Breakfast per night: single occupancy from £21.50
Bedrooms: 6 double, 1 twin, 3 triple
Bathrooms: 9 en-suite, 1 private

Parking for 10
Open: February–November
Cards accepted: Access, Visa

15 CRAGLANDS

🍽🍽🍽 HIGHLY COMMENDED

Penrith Road, Keswick, Cumbria CA12 4LJ Tel (01768) 774406

An excellent Victorian house situated in a quiet location on the outskirts of Keswick, overlooking the town, it offers splendid views of both Grisedale and Causey Pike to the front of the house, and Latrigg to the rear. You will receive a warm welcome in a relaxing and friendly atmosphere, together with a beautifully furnished and decorated interior. The dining room offers the very best of British cuisine using fresh local produce.

Bed & Breakfast per night: single occupancy from £25.00–£27.00; double room from £44.00–£50.00
Half board per person: £37.00–£42.00 daily; £240.00–£280.00 weekly

Evening meal 1900 (last orders 2000)
Bedrooms: 3 double, 1 twin
Bathrooms: 4 private
Parking for 5

Entries are cross referenced by number to the maps on pages 16–17

16 THE GRANGE COUNTRY HOUSE HOTEL   🛁🛁🛁🛁 HIGHLY COMMENDED
Manor Brow, Ambleside Road, Keswick, Cumbria CA12 4BA   Tel (017687) 72500

The Grange Country House Hotel is set in its own grounds overlooking Keswick-on-Derwentwater and the surrounding mountains. An elegant lakeland house built in the 1840s, The Grange is proudly owned by Duncan & Jane Miller. The hotel offers quality and comfort in a warm relaxing atmosphere, holds various awards and is featured in many of the leading guides. Lovely bedrooms, log fires and freshly prepared food. Unforgettable.

Bed & Breakfast per night: double room from
£69.00–£79.00
Half board per person: £43.00–£50.00 daily;
£297.50–£311.50 weekly
Evening meal 1930

Bedrooms: 7 double, 3 twin
Bathrooms: 10 en-suite
Parking for 13
Open: March–November
Cards accepted: Access, Visa

---

17 GREYSTONES   🛁🛁🛁 HIGHLY COMMENDED
Ambleside Road, Keswick, Cumbria CA12 4DP   Tel (01768) 773108

This small, comfortable, family-run hotel situated in a quiet area of Keswick is only a short walk from the town centre, lake and the Fells. All rooms are en-suite, tastefully furnished and include television, radio, tea/coffee making facilities and more. There is a comfortable residents' lounge, a separate dining room and a car park. Keswick is close to one of the most beautiful lakes and is ideally situated for the National Park, the Pennines and Hadrian's Wall.

Bed & Breakfast per night: single occupancy from £21.50;
double room from £41.00–£44.00
Half board per person: £34.00–£35.00 daily
Evening meal 1900 (last bookings 1400)

Bedrooms: 1 single, 5 double, 2 twin
Bathrooms: 7 private, 1 public
Parking for 9
Open: February–November

---

18 BRIDGE HOTEL   🛁🛁🛁🛁 HIGHLY COMMENDED
Buttermere, Cockermouth, Cumbria CA13 9UZ   Tel (01768) 770252   Fax (01768) 770252

An old 18th-century coaching inn, beautifully situated between two lakes in the Lakeland's loveliest valley. Superb unrestricted walking country and breathtaking scenery. Our no-smoking restaurant has a menu of daily freshly-prepared food complemented by a good selection of wines. There is a large, residents' lounge with a log fire where complimentary afternoon tea is served. Two well-stocked bars serve expertly kept real ales. Four-poster beds. Dogs welcome. Special breaks offered throughout the year. Self-catering available.

Half board per person: £45.00–£54.50 daily; £290.00
weekly
Lunch available: 1200–1430
Evening meal 1900 (last orders 2030)

Bedrooms: 2 single, 8 double, 12 twin
Bathrooms: 22 private
Parking for 60
Cards accepted: Access, Visa, Switch/Delta

19 SWINSIDE LODGE
 DE LUXE

Newlands, Keswick, Cumbria CA12 5UE Tel (017687) 72948

Swinside Lodge is a delightful Victorian house in a beautiful and tranquil corner of the Lake District, just beneath Cat Bells and a five-minute stroll from the shores of Derwentwater. Relax in this most comfortable and elegantly furnished house where you can enjoy superb award-winning food served by friendly staff in the candle-lit dining room. The hotel, which is personally run, is totally non-smoking and is unlicensed but please bring your own favourite wines. A warm welcome awaits you.

Bed & Breakfast per night: single occupancy from £36.00–£48.50; double room from £57.00–£80.00
Half board per person: £52.50–£76.00 daily
Evening meal 1930 (last orders 2000)

Bedrooms: 5 double, 2 twin
Bathrooms: 7 private
Parking for 12
Open: February–November

20 PICKETT HOWE
 DE LUXE

Buttermere Valley, Cockermouth, Cumbria CA13 9UY Tel (01900) 85444

Nestling peacefully beneath rugged lakeland peaks, this award-winning, 17th-century former farmhouse offers just eight non-smoking guests a unique holiday experience. Slate floors, oak beams and mullioned windows are enhanced by quality furnishings and antiques; the quaint bedrooms have jacuzzi baths and Victorian brass iron beds. The exceptional and extensive breakfast menu and well-balanced, beautifully presented dinners combined with caring, relaxed hospitality make Pickett Howe a perfect base for walking, touring or just relaxing!

Bed & Breakfast per night: double room £70.00
Half board per person: £51.00–£55.00 daily; £357.00 weekly
Evening meal 1915
Bedrooms: 3 double, 1 twin

Bathrooms: 4 en-suite
Parking for 4
Open: April–November
Cards accepted: Access, Visa

21 THE BORROWDALE GATES Country House Hotel & Restaurant
 HIGHLY COMMENDED

Grange-in-Borrowdale, Keswick, Cumbria CA12 5UQ Tel (01768) 777204 Fax (01768) 777254

Borrowdale Gates Hotel nestles peacefully in two acres of wooded gardens on the edge of the ancient hamlet of Grange. This charming lakeland house is set amidst the breath-taking scenery of the Borrowdale valley with panoramic views of the countryside. The bedrooms, of which six are on the ground floor, are tastefully decorated and furnished. The restaurant offers fine food, prepared by Chef/Patron Terry Parkinson, that is complemented by a carefully chosen wine list.

Half board per person: £48.50–£65.00 daily; £314.75–£400.00 weekly
Lunch available: 1215 (last orders 1330)
Evening meal 1900 (last orders 2045)
Bedrooms: 4 single, 9 double, 7 twin, 2 triple

Bathrooms: 22 en-suite
Parking for 40
Cards accepted: Access, Visa, Switch/Delta

22 GREENBANK COUNTRY GUEST HOUSE   ❦❦❦ HIGHLY COMMENDED
Borrowdale, Keswick, Cumbria CA12 5UY Tel (01768) 777215

Greenbank is a lovely Victorian house in a peaceful setting. Here you can enjoy magnificent views of Derwentwater and the Borrowdale Valley. There are ten comfortable well-appointed bedrooms, each with an en-suite bathroom. We particularly enjoy providing imaginatively-presented meals, with interesting menus using lots of local fresh produce.

Bed & Breakfast per night: single room from £25.00; double room from £44.00–£50.00
Half board per person: £34.00–£37.00 daily; £210.00–£231.00 weekly
Evening meal 1900 (last bookings 1700)

Bedrooms: 1 single, 6 double, 2 twin, 1 triple
Bathrooms: 10 en-suite
Parking for 15
Open: February–November

23 HAZEL BANK   ❦❦❦ HIGHLY COMMENDED
Rosthwaite, Borrowdale, Keswick, Cumbria CA12 5XB Tel (017687) 77248

Standing on an elevated site overlooking the village of Rosthwaite, there are unsurpassed views of the Borrowdale Valley and central lakeland peaks. The peaceful location makes Hazel Bank an ideal base for walkers, birdwatchers and lovers of the countryside, with direct access to many mountain and valley walks. The Victorian residence has been carefully and sympathetically converted to provide quality country house accommodation. Come and discover how enjoyable a stay in Borrowdale can be. Non-smokers only, please.

Half board per person: £43.00 daily; £265.00 weekly
Evening meal 1900 (last bookings 1900)
Bedrooms: 1 single, 2 double, 3 twin
Bathrooms: 6 en-suite

Parking for 12
Open: March–October
Cards accepted: Access, Visa

24 DALE HEAD HALL LAKESIDE HOTEL   ❦❦❦❦ HIGHLY COMMENDED
Thirlmere, Keswick, Cumbria CA12 4TN Tel (017687) 72478

With Helvellyn rising majestically behind, the hotel stands alone on the shores of Lake Thirlmere. At Dale Head Hall we offer a friendly home, a place of relaxation and beauty, set apart from the increasing pace of the modern world. Little can compare to a delicious dinner, prepared with love and care, particularly when wholesome ingredients come from the hotel's walled garden.

Half board per person: £49.00–£75.00 daily; £259.00–£441.00 weekly
Evening meal 1930 (last orders 2030)
Bedrooms: 6 double, 2 twin, 1 triple
Bathrooms: 9 private

Parking for 20
Cards accepted: Access, Visa, Delta

25 THE GRASMERE HOTEL

〰〰〰〰 HIGHLY COMMENDED

Grasmere, Ambleside, Cumbria LA22 9TA Tel (015394) 35277

An elegant Victorian lakeland stone-built country house set in the quiet location of Grasmere village, in an acre of secluded natural gardens bordered by the River Rothay. Renowned for our cuisine, our beautiful restaurant offers a four-course dinner with a varied choice of culinary delights that are imaginatively presented with only fresh produce used. A place for all seasons, The Grasmere Hotel extends a warm welcome and all the comfort you could wish for.

Bed & Breakfast per night: single room from
£25.00–£35.00; double room from £50.00–£70.00
Half board per person: £35.00–£52.00 daily;
£210.00–£315.00 weekly
Evening meal 1930 (last orders 2030)

Bedrooms: 1 single, 9 double, 2 twin
Bathrooms: 11 en-suite, 1 private
Parking for 14
Open: February–December
Cards accepted: Access, Visa

26 WOODLAND CRAG GUEST HOUSE

〰〰 HIGHLY COMMENDED

Howe Head Lane, Grasmere, Ambleside, Cumbria LA22 9SG Tel (01539) 435351

A warm welcome and an informal atmosphere are found in this delightful house, situated on the edge of Grasmere near Dove Cottage. Secluded but with easy access to all facilities, the accommodation has fine tastefully-decorated bedrooms, all with individual character and wonderful views of the lake, fells or gardens. Ideal for walking and centrally placed for the motorist (enclosed parking). All major outdoor activities are catered for nearby, including sailing, fishing, wind surfing and pony trekking. Totally non-smoking.

Bed & Breakfast per night: single room from
£23.00–£24.00; double room from £48.00–£50.00
Bedrooms: 2 single, 2 double, 1 twin

Bathrooms: 1 public, 3 en-suite showers
Parking for 5

27 LONG HOUSE

〰〰 HIGHLY COMMENDED

Great Langdale, Ambleside, Cumbria LA22 9JS Tel (015394) 37222

An early 17th-century cottage farmhouse enjoying a peaceful position near the foot of Langdale Pikes, with superb open mountain views and a beautiful garden and orchard to relax in. The cottage completely retains its original character with low beamed ceilings, original slate floors, stained-glass windows, beautiful oak hand-crafted doors and an inglenook fireplace. Pretty, fully-carpeted bedrooms with en-suite facilities. Central heating. Enclosed parking. Ideal walking country. Friendly and informal. Call Mrs. Wilkinson for a brochure.

Bed & Breakfast per night: double room from
£44.00–£50.00
Evening meal 1900 (last bookings 1100)
Bedrooms: 3 double

Bathrooms: 3 private
Parking for 6
Open: February–November
Cards accepted: Access, Visa, Switch/Delta

28 LANGDALE HOTEL & COUNTRY CLUB ♨♨♨♨♨ HIGHLY COMMENDED

Great Langdale, Ambleside, Cumbria LA22 9JB Tel (01539) 437302 Fax (01539) 437694

The beauty of the Langdale Valley and the grandeur of the Pikes is unforgettable, so too is the thirty-five acre estate of woodland, tarn and stream that is home to the Langdale Hotel & Country Club. So much to do and so much to remember: the scenery, the comfort, the good food, the excellent service and above all, guest membership of the Langdale Country Club – the social centre of this unique resort.

Bed & Breakfast per night: single occupancy from £80.00–£95.00; double room from £130.00–£160.00
Half board per person: £77.00–£99.00 daily;
£367.00–£444.00 weekly
Evening meal 1900 (last orders 2200)

Bedrooms: 41 double, 24 twin
Bathrooms: 65 private
Parking for 120
Cards accepted: Access, Visa, Diners, Amex

29 RIVERSIDE HOTEL ♨♨♨♨ HIGHLY COMMENDED

Under Loughrigg, Nr. Rothay Bridge, Ambleside, Cumbria LA22 9LJ Tel (01539) 432395 Fax (01539) 432395

Set within beautiful grounds on one of the loveliest lanes in England, the Riverside enjoys its own river frontages with woodland walks leading to Laughrigg Fell. Tastefully modernised throughout, our thoughtfully-furnished bedrooms all have en-suite facilities, some with spa baths. Our food is cooked with flair and imagination and served in a candle-lit atmosphere. We hope that at Riverside you will find a haven of peace and tranquillity in which to enjoy your holiday. No smoking in the dining room.

Bed & Breakfast per night: single occupancy from £40.00–£50.00; double room from £68.00–£80.00
Half board per person: £46.00–£50.00 daily;
£236.00–£308.00 weekly
Evening meal 1900 (last orders 2000)

Bedrooms: 8 double, 2 twin
Bathrooms: 10 en-suite
Parking for 20
Open: March–November
Cards accepted: Access, Visa

30 BORRANS PARK HOTEL ♨♨♨ HIGHLY COMMENDED

Borrans Road, Ambleside, Cumbria LA22 0EN Tel (015394) 33454

Peacefully situated in the heart of Lakeland, Borrans Park is the place to enjoy award-winning traditional home cooking and experience a truly memorable sweet trolley. Choose a fine wine from the extensive personally selected wine list and relax by the log fire or in the comfort of one of the four-poster bedrooms each with an en-suite spa bathroom. Special breaks are available all year. Complimentary membership of an exclusive nearby leisure club.

Bed & Breakfast per night: single occupancy from £29.00–£49.00; double room from £58.00–£78.00
Half board per person: £45.00–£55.00 daily;
£229.00–£325.00 weekly
Evening meal 1900 (last orders 1800)

Bedrooms: 9 double, 1 twin, 2 triple
Bathrooms: 12 private
Parking for 20
Cards accepted: Access, Visa

31 LAUREL VILLA ♛♛♛ HIGHLY COMMENDED
Lake Road, Ambleside, Cumbria LA22 0DB Tel (01539) 433240

Centrally situated in the heart of the Lake District, this elegant Victorian house, once visited by Beatrix Potter, is now personally run by resident proprietors, and is within easy walking distance of the village of Ambleside and Lake Windermere. Spacious, luxurious rooms are decorated in William Morris style, and all the bedrooms overlook the fells. Private car park.

Bed & Breakfast per night: single occupancy from £50.00; double room from £60.00–£80.00
Evening meal 1900 (last bookings 1700)
Bedrooms: 7 double, 1 twin

Bathrooms: 8 en-suite
Parking for 10
Cards accepted: Access, Visa

32 ROWANFIELD COUNTRY GUESTHOUSE ♛♛ HIGHLY COMMENDED
Kirkstone Road, Ambleside, Cumbria LA22 9ET Tel (015394) 33686

Set in idyllic tranquil countryside, three-quarters of a mile from Ambleside in central lakeland, Rowanfield enjoys fabulous panoramic lake and mountain views. This delightful period house with its country house decor is warm and welcoming. All the bedrooms are en-suite and individually and tastefully furnished. The chef/ patron, Philip Butcher, creates exciting evening meals from the finest fresh produce. Unlicensed, but own wine welcome. Superb location for exploring the whole Lake District area. No smoking.

Bed & Breakfast per night: double room from £48.00–£56.00
Half board per person: £39.00–£43.00 daily; £235.00–£252.00 weekly
Evening meal 1900 (last bookings 1700)

Bedrooms: 5 double, 1 twin, 1 triple
Bathrooms: 7 en-suite
Parking for 8
Open: March–December
Cards accepted: Access, Visa

33 THE REGENT HOTEL ♛♛♛♛ HIGHLY COMMENDED
Waterhead Bay, Ambleside, Cumbria LA22 0ES Tel (01539) 432254 Fax (01539) 431474

The Hewitts own and personally manage the hotel at peaceful Waterhead Bay on the shores of beautiful Lake Windermere. Highly commended for standards of comfort and cuisine, we offer the highest levels of traditional service, blended with every modern convenience. An indoor heated swimming pool in a delightful courtyard setting adds to your pleasure. Four-poster rooms available and flowers, champagne and chocolates make that extra special occasion.

Bed & Breakfast per night: single room from £40.00–£60.00; double room from £35.00–£54.50 per person
Half board per person: £35.00–£65.00 daily; £220.00–£350.00 weekly
Lunch available: 1200–1400

Evening meal 1900 (last orders 2030)
Bedrooms: 3 single, 9 double, 7 twin, 2 triple
Bathrooms: 21 private
Parking for 30
Cards accepted: Access, Visa

34 WATEREDGE HOTEL
中中中中 HIGHLY COMMENDED

Waterhead Bay, Ambleside, Cumbria LA22 0EP Tel (015394) 32332 Fax (015394) 32332

Wateredge is a delightfully-situated family-run hotel on the shores of Windermere, with gardens leading to the lake edge. It was developed from two 17th-century fishermen's cottages which are still part of the charm of the whole building. Relax in comfortable lounges overlooking the lake, or on our lakeside patio where teas and light lunches are served. In the evening, dine under oak-beams and enjoy exquisitely-cooked food. Cosy bar, pretty bedrooms and relaxed friendly service.

Bed & Breakfast per night: single room from £37.00–£51.00; double room from £58.00–£122.00
Half board per person: £49.00–£81.00 daily; £334.00–£539.00 weekly
Evening meal 1900 (last orders 2030)

Bedrooms: 3 single, 11 double, 8 twin, 1 triple
Bathrooms: 23 private
Parking for 25
Open: February–December
Cards accepted: Access, Visa, Amex, Switch/Delta

---

35 QUARRY GARTH COUNTRY HOUSE HOTEL AND RESTAURANT
中中中中 HIGHLY COMMENDED

Troutbeck Bridge, Windermere, Cumbria LA23 1LF Tel (015394) 43761 or (015394) 88282 Fax (015394) 46584

This gracious and mellow country house is set in eight acres of peaceful gardens near Lake Windermere. It is the home of Huw & Lynne Phillips, friendly and caring hosts who combine high standards with kindness and good humour. The lounge is comfortable, unpretentious and dotted with fresh flowers, books, magazines and guidebooks. Unmissable dinners of exceptional value are taken by candle-light in the restaurant where oak panelling and log fires underline the true country house ambience.

Bed & Breakfast per night: single room from £35.00–£45.00; double room from £70.00–£90.00
Half board per person: £45.00–£60.00 daily; £310.00–£345.00 weekly
Evening meal 1900 (last orders 2100)

Bedrooms: 1 single, 6 double, 2 twin, 1 triple
Bathrooms: 10 en-suite
Parking for 50
Cards accepted: Access, Visa, Diners, Amex, Switch/Delta

---

36 BORWICK LODGE
中中 HIGHLY COMMENDED

Outgate, Hawkshead, Ambleside, Cumbria LA22 0PU Tel (015394) 36332

Twice winner of the AWARD for 'Accommodation of the Highest Standards'. A leafy driveway entices you to a rather special 17th-century country house with magnificent panoramic lake and mountain views, quietly secluded in the heart of the Lakes. The beautiful en-suite bedrooms include 'Special Occasions' and 'Romantic Breaks' with king-size four-poster beds. Prize-winning home-made breads. Linda and Alan Bleasdale welcome you to this most beautiful corner of England. TOTALLY NON-SMOKING.

Bed & Breakfast per night: single occupancy from £18.00–£32.00; double room from £36.00–£64.00
Bedrooms: 2 double, 1 twin, 1 family room

Bathrooms: 4 en-suite
Parking for 8

37 GREY FRIAR LODGE COUNTRY HOUSE HOTEL   HIGHLY COMMENDED
Clappersgate, Ambleside, Cumbria LA22 9NE Tel (015394) 33158

A beautiful, lakeland-stone country house, ideally set in the heart of the Lake District between Ambleside and the Langdales, with superb river and mountain views and tasteful, well-appointed rooms. A warm, friendly and informal atmosphere is achieved by the Sutton family, complemented by exceptional hospitality and imaginative home cooking. Recommended by leading guides.

Bed & Breakfast per night: single occupancy from £27.00–£30.00; double room from £40.00–£61.00 Half board per person: £35.00–£45.50 daily; £215.00–£290.00 weekly Evening meal 1930 (last bookings 1900)

Bedrooms: 6 double, 2 twin
Bathrooms: 8 private
Parking for 12
Open: February–October

38 NANNY BROW COUNTRY HOUSE HOTEL   HIGHLY COMMENDED
Clappersgate, Ambleside, Cumbria LA22 9NF Tel (01539) 432036 Fax (01539) 432450

This elegant country house sits peacefully under Loughrigg Fell in five acres of gardens and woodland, with access onto the fell and also enjoys spectacular views of the River Brathay. The hotel is noted for its award-winning restaurant with a warm and friendly atmosphere. There are log fires on chilly evenings and fresh flowers are attended to daily. Bedrooms are individually designed and furnished in traditional quality. Croquet, fishing, spa bath, solarium, leisure club facilities, dogs accepted. Personally managed by the resident owners Michael and Carol Fletcher.

Bed & Breakfast per night: single occupancy from £45.00–£65.00; double room from £100.00–£130.00 Half board per person: £120.00–£160.00 daily (two people/double room); £346.00–£504.00 weekly (per person/double room) Evening meal 1930 (last orders 2030)

Bedrooms: 12 double, 4 twin, 3 triple
Bathrooms: 19 private
Parking for 22
Open: February–December
Cards accepted: Access, Visa, Amex

39 WHEELGATE COUNTRY HOUSE HOTEL   HIGHLY COMMENDED
Little Arrow, Torver, Coniston, Cumbria LA21 8AU Tel (01539) 441418

A delightful, 17th-century country house with a warm, relaxed atmosphere, situated in a peaceful rural location close to the heart of Lakeland. The hotel features exquisite individually-styled bedrooms and an enchanting oak-beamed lounge with log fires. In the intimate candle-lit restaurant the finest fresh local produce can be sampled. Breakfasts are delicious with an extensive buffet of cereals followed by a hearty grill. Quality service is guaranteed – a perfect and unforgettable experience. Totally non-smoking.

Bed & Breakfast per night: single room from £30.00–£32.50; double room from £50.00–£65.00 Half board per person: £40.50–£48.00 daily; £255.00–£297.50 weekly Evening meal 1930 (last bookings 1900)

Bedrooms: 1 single, 4 double, 3 twin
Bathrooms: 2 en-suite, 6 en-suite showers
Parking for 8
Open: February–November
Cards accepted: Access, Visa, Amex

40 FAYRER GARDEN HOUSE HOTEL   〰〰〰 HIGHLY COMMENDED

Upper Storrs Road, Bowness-on-Windermere, Windermere, Cumbria LA23 3JP   Tel (01539) 488195

Fayrer Garden House is beautifully situated in five acres of grounds overlooking Lake Windermere. The conservatory restaurant and elegant lounges all enjoy the vista over the lake to Claife Heights and Coniston Old Man beyond. Iain and Jackie have owned several hotels in the Lakes and have built a strong following of Jackie's imaginative cuisine. From the home-made soups to the delicious desserts, the accent is on serving the customer what they enjoy eating.

Bed & Breakfast per night: single occupancy from £30.00–£60.00; double room from £39.50–£90.00
Half board per person: £33.00–£59.00 daily
Evening meal 1930 (last orders 2000)
Bedrooms: 8 double, 3 triple

Bathrooms: 11 en-suite
Parking for 20
Cards accepted: Access, Visa, Amex

Gondola and the National Trust

THE NATIONAL TRUST understandably concerns itself with objects which can be preserved, kept in the *state* for which they were intended, kept in the *place* for which they were intended. This, in a sense, is exactly what has happened to *Gondola*, though, slightly unusually, one doesn't quite know where she will be at a given time – for *Gondola* is the National Trust's only steam yacht and she plies up and down Coniston Water for seven or so months each year.

Gondola's tale is typical of many National Trust stories. She was originally launched from Coniston Hall to sail on Coniston Water in 1859. A contemporary report in the *Illustrated London News* described her as 'a perfect combination of the Venetian Gondola and the English Steam Yacht' – and so she is: her prow and her low profile in the water both more clearly reminiscent of the Grand Canal than Coniston Water. She remained in service on the lake until 1937, when her hull became a houseboat and her boiler was used for the cutting of

timber in a saw mill. Twenty six years on, the violent winter storms of 1963 threw her aground, where she remained stranded.

By 1977 she was in a sorry state, but not yet beyond repair, and the lengthy business of restoring her to her past glory was begun. Appeals, and assistance from Vickers Shipbuilders in Barrow-in-Furness (the hull was manoeuvred there for a thorough overhaul), meant that repair work was completed by spring 1980. For the past 15 years she has been sailing the same waters, ferrying visitors the length of Coniston Water, one of the most beautiful, if not the wildest of the Lakes. One of the three stops on the lake is by Brantwood, where John Ruskin's house (complete with several of Turner's paintings, whose cause he championed) can be explored (not owned by the Trust). Ruskin, though not involved directly, was greatly influential in the setting up of the National Trust, which celebrates its centenary this year.

41 LINTHWAITE HOUSE HOTEL ✿✿✿✿ DE LUXE
Crook Road, Bowness-on-Windermere, Cumbria LA23 3JA Tel (015394) 88600 Fax (015394) 88601

A country house hotel, twenty minutes from the M6, situated in fourteen acres of peaceful hilltop grounds, overlooking Lake Windermere and breathtaking sunsets. The eighteen rooms have en-suite bathrooms, satellite television, radio, telephone and tea/coffee making facilities. The restaurant serves modern British food using local produce complemented by fine wines. There is a tarn for fly-fishing, croquet, golf practice hole and free use of nearby leisure spa. Romantic breaks feature a king-size double with canopy, champagne, chocolates and flowers.

Bed & Breakfast per night: single room from £69.00;
double room from £90.00–£160.00
Half board per person: £49.00–£100.00 daily;
£588.00–£1200.00 weekly
Lunch available: 1200–1330

Evening meal 1915 (last orders 2045)
Bedrooms: 1 single, 13 double, 4 twin
Bathrooms: 18 private
Parking for 30
Cards accepted: Access, Visa, Amex, Switch/Delta

42 THE BURN HOW GARDEN HOUSE HOTEL & MOTEL ✿✿✿✿ HIGHLY COMMENDED
Back Belsfield Road, Windermere, Cumbria LA23 3HH Tel (01539) 446226 Fax (01539) 447000

We offer comfort and superb service near the shore of Windermere, in spacious family chalets or elegant four-poster rooms all with private bathrooms, television, radio, and parking space. Many rooms have private balconies and four of the ground floor ones are suitable for wheelchairs. We serve first-class English and French cuisine and are acclaimed for our fine food. You also receive free use of a premier leisure club. It's that extra personal service that makes all the difference.

Bed & Breakfast per night: single room from
£46.00–£52.00; double room from £72.00–£98.00
Half board per person: £44.00–£65.00 daily;
£290.00–£360.00 weekly
Lunch available: 1230–1300

Evening meal 1900 (last orders 2030)
Bedrooms: 2 single, 8 double, 8 twin, 8 triple
Bathrooms: 26 private
Parking for 30
Cards accepted: Access, Visa, Amex, Switch/Delta

43 GILPIN LODGE COUNTRY HOUSE HOTEL & RESTAURANT ✿✿✿✿ DE LUXE
Crook Road, Windermere, Cumbria LA23 3NE Tel (015394) 88818 Fax (015394) 88058

Gilpin Lodge is a small family-run elegant, yet unpretentious, country house hotel and restaurant set in twenty acres of gardens and woodlands and close to the moors. Two miles from Lake Windermere and near the golf course, it has sumptuous bedrooms, some with four-posters. Fresh flowers, antiques and pictures abound. The food at Gilpin Lodge is a pleasant obsession! The wine list features over one-hundred-and-seventy wines, and the service is attentive and friendly.

Bed & Breakfast per night: single occupancy from
£50.00–£80.00; double room from £80.00–£120.00
Half board per person: £45.00–£75.00 daily;
£280.00–£490.00 weekly
Lunch available: 1200–1430

Evening meal 1900 (last orders 2045)
Bedrooms: 7 double, 1 twin, 1 triple
Bathrooms: 9 private
Parking for 40
Cards accepted: Access, Visa, Diners, Amex, Switch/Delta

44 LINDETH FELL COUNTRY HOUSE HOTEL ⚜⚜⚜⚜ HIGHLY COMMENDED
Windermere, Cumbria LA23 3JP Tel (015394) 43286 or 44287

A charming lakeland country house in magnificent gardens above Lake Windermere where you can wander through tranquil grounds enjoying brilliant views. Relax in stylish surroundings and delight in superb English cooking in a warm and friendly atmosphere, at highly competitive prices. Lawns are laid for tennis, croquet and putting, and Windermere Golf Club is one mile away. Good fishing is available free and interesting walks start from the door. Call for a brochure from the resident owners.

Bed & Breakfast per night: single room from £41.00–£57.50; double room from £79.00–£95.00
Half board per person: £49.50–£57.50 daily; £339.00–£380.00 weekly
Lunch available: 1230–1400 pre–booked

Evening meal 1930 (last orders 2030)
Bedrooms: 2 single, 5 double, 5 twin, 2 triple
Bathrooms: 14 en-suite
Parking for 20
Open: March–November

Cards accepted: Access, Visa

45 FIR TREES ⚜⚜ HIGHLY COMMENDED
Lake Road, Windermere, Cumbria LA23 2EQ Tel (015394) 42272 Fax (015394) 42272

Ideally situated midway between Windermere and Bowness villages, Fir Trees offers luxurious bed & breakfast in a Victorian guesthouse of considerable character and charm. Antiques and beautiful prints abound in the public areas, while the bedrooms are immaculately furnished and decorated. Breakfasts are simply scrumptious and the hospitality genuinely warm and friendly. As one might expect, Fir Trees is enthusiastically recommended by leading guides while providing exceptional value for money. (Evening meals are not available.)

Bed & Breakfast per night: single occupancy from £24.50–£30.50; double room from £39.00–£51.00
Bedrooms: 5 double, 1 twin, 1 triple

Bathrooms: 7 en-suite
Parking for 8
Cards accepted: Access, Visa, Amex

46 HAWKSMOOR ⚜⚜⚜ HIGHLY COMMENDED
Lake Road, Windermere, Cumbria LA23 2EQ Tel (01539) 442110

Ideally situated mid-way between and within easy walking distance of the villages of Bowness and Windermere. We offer traditional English home cooking and an optional evening meal (licensed). All rooms are en-suite, some with four-poster beds for that special occasion. Backed by woodland and a superb private car park with no steps or ramps. Some ground-floor rooms have level access to lounge and dining area. Off-season breaks, weekly rates or overnight stays welcome. Now in fourteenth year with same resident proprietors.

Bed & Breakfast per night: single occupancy from £20.00–£35.00; double room from £40.00–£62.00
Half board per person: £30.50–£41.50 daily; £205.00–£262.00 weekly
Evening meal 1830 (last bookings 1730)

Bedrooms: 7 double, 3 triple
Bathrooms: 10 en-suite
Parking for 12
Cards accepted: Access, Visa

47 BURROW HALL COUNTRY GUESTHOUSE ⚑⚑⚑ HIGHLY COMMENDED
Plantation Bridge, Kendal, Cumbria LA8 9JR Tel (01539) 821711

Built in 1648, Burrow Hall has been extended to provide modern comforts, including a television lounge, yet the principal lounge maintains original oak beams and a log fire. Paul and Honor Brind are congenial hosts who enjoy having guests in their home. The set main course for dinner is complemented by a mouth-watering range of starters and puddings and a small wine list. Breakfast is also impressive, offering a good selection of dishes.

Half board per person: £35.00–£37.00 daily;
£220.00–£235.00 weekly
Evening meal 2000 (last bookings 1900)
Bedrooms: 1 double, 2 twin

Bathrooms: 3 private
Parking for 8
Cards accepted: Access, Visa

48 CLARENCE HOUSE COUNTRY HOTEL AND RESTAURANT ⚑⚑⚑⚑ HIGHLY COMMENDED
Skelgate, Dalton-in-Furness, Cumbria LA15 8BQ Tel (01229) 462508 Fax 01229 467177

Clarence House is an elegant late Victorian mansion, luxuriously furnished to the taste of its owner, set in three acres of its own grounds overlooking a beautiful wooded valley. Seventeen centrally heated bedrooms luxuriously decorated, offer only the finest accommodation; dine in beautiful surroundings served by our friendly welcoming staff. Our à la carte five-course speciality and famous carvery offer even the most discerning diner a superb choice. "Quite simply the best."

Bed & Breakfast per night: single occupancy from
£45.00–£60.00; double room from £50.00–£80.00
Evening meal 1830 (last orders 2130)
Bedrooms: 14 double, 3 twin

Bathrooms: 17 en-suite
Parking for 40
Cards accepted: Access, Visa, Amex, Switch, Diners

49 HORNBY HALL COUNTRY HOUSE   Listed HIGHLY COMMENDED
Brougham, Penrith, Cumbria CA10 2AR Tel (01768) 891114 or Mobile (0831) 482108

Hornby Hall is a 16th-century farmhouse still with its original tower and spiral staircase. The house has been restored to provide comfortable accommodation; meals are served in the Great Hall, using fresh local food. We are ideally situated for trips to the Lakes, Dales, Hadrian's Wall and Carlisle which has a good shopping centre, interesting castle and a superb museum. Ride on the famous Carlisle–Settle railway or fish quietly on Hornby's own stretch of water.

Bed & Breakfast per night: single room from
£15.00–£28.00; double room from £52.00–£58.00
Half board per person: £28.00–£44.50 daily;
£186.00–£311.50 weekly
Evening meal 1900 (last orders 2100)

Bedrooms: 2 single, 2 double, 3 twin
Bathrooms: 2 en-suite, 3 private
Parking for 10
Cards accepted: Access, Visa

50 APPLEBY MANOR COUNTRY HOUSE HOTEL   HIGHLY COMMENDED
Roman Road, Appleby-in-Westmorland, Cumbria CA16 6JB   Tel (017683) 51571   Fax (017683) 52888

Probably the most relaxing and friendly hotel you'll ever stay at! Set amidst breathtaking beauty, you'll find high-quality accommodation; satellite television and video films; a splendid little indoor leisure club that has a small swimming pool, jacuzzi, steam-room, sauna and sunbed; magnificent lounges, and great food in the award-winning restaurant – all in a genuine country house. Golf, squash, horse-riding and all the delights of the Lake District and Yorkshire Dales are close by.

Bed & Breakfast per night: single occupancy from £58.00–£64.00; double room from £86.00–£98.00 Half board per person: £49.50–£72.00 daily; £297.00–£432.00 weekly Lunch available: 1200–1400 (but flexible)

Evening meal 1900 (last orders 2100) Bedrooms: 11 double, 11 twin, 1 triple, 7 family rooms Bathrooms: 30 en-suite Parking for 51 Cards accepted: Access, Visa, Diners, Amex, Switch/Delta

51 MEABURN HILL FARM   Listed HIGHLY COMMENDED
Meaburn Hill, Maulds Meaburn, Penrith, Cumbria CA10 3HN   Tel (01931) 715205   Fax (01931) 715205

Escape to a hidden valley and relax at our beautifully-restored, 16th-century Yeomans farmhouse, quietly situated near Appleby-in-Westmorland. Lovely antique-furnished rooms overlook the tranqil river and village green. Sink into chairs in front of a roaring fire to enjoy afternoon tea and a good book. Awake refreshed to relish a superb breakfast and ever-changing colours of our little valley lost in Eden. Totally non-smoking.

Bed & Breakfast per night: double room from £38.00–£44.00 Bedrooms: 2 double, 1 twin (all with private facilities)

Bathrooms: 3 private Parking for 3 Open: April–November

52 AUGILL HOUSE FARM   HIGHLY COMMENDED
Brough, Kirkby Stephen, Cumbria CA17 4DX   Tel (017683) 41305

A hill farm in the Eden Valley, ideal for visiting the Lakes, Dales and Northern Pennines. In our lovely conservatory overlooking the garden you can start the day with a super breakfast and return in the evening to a complimentary glass of sherry. Savour the delights of fresh salmon, trout, local beef, lamb or pork, and real old-fashioned puddings. Stay with us and be spoilt – you won't be disappointed!

Half board per person: £29.00 daily; £175.00–£185.00 weekly Evening meal 1900

Bedrooms: 2 double, 1 twin Bathrooms: 3 en-suite Parking for 6

53 HIPPING HALL
⬙⬙⬙ HIGHLY COMMENDED

Cowan Bridge, Kirkby Lonsdale, Cumbria LA6 2JJ Tel (01524) 271187 Fax (01524) 272452

Hipping Hall is a 17th-century country house, set in four acres of walled gardens, on the Cumbria/Yorkshire border and an ideal location from which to tour both the Lakes and Dales. With comfortable well-equipped en-suite rooms, most furnished with antiques, guests dine together in informal house-party style in the Great Hall. All dishes are freshly prepared with home and local produce. Private house-parties arranged for five/seven couples from October to April. Special-break rates available all year.

Bed & Breakfast per night: single occupancy from £62.00;
double room from £78.00
Half board per person: £52.50 daily
Evening meal 2000 (last bookings 2000)
Bedrooms: 5 double, 2 twin

Bathrooms: 7 en-suite
Parking for 12
Open: February–December
Cards accepted: Access, Visa, Amex

54 DERVAIG GUEST HOUSE
⬙⬙ HIGHLY COMMENDED

1 North Road, Berwick-upon-Tweed, Northumberland TD15 1PW Tel (01289) 307378

Dervaig is a superb Victorian house set in beautiful gardens in a quiet part of town. The house is immaculate, retaining many original features, and is furnished with traditional and antique furniture. Bedrooms are large: all have television, armchairs, tea/coffee making facilities, etc. Guests are welcome to enjoy the lovely gardens and fishpond. Breakfasts are served in the elegant dining room which features an interesting plate collection. Gentle five-minute stroll into town along the banks of the River Tweed. Two minutes from Berwick-upon-Tweed railway station.

Bed & Breakfast per night: single occupancy from
£20.00–£30.00; double room from £35.00–£50.00
Bedrooms: 2 double, 2 twin, 1 triple

Bathrooms: 3 private, 2 private showers
Parking for 8

55 MARSHALL MEADOWS COUNTRY HOUSE HOTEL
⬙⬙⬙⬙ HIGHLY COMMENDED

Berwick-upon-Tweed, Northumberland TD15 1UT Tel (01289) 331133 Fax (01289) 331438

The most northerly hotel in England, this elegant Georgian mansion house is set in fifteen acres of woodland and pastures, within ten minutes drive from the heart of Berwick. We offer a family restaurant, a superb à la carte restaurant, comfortable bar and residents' lounge with open log fires overlooking the patio, a croquet lawn and petanque pistes. For the more active there is also an all-weather tennis court and woodland walks. All rooms are individually designed with en-suite facilities. Special break packages available.

Bed & Breakfast per night: single room from £55.00;
double room from £68.00
Half board per person: £50.00–£50.00 daily; £45.00–£45.00
weekly
Evening meal 1900 (last orders 2200)

Bedrooms: 3 single, 6 double, 9 twin
Bathrooms: 18 en-suite
Parking for 50
Cards accepted: Access, Visa

56 MIDDLE ORD MANOR HOUSE

≋≋ DE LUXE

Middle Ord Farm, Berwick-upon-Tweed, Northumberland TD15 2XQ Tel (01289) 306323

Mrs Gray offers quality accommodation within her Grade II listed farmhouse on a working farm with a very comprehensive breakfast menu served in a gracious dining-room. Two residents lounges (one no smoking) and secluded gardens with all day access. The en-suite or handbasin-only bedrooms include a four-poster bedroom if desired. Come and enjoy the ambience of such a high standard in our truly friendly home. Sorry, no children or pets.

Bed & Breakfast per night: single occupancy from £18.00–£23.00; double room from £36.00–£46.00
Bedrooms: 2 double, 1 twin

Bathrooms: 2 en-suite, 1 private
Parking for 3
Open: April–October

Berwick-upon-Tweed Superlatives and Peculiarities

BERWICK-UPON-TWEED has a clutch of superlatives and peculiarities to its name. First is its geographical position; the most northerly town in England, it is, remarkably, further north than Port Ellen on the Hebridean island of Islay, and further west than Poole in Dorset. Berwick is also cut off from the county which bears its name: Berwickshire lies in Scotland. The town's football team even plays in the Scottish league.

Berwick's history is intractably bound up with the struggle between England and its neighbour to the north. Between 1147 and 1482 the town changed hands on no less than 13 occasions, so it might not be too surprising that Queen Victoria should officially be called 'Queen of Great Britain, Ireland, Berwick-upon-Tweed and the British Dominions beyond the seas'. This, claimed Peterborough in a 1935 edition of the *Daily Telegraph,* was how she signed the declaration of war against Russia in 1854. The ensuing peace treaty two years later, apparently made no mention of Berwick, leaving the town at war with Russia until this oversight was rectified by the Foreign Office in 1914, concluding Berwick's 'Sixty Years' War'.

Had there been any truth in the story – Victoria never signed herself as reported – Berwick would have been admirably prepared for a Russian invasion. Because Elizabeth I was fearful of a combined Scots–French force, the town walls, the most complete from the 16th century in northern Europe, were comprehensively fortified, but never actually saw a shot fired in anger, hence their amazing state of preservation. Within the walls lie the greatest concentration of preserved buildings (for a town of its size) anywhere in England.

Amongst the listed buildings are the first purpose-built barracks (designed by the architect-cum-playwright, Vanbrugh) and Holy Trinity Church (1652) one of only two surviving churches built during the Commonwealth Period.

One other peculiarity of Berwick is the fact that this church, built in restrained Puritan style with neither tower nor steeple, resembles a town hall, while Berwick's town hall, complete with spire and peal of bells, resembles a church...

The town walls, Berwick-upon-Tweed

57 TREE TOPS

~~~ DE LUXE

The Village Green, East Ord, Berwick-upon-Tweed, Northumberland TD15 2NS Tel (01289) 330679

Come and be pampered in our spacious, single-storey home of character, elegantly furnished, in a peaceful village just two miles from Berwick. Enjoy wonderful home cooking and fresh garden produce. Breakfasts with extensive choice and candle-lit dinners are served in a licensed dining-room overlooking a superb mature garden with croquet lawn, summer-houses and stream. This haven of tranquillity and personal service features residents' lounge and beautiful en-suite bedrooms. Sorry, no smoking, children or pets.

Bed & Breakfast per night: single occupancy from £26.00–£28.00; double room from £42.00–£46.00
Half board per person: £34.00–£36.00 daily;
£222.00–£236.00 weekly
Evening meal 1900 (last orders 1700)

Bedrooms: 1 double, 1 twin
Bathrooms: 2 en-suite
Parking for 4
Open: April–October

58 TILLMOUTH PARK HOTEL

~~~~ HIGHLY COMMENDED

Cornhill-on-Tweed, Northumberland TD12 4UU Tel (01890) 882255 Fax (01890) 882540

A secluded country mansion set in fifteen acres of mature parkland, Tillmouth Park typifies a more leisured age, and is an ideal centre for country pursuits, fishing, shooting and, of course, golf. All our en-suite bedrooms are individually furnished to the highest standards and our spacious public rooms have open log fires burning to create a relaxing ambience. Our library restaurant offers fresh local produce which is complemented by our extensive wine list.

Bed & Breakfast per night: single occupancy from £62.50–£75.00; double room £115.00–£135.00
Half board per person: £79.00–£87.50 daily
Lunch available: 1200–1345
Evening meal 1930 (last orders 2045)

Bedrooms: 6 double, 6 twin, 1 triple
Bathrooms: 13 private
Parking for 50
Cards accepted: Access, Visa, Diners, Amex

59 BLUE BELL HOTEL

~~~~ HIGHLY COMMENDED

Market Place, Belford, Northumberland NE70 7NE Tel (01668) 213543 Fax (01668) 213787

Perfectly situated between Northumberland's beautiful coastline and the magnificent national parks of the Cheviot Hills, this former coaching inn makes the ideal base for discovering the Northern Border region. Known for its excellent food and delightful en-suite bedrooms, the Blue Bell offers a choice of three restaurants and two bars with efficient, friendly service. Privately owned for the past eight years, the hotel has been extensively refurbished to provide superb accommodation for the discerning visitor.

Bed & Breakfast per night: single room from £38.00–£42.00; double room from £35.00–£46.00
Half board per person: £46.00–£58.00 daily;
£300.00–£400.00 weekly
Lunch available: 1200–1400

Evening meal 1830 (last orders 2100)
Bedrooms: 1 single, 8 double, 8 twin
Bathrooms: 17 en-suite
Parking for 10
Cards accepted: Access, Visa, Amex

60 WAREN HOUSE HOTEL

👑👑👑👑 HIGHLY COMMENDED

Waren Mill, Belford, Northumberland NE70 7EE Tel (01668) 214581 Fax (01668) 214484

A traditional 18th-century country house set in six acres of well-tended, wooded grounds and a walled garden, on the edge of Budle Bay overlooking Holy Island. Anita & Peter Laverack have created a haven of peace and tranquillity for adults who enjoy good food, wine and excellent accommodation. The magnificent spacious dining room overlooks Lindisfarne, while the drawing room looks over the Cheviot Hills. The service from local staff is friendly, efficient and discreet.

Bed & Breakfast per night: single occupancy from £74.00–£94.00; double room from £104.00–£154.00
Half board per person: £74.50–£99.50 daily; £862.00–£1162.00 weekly
Evening meal 1900 (last orders 2030)

Bedrooms: 3 double, 2 twin, 2 double suites
Bathrooms: 7 en-suite
Parking for 25
Cards accepted: Access, Visa, Diners, Amex, Switch/Delta

Cragside

CRAGSIDE is an odd combination of whimsical romanticism and solid Victorian practicality. Perched on the rocky Northumbrian hillside like some medieval Bavarian castle, it was, in fact, the most modern house of its day, the first in the world to be lit by water-generated electricity.

Cragside's creator was the great Victorian inventor, engineer and gunmaker, William Armstrong. It was not until 1863 when Armstrong was 52 years old, that he could spend sufficient time away from his business near Newcastle to build a summer retreat in the Debdon Valley. The spot chosen for the house was a dramatic one; a vast bare rocky hillside with the Debdon burn running far below. The original building was relatively modest, but as Armstrong spent more time there, he began to enlarge it in a piecemeal way. It is a testament to the skill (and patience) of the architect, Richard Norman Shaw, that after 15 years of gradual additions, the final building is such a unified, if somewhat eccentric-looking whole.

The design of the house was influenced in part by the technological innovations that Armstrong insisted on bringing to Cragside. When a water shortage occurred in 1865, for example, he arranged for the Debdon burn to be dammed in order to form a reservoir, then had a hydraulic ram installed to pump water to a tank at the top of the house. The house was fitted with every labour-saving device possible, including a special water-powered engine to turn the spits in the kitchen and a hydraulic lift to carry coal to the top of the house. In around 1878 the first electric lights were installed to illuminate pictures in the new gallery; two years later

lamps were fitted throughout the house.

Armstrong lived at Cragside until his death (aged 90) in 1900 and almost until the day he died he continued to plan further innovations for the house (tel. 01669 20333).

William Armstrong with his first wife and children

61 NORTH COTTAGE

HIGHLY COMMENDED

Birling, Warkworth, Morpeth, Northumberland **NE65 0XS Tel (01665) 711263**

Situated on the outskirts of the historic coastal village of Warkworth, North Cottage is an ideal base from which to explore Northumberland with its superb beaches, castles, scenery and golf courses. Our ground floor en-suite bedrooms have colour television, hospitality trays, central heating and electric overblankets. A full breakfast is served in the dining room and there is a sitting room to relax in, or a large well-kept garden to wander around in. Weekly rates available. Totally non-smoking.

Bed & Breakfast per night: single room from £17.00–£18.00; double room from £34.00–£36.00
Bedrooms: 1 single, 2 double, 1 twin

Bathrooms: 3 en-suite, 1 public
Parking for 8

62 LINDEN HALL HOTEL AND HEALTH SPA

DE LUXE

Longhorsley, Morpeth, Northumberland **NE65 8XF Tel 01670 516611 Fax 01670 788544**

Linden Hall is a superb Georgian Country House set in four-hundred-and-fifty acres just twenty minutes north of Newcastle-upon-Tyne. All fifty bedrooms are individually furnished, some with four-poster beds. The award-winning Dobson Restaurant uses the finest of local produce, with the Old Granary Restaurant and Linden Pub offering a more relaxed alternative. Leisure facilities include indoor swimming pool, fitness room, beauty spa, steam room, snooker, fishing, croquet and putting.

Bed & Breakfast per night: single room from £97.50–£102.50; double room from £125.00–£260.00
Half board per person: £77.50–£95.00 daily; £542.50–£665.00 weekly
Evening meal 1900 (last orders 2130)

Bedrooms: 9 single, 20 double, 17 twin, 4 triple
Bathrooms: 50 en-suite
Parking for 300
Cards accepted: Access, Visa, Amex, Switch/Delta, Diners

63 WESTFIELD HOUSE

HIGHLY COMMENDED

Bellingham, Hexham, Northumberland **NE48 2DP Tel (01434) 220340**

Good old-fashioned hospitality in a peaceful setting. If beautiful bedrooms, including a four-poster, cosy fire-side and candle-lit dinners and a true welcome are for you, then come and be spoilt! This is real get-away-from-it-all country, where three cars make a traffic jam. Within visiting distance are hills, lakes, forest, sea beaches and castles, and the ancient Hadrian's Wall and Armstrong's Cragside are also there to visit. Partake in October–April's three-nights-for-the-price-of-two break (Easter excluded). A non-smoking establishment.

Bed & Breakfast per night: single occupancy from £18.00–£26.00; double room from £36.00–£52.00
Half board per person: £32.00–£40.00 daily; £218.00–£270.00 weekly
Evening meal 1930

Bedrooms: 2 double, 2 twin, 1 family room
Bathrooms: 2 en-suite, 1 public
Parking for 8
Cards accepted: Access, Visa

64 WEST CLOSE HOUSE

Hextol Terrace, Hexham, Northumberland NE46 2AD Tel (01434) 603307

🌊🌊 HIGHLY COMMENDED

Situated in a quiet leafy cul-de-sac only a ten-minute stroll from the centre of historic Hexham, West Close House is a charming detached 1920s villa, lovingly maintained and tastefully furnished. All bedrooms, the dining room and the elegant drawing room overlook the delightfully secluded gardens which feature a revolving summer-house. Careful attention to detail, wholesome food, warm hospitality and every comfort ensure a memorable stay. A non-smoking establishment.

Bed & Breakfast per night: single room from £17.50–£19.00; double room from £35.00–£46.00
Bedrooms: 2 single, 1 double, 1 triple

Bathrooms: 1 en-suite, 1 public
Parking for 5

Pele Towers

NORTHUMBERLAND, on the border between Scotland and England, is frontier country. For centuries it was the scene of border conflict with its far from friendly neighbour, and peace finally arrived only with the Act of Union in 1707. Its wild and lawless nature had a dramatic effect upon its architecture; for centuries it was crucial that every dwelling place was fortified against hostile invaders and as a result the county abounds in fortresses and castles of all varieties.

A large proportion of these fortified buildings was constructed in the 14th century. In 1296 Edward I had begun a campaign which was the start of three centuries of hostilities

between England and Scotland. After the Scottish victory at Bannockburn in 1314 the Northumbrians felt particularly vulnerable. The nobility built or strengthened their castles, but the lesser nobility built pele towers. These fulfilled the role of a small manor house in the Northumbrian village, but because of the need for protection, they were built four square and strongly fortified, with immensely thick walls, small impenetrable windows, and crenelated battlements.

At Belsay Hall (EH), about 10 miles north-west of Newcastle, the ruins of an earlier Jacobean mansion adjoin a magnificent pele tower. The town of Corbridge boasts two pele towers. As at Belsay, one, built in about 1600, is part of Low Hall, an impressive Jacobean house at the east end of Main Street. The other is much older, dating from around 1300. Now a tourist information centre, it stands near St Andrew's Church, and was originally built to protect the local clergyman. There are several of these so called 'parsons' peles' in Northumberland; another particularly fine example is at Elsdon, which, although modernised, continued to be used as a rectory until 1962.

Belsay Castle, Northumberland

65 LOW STEAD

Wark, Hexham, Northumberland NE48 3DP Tel (01434) 230352

HIGHLY COMMENDED

Low Stead was formally a 16th-century bastle house (fortified farmhouse) and is now a haven of peace set deep in unspoilt countryside in the National Park, between Hadrian's Wall and Kielder. Imaginatively-produced meals are served in the oak-beamed dining room. The call of the curlew and the sheep on the fells are the loudest sounds to be heard. Solitude, history and comfort combine to create Low Stead's unique atmosphere. Packed lunches available. A non-smoking house.

Bed & Breakfast per night: single occupancy from £22.50–£25.00; double room from £45.00
Half board per person: £36.00–£38.50 daily; £223.50–£223.50 weekly

Evening meal 1900 (last orders 2000)
Bedrooms: 1 double, 1 twin
Bathrooms: 2 en-suite
Parking for 6

66 NEW KENT HOTEL

HIGHLY COMMENDED

127 Osborne Road, Jesmond, Newcastle upon Tyne, Tyne and Wear NE2 2TB Tel (0191) 281 1083 Fax (0191) 281 3369

Why not enjoy the renowned warm Geordie hospitality whilst combining the old and new: visit historic castles, cathedrals or Hadrian's Wall or spend a day in Europe's finest and largest indoor shopping centre. View areas of outstanding natural beauty in Northumbria's National Park including Kielder Forest, and enjoy water sports facilities in Europe's biggest man-made forest and reservoir complex. See wonderful coastal areas including Holy Island, Bamburgh Castle or tour the picturesque border country with its many stately homes.

Bed & Breakfast per night: single room from £29.00–£69.00; double room from £59.00–£79.00
Evening meal 1830 (last orders 2230)
Bedrooms: 16 single, 9 double, 3 twin, 4 triple

Bathrooms: 32 private
Parking for 45
Cards accepted: Access, Visa, Diners, Amex, Switch/Delta

67 BEE COTTAGE FARM

HIGHLY COMMENDED

Castleside, Consett, County Durham DH8 9HW Tel (01207) 508224

A working farm set in peaceful surroundings with access to quiet pleasant walks and unspoilt views. Visitors are welcome to help with the animals that are mainly baby calves, lambs, etc. The farm is ideally situated for visits to Beamish Museum, Durham Cathedral, Hadrian's Wall or as an overnight break in a long journey. There are some ground-floor rooms, a tearoom open daily between 1100 and 1800, and an evening meal is available. No smoking in main farmhouse.

Bed & Breakfast per night: single room from £22.00; double room from £36.00
Half board per person: £33.00 daily; £230.00 weekly
Evening meal 1915 (last orders 2130)

Bedrooms: 1 single, 3 double, 2 twin, 1 triple, 2 family rooms
Bathrooms: 4 en-suite, 3 public
Parking for 20

68 CRAKEMARSH
Listed HIGHLY COMMENDED

Mill Lane, Plawsworth Gate, Chester-Le-Street, County Durham DH2 3LG Tel (0191) 371 2464

Crakemarsh is a lovely dormer bungalow with panoramic views, voted the 1990 ETB 'Guesthouse of the Year'. All rooms have colour television, hot and cold running water, tea/coffee making facilities; a comfortable television lounge offers relaxing scenic views over the local countryside. Crakemarsh is ideally located for visiting the historic city of Durham, Beamish Museum and many more places of interest and is just a short journey away from the Northumbria coastline.

Bed & Breakfast per night: single occupancy from £23.00–£25.00; double room from £35.00–£35.00. Evening meal 1800 (last orders 1900)

Bedrooms: 1 double, 1 triple
Bathrooms: 1 private shower
Parking for 4

69 BRECKON HILL COUNTRY GUEST HOUSE
HIGHLY COMMENDED

Westgate-in-Weardale, County Durham DL13 1PD Tel (01388) 517228

Located high in the North Pennines with stunning views over Weardale, our guest house is a tranquil resting place. We offer good wholesome foods and wines in our comfortable dining room, served with our personal care and consideration. Our walled garden, filled with herbaceous flowers and shrubs, awaits your leisurely tread on its meandering paths. The cool dappled light of the conservatory is a welcoming refuge after a day's exploring this beautiful region. No smoking.

Bed & Breakfast per night: single occupancy from £27.00; double room from £40.00. Half board per person: £34.00 daily; £212.00 weekly. Evening meal 1900

Bedrooms: 3 double, 3 twin
Bathrooms: 6 en-suite
Parking for 6

70 WESTGATE HOUSE
HIGHLY COMMENDED

Westgate-in-Weardale, Bishop Auckland, County Durham DL13 1LW Tel (01388) 517564

Deep in the North Pennines' area of outstanding natural beauty is Westgate House, an elegant Victorian country home with a large secluded garden on the banks of the River Wear. In an informal atmosphere, guests may relax in between visiting the many and varied delights of Northumbria. We offer North Country hospitality and a menu featuring local game and produce. We welcome dogs and well-behaved children.

Bed & Breakfast per night: single occupancy from £20.00; double room from £40.00. Half board per person: £32.00 daily; £201.60 weekly. Evening meal 1900

Bedrooms: 1 double, 2 twin
Bathrooms: 2 private, 1 private shower
Parking for 4
Open: April–September

71 GREENHEAD COUNTRY HOUSE HOTEL

〜〜 HIGHLY COMMENDED

Fir Tree, Crook, County Durham DL15 8BL Tel (01388) 763143

Greenhead Hotel is perfectly situated at the centre of rural Durham countryside and at the foot of Weardale, just fifteen minutes from Durham city, surrounded by open fields and woodland. The tranquillity of Greenhead is complemented by the fact that only private resident guests are catered for (no public bars or disco's). The accolades, describing why Greenhead offers something special in the way of service and accommodation, can be seen in our full-colour brochure.

Bed & Breakfast per night: single room £35.00; double room £45.00–£50.00
Bedrooms: 1 single, 4 double, 2 twin, 1 four-poster (2 ground-floor garden rooms available)

Bathrooms: 6 private
Parking for 15
Cards accepted: Access, Visa

Saint Cuthbert and Early Christianity

'**H**ALF CHURCH OF GOD, half castle 'gainst the Scot' goes the old saying about Durham. This potent mixture of spirituality and violent struggle also serves as an accurate description of the early years of Christianity in the north-east of England, and is the reason for Durham's magnificent cathedral, perched high on a rock almost encircled by a loop of the River Wear.

Aidan, created Bishop of Northumbria in 635, and his successor, Cuthbert, both exerted great influence on the spread of Christianity. Northumbria's religious

headquarters were on the tidal island of Lindisfarne, and it seems probable that during Cuthbert's time as bishop he oversaw one of the crowning achievements of the first millennium, the exquisitely ornate Lindisfarne Gospels. Cuthbert, perhaps the most spiritual of early English saints, found even the remoteness of Lindisfarne too worldly, and after 12 years he escaped to the greater isolation of the Farne Islands. For his last years he lived the hermit's life, his befriending of the native eider ducks doubtless leading to his reputation as the English St Francis. (To this day, they are known as 'cuddy ducks' in his honour.) A 14th-century chapel built to the memory of the saint, as well as his ducks, can still be seen on Inner Farne.

Cuthbert's body, brought back to Lindisfarne for burial, soon gained the status of a valued relic. When the Danes began raiding the north-east coast in the 8th century the monks forsook their exposed religious outpost for the inland stronghold of Norham, on the Tweed near Berwick – and they took Cuthbert with them. And there he probably stayed until the latter half of the 10th century, when Danish raids threatened the monks' safety once again. So began an unhappy century of wandering in which the Lindisfarne monks traipsed around Northumbria, before eventually lighting upon the bend in the River Wear, where the much-travelled bones now rest.

The saint's tomb is now a simple affair – a plain slab inscribed with the name 'CUTHBERTUS' – after the original was destroyed in the Reformation.

The Inscription on St. Cuthbert's Tomb – Durham Cathedral

72 THE BRACKEN GUEST HOUSE

HIGHLY COMMENDED

Bank Foot, Shincliffe, Durham, County Durham DH1 2PB   Tel (0191) 386 2966

The Bracken Guest House is a two-minute drive from Durham city centre, on the A177. We provide private parking in our own grounds with a residents' lounge/bar. All our rooms are en-suite and disabled facilities are now available. Customer satisfaction is our priority.

Bed & Breakfast per night: single room from
£25.00–£35.00; double room from £40.00–£60.00
Half board per person: £35.00–£45.00 daily;
£230.00–£350.00 weekly

Evening meal 1900 (last orders 2030)
Bedrooms: 1 single, 5 double, 1 twin
Bathrooms: 7 private
Parking for 12

73 GLENDALE

HIGHLY COMMENDED

Cotherstone, Barnard Castle, County Durham DL12 9UH   Tel (01833) 650384

A delightful bed & breakfast in a beautiful home, with separate dining and sitting rooms, and three double en-suite bedrooms that have tea-making, television, hairdryers and full central heating. Full of character, comfort and personal attention, and situated in superb gardens in a quiet rural setting, with open views on all sides. There are also many choices of quality eating-out places. No pets; no children under 10. Call or write to David or Morlene Rabbitts for a brochure. No smoking.

Bed & Breakfast per night: single occupancy from
£18.00–£22.00; double room from £30.00
Bedrooms: 3 double

Bathrooms: 3 private, 1 public
Parking for 4

74 ELDON HOUSE

HIGHLY COMMENDED

East Green, Heighington, Darlington, County Durham DL5 6PP   Tel (01325) 312270

This is a 17th-century house with spacious bedrooms, overlooking the village green, with a large garden and tennis court. There is ample parking. Easy to find and convenient, it is situated six miles from Darlington railway station, twelve miles from Teesside Airport, three miles from A1(M), and three miles from Newton Aycliffe.

Bed & Breakfast per night: single occupancy from
£25.00–£30.00; double room from £35.00–£40.00
Bedrooms: 3 twin

Bathrooms: 1 en-suite, 2 private
Parking for 6

75 HEADLAM HALL HOTEL

HIGHLY COMMENDED

Headlam, Gainford, Darlington, County Durham DL2 3HA Tel (01325) 730238 Fax (01325) 730790

Set in four acres of grounds and gardens, Headlam Hall offers twenty six en-suite bedrooms, all furnished to high standards. There are two suites, three family rooms and ten four-poster bedrooms; leisure facilities available for guests' include an indoor heated swimming pool, sauna, snooker room, tennis court and fishing. The property is situated in rural surroundings within attractive farmland. Secluded yet easily accessible from motorways and main transport links. A family business offering value and individuality.

Bed & Breakfast per night: single occupancy from £55.00–£75.00; double room from £70.00–£90.00. Half board per person: £53.00–£73.00 daily; £43.00–£63.00 per night weekly
Evening meal 1930 (last orders 2200)

Bedrooms: 16 double, 6 twin, 4 triple
Bathrooms: 26 private
Parking for 60
Cards accepted: Access, Visa, Diners, Amex, Switch/Delta

76 OLD BREWERY GUEST HOUSE

HIGHLY COMMENDED

29 The Green, Richmond, North Yorkshire DL10 4RG Tel (01748) 822460 Fax (01748) 825561

Nestling on the green just off the town centre, close to the River Swale and with marvellous views of the castle high above, The Old Brewery Guest House has a really attractive location. Once an old inn, it has been fully re-furbished in a luxurious Victorian style capturing the essence of a bygone age, whilst retaining all the modern comforts. Pre-theatre snacks for the early Georgian Theatre Royal bookings, packed lunches and evening dinners are available.

Bed & Breakfast per night: single occupancy from £28.00; double room from £38.00–£45.00
Half board per person: £34.00–£37.50 daily

Evening meal 1930 (last bookings 1730)
Bedrooms: 4 double, 1 twin
Bathrooms: 5 private

77 WHASHTON SPRINGS FARM

HIGHLY COMMENDED

Richmond, North Yorkshire DL11 7JS Tel (01748) 822884

If you are looking for a quiet, peaceful stay in beautiful surroundings amidst breathtaking scenery, Gordon & Fairlie Turnbull offer you a warm welcome to their lovely stone-built Georgian farmhouse, three miles from historic Richmond, the gateway to the Dales. Why not start your day with a real farmhouse breakfast and return in the evening to a cosy log fire and delicious home-cooked dinner, using the pick of home-grown and local produce whenever possible?

Bed & Breakfast per night: single occupancy from £26.00–£28.00; double room from £40.00–£44.00
Half board per person: £32.00–£34.00 daily;
£200.00–£210.00 weekly
Evening meal 1900 (last bookings 1400)

Bedrooms: 5 double, 1 twin, 2 triple
Bathrooms: 8 en-suite
Parking for 10
Open: February–December

78 BURGOYNE HOTEL

 DE LUXE

Reeth, Richmond, North Yorkshire DL11 6SN Tel (01748) 884292 Fax (01748) 884292

This listed building has been transformed into an owner-operated small hotel where service is of paramount importance in this lovely setting with unique hospitality. Peaceful and relaxing with beautifully appointed bedrooms and panoramic views, it is ideal for grouse shooting, trout fishing, touring the Northern Dales of Yorkshire, and personalised walking tours. There is ample choice of the highest quality English home cooking using local produce with a personally selected wine list. All diets are catered for.

Bed & Breakfast per night: single occupancy from £55.00–£65.00; double room from £60.00–£75.00
Half board per person: £76.00–£86.00 daily
Evening meal 1930 (last orders 2030)
Bedrooms: 6 double, 2 twin

Bathrooms: 5 en-suite, 3 private
Parking for 6
Open: February–December
Cards accepted: Access, Visa

79 HIGH GREEN HOUSE

HIGHLY COMMENDED

Thoralby, Leyburn, North Yorkshire DL8 3SU Tel (01969) 663420

High Green House offers the discerning visitor comfort, a warm friendly atmosphere and excellent home cooking. The house, a Georgian property, is situated on the edge of Thoralby village green and in the heart of the Yorkshire Dales National Park. There are wide views to enjoy across Bishopdale – a quiet dale just off Wensleydale – and a walled garden to the rear in which to relax. It is an excellent centre for touring and walking in the Dales. A non-smoking establishment.

Bed & Breakfast per night: double room from £40.00–£52.00
Half board per person: £33.50–£40.00 daily; £221.00–£266.00 weekly
Evening meal 1900

Bedrooms: 2 double, 1 twin
Bathrooms: 2 en-suite, 1 private
Parking for 4
Open: April–October
Cards accepted: Access, Visa

80 HAYLOFT SUITE

HIGHLY COMMENDED

Foal Barn, Spennithorne, Leyburn, North Yorkshire DL8 5PR Tel (01969) 22580

A two-hundred-year-old barn, set around a picturesque garden courtyard in a tranquil village by the River Ure, this cottage suite is for the exclusive use of one party of up to four people and offers privacy, peace and comfort. Climb up old stone steps at the private entrance to your own beamed lounge with an open fire. A freshly-cooked breakfast of your choice will be served. Two miles from Leyburn market town and the historical town of Middleham.

Bed & Breakfast per night: single occupancy from £22.00; double room from £44.00
Bedrooms: 1 double, 1 twin

Bathrooms: 1 private
Parking for 1

81 MILLERS HOUSE HOTEL

≋≋≋≋ HIGHLY COMMENDED

Middleham, Wensleydale, North Yorkshire DL8 4NR Tel 0969 22630 (01969 622630 from March) Fax 0969 23570 (01969 623570 from March)

An award-winning luxury hotel set in the historic village of Middleham in the heart of Herriot's Yorkshire Dales where the owners emphasise personal care and attention to detail. The renowned restaurant uses quality local produce, including home-grown herbs and vegetables, and provides an original selection of dishes, including vegetarian choices. Elegant, individually-furnished en-suite rooms, including a luxury four-poster, are decorated in keeping with the Georgian period. Gourmet Wine Weekends, Racing Breaks, Christmas and New Year celebrations are a must. Yorkshire & Humberside Tourist Board 'Hotel of the Year' runner-up.

Bed & Breakfast per night: single room from £34.00–£67.00; double room from £68.00–£85.00	Bedrooms: 1 single, 3 double, 3 twin
Half board per person: £52.50–£62.00 daily; £340.00–£400.00 weekly	Bathrooms: 6 en-suite, 1 private
Evening meal 1915 (last orders 2030)	Parking for 8
	Open: February–December
	Cards accepted: Access, Visa

Wensleydale Cheese

FEW ENGLISH CHEESES can still claim to be both made in the place after which they are named and to use milk from the surrounding area, but Wensleydale is one. Cheese has been made in Wensleydale since the 12th century – and probably even before. It is thought that the original recipe was brought over with the French order of Cistercian monks who built their monastery first at Fors and later at Jervaulx in Lower Wensleydale. For 400 years the monks of Jervaulx continued to make their special cheese. By the time the dissolution forced them to leave, the local farmers' wives had picked up their skills and continued to make cheese in their own dairies and farmhouses. Apart from a change from sheep's to cows' milk in the 17th century, the method is thought to have changed little.

A commercial creamery was first set up in Hawes in 1897 (tel. 01969 667727). It has had something of a troubled history and as recently as 1992 it attracted much media attention when its closure seemed imminent. Adding insult to injury was the announcement that the manufacture of Wensleydale cheese had been transferred to Yorkshire's ancient rival, Lancashire!

The workforce refused to be defeated, however, and the Hawes creamery was finally saved by a management buyout. Since 1994 it has opened to the public and you can watch the long and complicated process of cheese production from viewing galleries above the workfloor. There are a number of stages, each requiring accurate timing and judgement. As the milk gradually sours and coagulates the curds are continually cut, ripped and shredded to expel moisture. Once it has become fairly solid it is packed into moulds which are pressed in a cheese press. The resulting cheese is either sent off to the shops immediately or allowed to mature, creating a stronger fuller flavour.

18th-century cheese making

Mary Evans Picture Library

82 WATERFORD HOUSE

HIGHLY COMMENDED

19 Kirkgate, Middleham, Leyburn, North Yorkshire DL8 4PG Tel (01969) 22090 Fax (01969) 24020

A beautiful traditional stone-built Georgian residence overlooking the market square. Spacious beamed bedrooms, including a four-poster, exquisitely decorated in keeping with the period atmosphere with tea/coffee, fresh milk, sherry, fresh fruit, television, radio, hairdryers and more. The very select restaurant has an à la carte menu that changes daily and over seven hundred vintage wines, many from the 50s and 60s. Many antiques, including a baby grand piano, add to the charm. Somewhere special in the Yorkshire Dales and Herriot country.

Bed & Breakfast per night: single occupancy from £40.00–£50.00; double room from £55.00–£75.00
Half board per person: £45.00–£55.00 daily
Lunch available: 1230–1430
Evening meal 1900 (last orders 2200)

Bedrooms: 3 double, 1 triple, 1 family room
Bathrooms: 3 en-suite, 1 private, 1 en-suite shower
Parking for 8
Cards accepted: Access, Visa, Diners

83 HILLTOP COUNTRY GUEST HOUSE

HIGHLY COMMENDED

Starbotton, Skipton, North Yorkshire BD23 5HY Tel (01756) 760321

Hilltop overlooks the unspoilt village of Starbotton in the heart of the Yorkshire Dales National Park. Superb hill and riverside walks lead from the beck-side gardens of this 17th-century listed farmhouse. Immaculate bedrooms with splendid views and log fires, plus a lively bar all combine with attentive service to create the relaxed air of a country house-party. Menus are chosen from the proprietors' best selling cookery book for candle-lit dinners served in the oak beamed dining room.

Bed & Breakfast per night: double room £58.00
Evening meal 1900
Bedrooms: 2 double, 2 twin, 1 family room

Bathrooms: 5 en-suite
Parking for 7
Open: March–November

84 AMERDALE HOUSE HOTEL

HIGHLY COMMENDED

Arncliffe, Skipton, North Yorkshire BD23 5QE Tel (01756) 770250

Arncliffe, the principal village in Littondale, is a conservation area in the heart of the Yorkshire Dales National Park. Footpaths leave the village for neighbouring Wharfedale, Malhamdale and Langstrothdale, and Pen-Y-Ghent is at the head of the valley. Amerdale House Hotel enjoys open views of the dale and is a haven for those who wish to relax and enjoy the comfort, the caring hospitality and the fine food and wines that make the hotel unique in the Yorkshire Dales.

Half board per person: £53.50–£56.50 daily; £360.50–£381.50 weekly
Evening meal 1900 (last orders 2030)
Bedrooms: 7 double, 3 twin, 1 triple

Bathrooms: 7 private, 4 private shower
Parking for 20
Open: March–November
Cards accepted: Access, Visa

85 LANGCLIFFE COUNTRY GUEST HOUSE 〰〰〰 COMMENDED

Kettlewell, Skipton, North Yorkshire BD23 5RJ Tel (01756) 760243

A traditional Dales stone house in its own grounds with panoramic views, a beautiful garden, and its own car park. Open all year, we have delightful spacious and light en-suite bedrooms, a lounge with a log fire and a conservatory restaurant with unspoilt views, serving home-made food using fresh local produce. Wheelchair access and adapted room. A warm friendly welcome.

Bed & Breakfast per night: single occupancy from £35.00–£40.00; double room from £45.00–£55.00 Half board per person: £39.00–£42.50 daily; £260.00–£285.00 weekly Evening meal 1900 (last orders 2030)

Bedrooms: 2 double, 2 twin, 1 family room Bathrooms: 5 private, 1 private shower Parking for 7 Cards accepted: Access, Visa

Clints and Grikes

LIMESTONE, the predominant stone of much of the Pennines is a hard, sharp rock used widely for house-building and dry-stone walls. Because it is more easily dissolved by water than almost any other commonly occurring rock, limestone gives rise to countryside often characterised by spectacular caverns and underground rivers. Other geological oddities include clints and grikes, which together make up the remarkable phenomenon of a limestone pavement.

Roughly 15,000 years ago, when England was in the grip of the last Ice Age, glaciers scraped the soil from the limestone, exposing the flat surface of the rock to rainwater. As this ran off, it created small runnels which, over time, were eroded into deep slits – or grikes. The rocks left between this network of chasms – the clints – look like large irregular paving stones. They vary in size considerably, and have frequently broken away from the stone beneath, so allowing the

clints to move, sometimes emitting a sinister rumble as you walk on them. If you have trouble remembering which is which, you may wish to think of 'clints clanking' as they move.

The best limestone pavements are to be found in the Yorkshire Dales National Park, most notably at the top of Malham Cove, where the grikes seem to have got the better of the clints, which tend to be rather small and numerous. Other dramatic pavements include the southern spur of Whernside (Scales Moor) and the north-western edge of Ingleborough, both not far from Ingleton in the western Dales. Smaller examples crop up all over this part of the Dales, together with disappearing and reappearing rivers, extensive cave systems and spectacular waterfalls, all typical features of limestone scenery.

Limestone Pavement – Malham, North Yorkshire

86 MANOR HOUSE
De Luxe

Rylstone, Skipton, North Yorkshire BD23 6LH Tel (01756) 730226

This Yorkshire & Humberside White Rose award-winner for the 1994 Bed & Breakfast of the Year is a south-facing, stone-built Manor House which is an excellent base from which to explore the Yorkshire Dales and enjoy the luxury and comforts of a traditional Country House. Surrounded by wonderful countryside, there are several walks starting from the garden. The well-known and award-winning Angel Inn Bar Brasserie & Restaurant at Hetton is only half a mile away.

Bed & Breakfast per night: double room from £50.00–£70.00
Bedrooms: 1 double, 1 twin

Bathrooms: 2 en-suite
Parking for 6

87 DEVONSHIRE ARMS COUNTRY HOUSE HOTEL
De Luxe

Bolton Abbey, Skipton, North Yorkshire BD23 6AJ Tel (01756) 710441 Fax (01756) 710564

Surrounded by the Yorkshire Dales' peace and beauty, Chatsworth antiques add to the country house atmosphere, which is complemented by refreshingly good service and an award-winning restaurant. As well as a choice of outdoor activities, themed or activity breaks, the Devonshire Club offers a range of leisure, health, beauty and therapy facilities. The Devonshire is '92, '93 and '94 Yorkshire & Humberside Tourist Board 'Hotel of the Year' and a '93 English Tourist Board Silver award-winner.

Bed & Breakfast per night: single occupancy from £95.00–£105.00; double room from £120.00–£150.00
Lunch available: 1200–1400
Evening meal 1900 (last orders 2145)

Bedrooms: 21 double, 19 twin
Bathrooms: 40 en-suite
Parking for 150
Cards accepted: Access, Visa, Diners, Amex

88 KNABBS ASH
Highly Commended

Skipton Road, Felliscliffe, Harrogate, North Yorkshire HG3 2LT Tel (01423) 771040 Fax (01423) 771515

A converted stone farmhouse where a warm welcome is always assured, the property has been arranged internally to provide visitors with their own lounge and dining facilities together with three en-suite bedrooms. Knabbs Ash is a family-run bed & breakfast, situated some six miles west of Harrogate, set back from the A59 Skipton Road. Within an area of natural beauty, visitors can enjoy panoramic views of the Nidderdale Valley. A non-smoking household.

Bed & Breakfast per night: single occupancy from £25.00; double room from £40.00
Bedrooms: 2 double, 1 twin

Bathrooms: 3 en-suite
Parking for 6

89 BALMORAL HOTEL & HENRY'S RESTAURANT 🜚🜚🜚🜚 HIGHLY COMMENDED

Franklin Mount, Harrogate, North Yorkshire HG1 5EJ Tel (01423) 508208 Fax (01423) 530652

Keith and Alison Hartwell, the owners and managers, have built a reputation for providing a rather special hotel with the most desirable accommodation in Harrogate: nine four-poster bedrooms and three suites. Henry's, the award-winning restaurant, is open to non-residents and has an extensive cellar. It is ideal for business/conference dinners as it is only a three-minute walk from the Conference and Exhibition Centre. Car park available.

Bed & Breakfast per night: single room from £35.00–£82.00; double room from £60.00–£155.00
Evening meal 1900 (last orders 2100)
Bedrooms: 5 single, 11 double, 4 twin

Bathrooms: 20 private, 1 private shower
Parking for 20
Cards accepted: Access, Visa, Amex

---

90 NUMBER TWENTY SIX 🜚🜚🜚 HIGHLY COMMENDED

26 Harlow Moor Drive, Harrogate, North Yorkshire HG2 0JY Tel (01423) 524729 Fax (01423) 524729

A superb Victorian townhouse overlooking valley gardens. This is an ideal setting, being a short walk from Harrogate centre with parks and woodland on the doorstep. Beautifully decorated throughout, the atmosphere is warm and welcoming – we like our guests to feel really at home. We provide delicious meals at times to suit your schedule. Harrogate is a wonderful base for exploring North Yorkshire. No smoking.

Bed & Breakfast per night: single occupancy from £25.00; double room from £40.00–£45.00
Half board per person: £30.00–£35.00 daily
Evening meal 1900 (last bookings 1600)

Bedrooms: 2 double, 1 twin
Bathrooms: 2 en-suite
Parking for 3

---

91 THE BOAR'S HEAD COUNTRY HOTEL 🜚🜚🜚🜚 HIGHLY COMMENDED

Ripley, Harrogate, North Yorkshire HG3 3AY Tel (01423) 771888 Fax (01423) 771509

Overlooking the cobbled square and village stocks, this historic country house is set at the heart of the Ripley Castle estate. The welcoming de luxe bedrooms with king-size beds are individually designed by Lady Ingilby, and the award-winning restaurant offers the best English cuisine and a fine selection of international wines. The Bistro specialises in pasta and salads and serves a range of Yorkshire ales. Residents enjoy complimentary admission to the glorious grounds and gardens of the Ripley Estate.

Bed & Breakfast per night: single occupancy from £70.00–£95.00; double room from £85.00–£105.00
Half board per person: £65.00–£75.00 daily; £390.00–£450.00 weekly
Lunch available: 1200–1400

Evening meal 1900 (last orders 2130)
Bedrooms: 5 double, 20 twin
Bathrooms: 25 en-suite
Parking for 43
Cards accepted: Access, Visa, Amex

92 PRIMROSE COTTAGE

Listed HIGHLY COMMENDED

Lime Bar Lane, Grafton, York, North Yorkshire YO5 9QJ Tel (01423) 322835 or (01423) 322711 Fax (01423) 323985

A warm friendly welcome awaits at Primrose Cottage, situated between York and Ripon and one mile east of the A1. Comfortable bedrooms with wash-basins and tea/coffee facilities, two bath/shower rooms, a spacious television lounge and a sheltered garden with patio and barbecue for guests' use. Ample parking. Two local inns, a short walk away, serve excellent food. Ideally situated just fifteen minutes north of York, with Ripon, Harrogate and the Yorkshire Dales within easy distance.

Bed & Breakfast per night: double room from
£28.00–£30.00
Bedrooms: 1 double, 2 twin

Bathrooms: 2 bath/shower rooms
Parking for 11

---

93 OLD FARMHOUSE COUNTRY HOTEL & RESTAURANT

HIGHLY COMMENDED

Raskelf, York, North Yorkshire YO6 3LF Tel (01347) 821971 Fax (01347) 822392

An old farmhouse, this small comfortable hotel is ideally situated for the Moors, Dales and York, which is just fifteen miles south. A warm welcome from the resident chef/proprietors, who will provide you with huge Yorkshire breakfasts, home-baked bread, splendid dinners, a speciality English cheese board, fine wines, malt whiskies and en-suite rooms with central heating, television, direct dial phone and a hospitality tray. Short Winter Breaks at reduced rates available. Ring for a brochure and sample menu.

Half board per person: £41.00–£46.00 daily;
£266.00–£301.00 weekly
Evening meal 1900 (last orders 2030)
Bedrooms: 6 double, 1 twin, 3 triple

Bathrooms: 10 private
Parking for 12
Open: February–December

---

94 HALFWAY HOUSE

DE LUXE

Easingwold Road, Crayke, York, North Yorkshire YO6 4TJ Tel (01347) 822614 Fax (01347) 822942

An accent on luxurious surroundings, peaceful countryside and welcoming care is the over-riding feature. Romantic candle-lit dinners, featuring fresh seasonal ingredients, are served in the beautiful oak-panelled dining room. Our all-weather tennis court is there for the energetic, and York, the North Yorkshire Moors, golf and fishing are close by. Feel relaxed and completely pampered....

Bed & Breakfast per night: single occupancy from £40.00;
double room from £60.00–£65.00
Half board per person: £58.00–£60.50 daily;
£375.00–£396.00 weekly
Evening meal 2000

Bedrooms: 2 double, 1 twin
Bathrooms: 3 en-suite
Parking for 13
Cards accepted: Access, Visa

95 FEVERSHAM ARMS HOTEL

🏰🏰🏰🏰 HIGHLY COMMENDED

1 High Street, Helmsley, York, North Yorkshire YO6 5AG Tel (01439) 770766 Fax (01439) 770346

Rebuilt by the Earl of Feversham in 1855 and owned and managed by the Argues family since 1967, this historic coaching inn has been elegantly modernised, retaining its old charm. It is situated on the edge of the North York Moors National Park, central to the Dales, the east coast and the city of York. The award-winning restaurant and wine list, candle-lit dinners, open fires and friendly atmosphere will make your stay an occasion to remember.

Bed & Breakfast per night: single room from £55.00–£65.00; double room from £70.00–£80.00
Half board per person: £40.00–£49.00 daily; £280.00–£343.00 weekly
Evening meal 1900 (last orders 2130)

Bedrooms: 1 single, 7 double, 7 twin, 3 triple
Bathrooms: 18 en-suite
Parking for 30
Cards accepted: Access, Visa, Diners, Amex

96 GREENACRES COUNTRY GUEST HOUSE

🏰🏰 HIGHLY COMMENDED

Amotherby, Malton, North Yorkshire YO17 0TG Tel (01653) 693623 Fax (01653) 693623

A quiet country guesthouse, set in over two-and-a-half acres of gardens and woodlands, with an indoor heated swimming pool. All the bedrooms are en-suite with colour television, tea making and hairdryers. Situated in central Ryedale, it is an ideal base for York, the North Yorkshire Moors and the East Coast. Colour brochure and details on request. Closed mid-November to March.

Bed & Breakfast per night: single room from £23.50–£26.50; double room from £47.00–£53.00
Half board per person: £35.50–£38.50 daily; from £228.00 weekly
Evening meal 1900 (last bookings 1900)

Bedrooms: 1 single, 3 double, 3 twin, 1 triple, 1 family room
Bathrooms: 9 private
Parking for 15
Open: March–November
Cards accepted: Access, Visa

97 NEWSTEAD GRANGE

🏰🏰🏰 HIGHLY COMMENDED

Norton, Malton, North Yorkshire YO17 9PJ Tel (01653) 692502 Fax (01653) 696951

The Grange is an elegant Georgian country house set in two-and-a-half acres of gardens and grounds with delightful views of the North Yorkshire Moors and Wolds. The style of the house is tastefully enhanced by antique furniture, open log fires burn in cooler weather and the bedrooms are individually furnished. The proprietors personally prepare the meals from the produce in the organic kitchen garden and fresh local produce, to a very high standard. Totally non-smoking.

Bed & Breakfast per night: single occupancy from £33.00–£38.00; double room from £59.00–£69.00
Half board per person: £35.00–£48.00 daily; £225.00–£290.00 weekly
Evening meal 1930

Bedrooms: 4 double, 4 twin
Bathrooms: 8 en-suite
Parking for 15
Open: February–December
Cards accepted: Access, Visa

98 GILL HOUSE FARM

🌊🌊🌊 HIGHLY COMMENDED

Tockwith Road, Long Marston, York, North Yorkshire YO5 8PJ Tel (01904) 738379 or Mobile 0850 511140

A peaceful period farmhouse set in glorious countryside overlooking the Vale of York on a five-hundred-acre family farm with horses, cattle, sheep and working sheepdogs. The historic battle ground of Marston Moor is on our doorstep. We pride ourselves on our warm welcome and top-quality service. Our guests' wishes are our prime concern. No smoking in the house.

Bed & Breakfast per night: single occupancy from £30.00; double room from £40.00
Bedrooms: 2 double, 1 triple, 1 family room

Bathrooms: 4 en-suite
Parking for 5

99 MIDDLETHORPE HALL

🌊🌊🌊🌊 DE LUXE

Bishopthorpe Road, York, North Yorkshire YO2 1QB Tel (01904) 641241 Fax (01904) 620176

Standing in twenty-six acres of gardens and parkland close to the heart of the city, Middlethorpe Hall is a distinguished William III house, built in 1699, which has been completely restored and carefully furnished with antiques and fine paintings. Elegant, individually-designed bedrooms and suites are situated in the house and adjacent classical courtyard. Two restaurants offer formal and informal dining. Middlethorpe is ideally situated for discovering the ancient city of York as well as exploring stately homes and the magnificent scenery of the Yorkshire dales and moors.

Bed & Breakfast per night: single room from £92.95–£108.95; double room from £134.90–£148.90
Half board per person: £120.75–£148.90 daily
Lunch available: 1230–1345 (last orders)
Evening meal 1930 (last orders 2145)

Bedrooms: 8 single, 8 double, 12 twin, 2 triple
Bathrooms: 30 private
Parking for 70
Cards accepted: Access, Visa, Amex, Diners

100 YORK PAVILION HOTEL

🌊🌊🌊🌊 HIGHLY COMMENDED

45 Main Street, Fulford, York, North Yorkshire YO1 4PJ Tel (01904) 622099 Fax (01904) 626939

Situated just two miles from the city centre, this privately owned and run Georgian hotel, with the atmosphere of an English country house, offers a haven of peace and tranquillity. The unique decorative style of the Pavilion is wonderfully complemented by the award-winning cuisine, a well-stocked cellar and friendly, efficient but informal service. A perfect place to relax and unwind.

Bed & Breakfast per night: single room from £75.00; double room from £95.00
Half board per person: £57.00–£72.60 daily
Evening meal 1830 (last orders 2130)
Bedrooms: 1 single, 13 double, 7 twin, 2 family rooms

Bathrooms: 23 en-suite
Parking for 45
Cards accepted: Access, Visa, Diners, Amex, Switch/Delta

101 VALLEY VIEW FARM

Old Byland, York, North Yorkshire YO6 5LG Tel (01439) 6221

≋≋ HIGHLY COMMENDED

Friendly, relaxed Yorkshire hospitality in our well-appointed, tastefully-furnished home with open fires and pretty en-suite bedrooms with tea/coffee, television and more. Hearty country breakfasts of delicious traditional farmhouse fare and a good wine list. All this is surrounded by a peaceful cottage garden with beautiful views. Wonderful marked walks to the North Yorkshire Moors – the driest national park in England. Call now and make a booking, or request our colour brochure for more details.

Bed & Breakfast per night: single room from £22.00–£25.00; double room from £40.00–£50.00
Half board per person: £32.00–£37.00 daily; £224.00–£259.00 weekly
Evening meal 1900

Bedrooms: 1 double, 2 twin, 1 family room
Bathrooms: 4 en-suite
Parking for 4
Cards accepted: Access, Visa

Snickelways of York

AS YET, the English dictionary knows no such word as snickelway. Nor, indeed, does a dialect dictionary, though at least this has 'snicket'. 'Snickelway' is, in fact, an amalgam of '*snicke*t', 'ginn*el*' and alley-*way*, all three of which have broadly similar meanings, and was coined in 1983 by one Mark W Jones, a resident of York.

Snickelways have a distinctive feel to them, and are characterised by being narrow passageways which offer a short-cut from one street to another. Most are old – medieval in origin – and many give views of York's finest buildings, but since almost all pre-date the age of the car, perhaps their chief virtue is that they offer an escape from the noise and commotion of motorised transport. (Not that past generations were reluctant to wheel their carts down these snickelways; notches at axle height are a frequent sight.) These notches actually provide a clue to the origin of these intriguing thoroughfares, as does their convergence on St Sampson's Square, for until 1835 this was the site of York's market, and stall-holders' and shoppers' short-cuts over time became snickelways.

Their very names reveal their history: Mad Alice Lane (between Swinegate and Low Petergate) was so called after one Alice Smith who lived here and who was hanged at York Castle in 1825; Hornpot Lane (near by) was where horns were made in the 14th century; Coffee Yard, between Grape Lane and Stonegate, was the site of an old coffee-roasting oven; while the most famous of York's snickelways, The Shambles, recalls not any state of great disorder, but the butchers shops which were once concentrated here (a "shamble" was a table used by a meat vendor). Perhaps the most intriguing name of all belongs to a (very) short street rather than a snickelway, but it is too good to leave out: Whip-ma-whop-ma-gate. Theories of its derivation abound, and include one claim that it was connected to the chastisement of disobedient medieval wives. This seems no less plausible than any other...

A Walk Around the Snickleways of York combines all these various idiosyncratic passageways into a meandering route past York Minster, York Castle, across The Shambles, to the Jorvik Museum, beside the oldest houses in York (Lady Row), never treading the same ground twice.

102 ARNDALE HOTEL

HIGHLY COMMENDED

290 Tadcaster Road, York, North Yorkshire YO2 2ET Tel (01904) 702424

A delightful Victorian house overlooking York's famous race-course with beautiful enclosed walled gardens giving a country house atmosphere within the city. The spacious elegant lounge, complete with antiques, fresh flowers, paintings and a small bar, exudes the charm of a bygone age. The outstanding, thoughtfully-equipped bedrooms are all en-suite. Many bathrooms are Victorian with modern whirlpool baths. Antique half-tester/four-poster beds give an aura of nostalgic luxury. Substantial English breakfast. Large enclosed walled car park.

Bed & Breakfast per night: single occupancy from £29.00–£39.00; double room from £45.00–£55.00
Bedrooms: 6 double, 2 twin, 1 triple

Bathrooms: 9 en-suite
Parking for 20

103 DEAN COURT HOTEL

HIGHLY COMMENDED

Duncombe Place, York, North Yorkshire YO1 2EF Tel (01904) 625082 Fax (01904) 620305

Superbly situated in the shadow of York Minster, the hotel has an unrivalled position in the heart of York. This historic city's main attractions are within walking distance and many tours to Castle Howard, the moors and dales can be arranged by the hotel. Renowned for very friendly service, it boasts an elegant restaurant offering excellent modern food and a delightful tea-room conservatory as well as comfortable lounges. Secure car park with valet service.

Bed & Breakfast per night: single room from £65.00–£75.00; double room from £100.00–£125.00
Lunch available: 1230–1400
Evening meal 1900 (last orders 2130)
Bedrooms: 18 single, 8 double, 10 twin, 4 triple, 2 family rooms

Bathrooms: 41 private
Parking for 30
Cards accepted: Access, Visa, Diners, Amex, Switch/Delta

104 23 ST MARYS

HIGHLY COMMENDED

Bootham, York, North Yorkshire YO3 7DD Tel (01904) 622738

Situated near the heart of the city in a peaceful location to suit the most discerning visitor, "23" is a haven for those who appreciate the elegance and service of a bygone era but with the comforts and individuality of today. Each en-suite bedroom has its own special character furnished with thoughtfulness and care. Rest assured you will be provided with every comfort within our home.

Bed & Breakfast per night: single room from £30.00–£32.00; double room from £48.00–£60.00
Bedrooms: 2 single, 6 double, 1 triple

Bathrooms: 9 en-suite
Parking for 3

105 JUDGES LODGING

☗☗☗☗ HIGHLY COMMENDED

9 Lendal, York, North Yorkshire YO1 2AQ Tel (01904) 623587 or (01904) 638733 Fax (01904) 679947

This early Georgian townhouse, built c1710 and formerly the residence of the Assize court judges, is a Grade I listed building of architectural and historical importance. Set in the very heart of the city, it provides an excellent base to explore the historic city of York. The hotel has twelve en-suite individually furnished rooms, some with four-poster beds, and its own secure private parking for residents. Enjoy candle-lit dinners in the elegant dining rooms.

Bed & Breakfast per night: single room from £65.00–£75.00; double room from £85.00–£130.00
Half board per person: £52.45–£84.95 daily; £472.18–£535.18 weekly
Evening meal 1830 (last orders 2130)

Bedrooms: 2 single, 5 double, 2 twin, 2 triple
Bathrooms: 12 en-suite
Parking for 12
Cards accepted: Access, Visa, Diners, Amex, Switch/Delta

106 HOLMWOOD HOUSE HOTEL

☗☗ HIGHLY COMMENDED

112-114 Holgate Road, York, North Yorkshire YO2 4BB Tel (01904) 626183 Fax (01904) 670899

Close to the city walls, an elegant listed Victorian town house offering a feeling of home with a touch of luxury. All the en-suite bedrooms are different in size and decoration, some with four-poster beds and one has a spa bath; a large proportion of the rooms are set aside for non-smokers. Imaginative breakfasts are served to the sound of gentle classical music. The inviting sitting room, with its open fire, highlights the period style of the house. Car park; on the A59.

Bed & Breakfast per night: single occupancy from £40.00–£50.00; double room from £50.00–£65.00
Bedrooms: 9 double, 2 twin, 1 triple

Bathrooms: 12 en-suite
Parking for 8
Cards accepted: Access, Visa

107 BARFF LODGE

☗☗ HIGHLY COMMENDED

Mill Lane, Brayton, Selby, North Yorkshire YO8 9LB Tel (01757) 213030

Spectacularly positioned and featuring a central courtyard, this unique bungalow was designed and built by the owners. Pleasingly-priced accommodation with private access to all the rooms, offers the discerning guest unequalled quality and the personal attention of the owners. The peaceful countryside location belies the easy accessibility to major roads (M62 is six miles and the A19 Selby/Doncaster is half-a-mile away). Adjacent to Selby Golf Club, there are excellent modestly-priced places to eat nearby. Totally non-smoking.

Bed & Breakfast per night: single occupancy from £25.00; double room from £36.00
Bedrooms: 2 double, 1 twin

Bathrooms: 3 en-suite
Parking for 4
Cards accepted: Access, Visa

108 DUNSLEY HALL

≋≋≋ HIGHLY COMMENDED

Dunsley, Whitby, North Yorkshire YO21 3TL Tel (01947) 893437 Fax (01947) 893505

An elegant country hall in four acres of grounds, three miles north of Whitby in the North Yorkshire Moors National Park. Warm and relaxing, friendly service and good food. All the rooms are en-suite with toiletries and hairdryers, full central heating and open fires; there is also an indoor heated swimming pool, billiard/snooker room, gym, tennis court and putting green. An ideal touring centre for the heritage coast, moors and Captain Cook country.

Bed & Breakfast per night: single occupancy from £36.50–£46.50; double room from £73.00–£83.00 Half board per person: £51.50–£61.50 daily; £325.00–£340.00 weekly Evening meal 2000 (last orders 1900)	Bedrooms: 5 double, 2 twin Bathrooms: 7 en-suite Parking for 10 Cards accepted: Access, Visa	

109 BELMONT

Listed HIGHLY COMMENDED

Ruswarp Bank, Whitby, North Yorkshire YO21 1NF Tel (01947) 602519

A warm welcome awaits you at this beautiful old manor house standing in its own grounds and overlooking the village of Ruswarp and picturesque River Esk. Two well-appointed spacious bedrooms, one with a beautiful large four-poster bed and the other with twin-beds and a balcony (the rooms share a bathroom with shower, fitted out in mahogany), guests' lounge with television and attractive dining room. Handy for the Moors, beaches, North Yorkshire Moor Steam Railway. Goathland and Heartbeat are filmed here. Dedicated to excellence in hospitality. A non-smoking establishment.

Bed & Breakfast per night: four-poster bedroom from £18.00 per person; twin-bedded room from £16.00 per person; single room from £.15.00 Bedrooms: 1 double, 1 twin, 1 single	Bathrooms: 1 public Parking for 3 Open: March–November

The Hand of Glory

AT THE PANNETT MUSEUM (tel. 01947 602 908) in Whitby is a strange and sinister exhibit. Blackened and shrivelled by time, baked as hard as a rock, it is a human hand. Popularly known as Hands of Glory, this and many other amputated hands were believed to have supernatural powers and were used by thieves to protect themselves from discovery while they worked.

The Hand of Glory was a human hand, usually cut from an executed criminal, preserved in accordance with a special recipe.

Bearing aloft his charm, the thief would make his way to the house he planned to rob, sure in his belief that he would be able to carry out his work unhindered. If his victims were asleep, the hand would ensure they stayed asleep; if they were awake, they would be transfixed to the spot with fear or hypnotised by the flame of a candle, stuck between the fingers of the hand. To be on the safe side, the thief took the precaution of reciting a special rhyme. History does not relate how many thefts were carried out in this way, but it is likely that the fearsome reputation of the Hand of Glory meant that its effect on innocent householders was exactly as folklore predicted.

110 WREA HEAD COUNTRY HOTEL ⛁⛁⛁⛁ HIGHLY COMMENDED

Barmoor Lane, Scalby, Scarborough, North Yorkshire YO13 0PB Tel (01723) 378211 or (01723) 371780

Turn left at the duck pond in the village of Scalby and you will find this delightful country house hidden at the end of the drive, in acres of landscaped gardens and grounds with panoramic views. Wrea Head has individual charm and character with oak panelling, open fires, a myriad of books and fine paintings and is well-known for its fine food and wines. When you choose Wrea Head you will find a relaxing, friendly and welcoming stay.

Bed & Breakfast per night: single room from £49.50–£59.50; double room from £99.00–£119.00 Half board per person: £57.50–£67.50 daily; £345.00–£405.00 weekly Lunch available: 1230–1400	Evening meal 1900 (last orders 2115) Bedrooms: 4 single, 8 double, 6 twin, 1 triple, 2 family rooms Bathrooms: 21 private Parking for 101	Cards accepted: Access, Visa, Diners, Amex ⛁⛁⛁⛁⛁⛁⛁⛁⛁⛁⛁ ⛁⛁⛁⛁⛁⛁⛁⛁[SP][晶][T]

Medieval and Georgian Beverley

THE MAJESTIC twin towers of Beverley Minster rise proudly from the surrounding flat pastureland and, visible from miles around, are the most obvious sign of the town's medieval prosperity. At the northern end of the main street lies 14th-century St Mary's Church, originally only a chapel for the larger building but now a church in its own right. Other highlights include an ornate early 18th-century market cross and the 15th-century North Bar. This charming brick structure complete with crow-stepped battlements, built in 1409–10, is the only remaining of five gates in the town walls, which have also disappeared. North Bar Street Without, the street beyond North Bar, is a broad, pleasant thoroughfare with fine Georgian buildings. The fruits of 18th-century wealth can be seen in The Guildhall (established 1500, rebuilt in 1753) where there is a marvellous stucco ceiling.

However, it is for its medieval churches that Beverley is famous. The Minster's exterior, with its elegant twin towers, shows a remarkable continuity of style, despite construction spanning two centuries from about 1220. The glowing golden stone, the medieval stained-glass in the east window, the exquisite skill of the 14th-century stonemason's art as displayed in the magnificently ornate Percy Tomb and the largest number (68) of misericords in England all combine to make Beverley Minster, some believe, the most beautiful church in the entire country.

Misericords – narrow ledges on the underside of a choir stall on which the occupant can support him or herself while standing – were often carved in whimsical fashion. The church of St Mary's, with its unique roof paintings of 40 English kings (1445) and its gloriously detailed stone carving, has some remarkable misericords. One depicts the solution to a riddle, well-known in the 15th century: a king asks a subject to come neither walking nor riding; neither dressed nor naked; neither out of the road nor in the road; and bringing something that is a gift and no gift. The misericord shows a man half-riding on a goat, with one foot on the ground, his nakedness covered only by a net, and with a hare under his arm which will jump away when presented.

The twin towers of Beverley Minster

111 WREA HEAD HOUSE

🏵🏵 HIGHLY COMMENDED

Wrea Head Farm, Barmoor Lane, Scalby, Scarborough, North Yorkshire YO13 0PB Tel (01723) 375844 Fax (01723) 500274

A really warm welcome awaits you at our country house which is set in beautiful countryside on the edge of the North Yorkshire Moors National Park. From the gardens there are panoramic views to the sea and Scarborough Castle. All bedrooms are en-suite with television and tea/coffee making facilities. Enjoy a traditional English breakfast with individual diets catered for. A superb thirty six by eighteen foot indoor heated swimming pool, sauna and jacuzzi await you. No smoking in the house, please. Your hosts: Andrea and Chris Wood.

Bed & Breakfast per night: double room from £48.00–£60.00
Bedrooms: 2 double, 1 twin
Bathrooms: 3 en-suite

Parking for 50
Open: March–October
Cards accepted: Access, Visa

112 BURTON LODGE HOTEL

🏵🏵🏵 HIGHLY COMMENDED

Brandesburton, Driffield, North Humberside YO25 8RU Tel (01964) 542847 Fax (01964) 542847

Standing in over two acres of grounds this delightful country hotel lies in rural surroundings adjoining an 18-hole parkland golf course (reduced green fees for guests). The ten bedrooms are all en-suite with a television, telephone and tea/coffee making facilities. There is a comfortable cocktail lounge with an open fire and a charming dining room offering fine English cooking. The hotel lies at the southern edge of the village of Brandesburton on the A165, eight miles from Beverley.

Bed & Breakfast per night: single room from £30.00–£35.00; double room from £40.00–£45.00
Half board per person: £32.00–£42.00 daily; £210.00–£280.00 weekly
Evening meal 1900 (last orders 2100)

Bedrooms: 2 single, 2 double, 3 twin, 2 triple
Bathrooms: 9 private
Parking for 15
Cards accepted: Access, Visa, Amex

113 ROWLEY MANOR

🏵🏵🏵🏵 HIGHLY COMMENDED

Little Weighton, Cottingham, North Humberside HU20 3XR Tel (01482) 848248 or (01482) 843132 Fax (01482) 849900

Situated in the Yorkshire wolds within five minutes of the M62/63, Rowley Manor provides a haven from the pressures of the modern world. This unique situation makes it equally suitable for business visits to Hull and Beverley or relaxed weekends, with the attractions of York and beautiful coastline within easy reach. Our excellent restaurant specialises in fresh produce and fresh-fish dishes and is complemented by an extensive wine list.

Bed & Breakfast per night: single room from £55.00–£65.00; double room from £70.00–£90.00
Half board per person: £75.00–£85.00 daily; £525.00–£595.00 weekly
Evening meal 1900 (last orders 2200)

Bedrooms: 3 single, 9 double, 4 twin
Bathrooms: 16 en-suite
Parking for 100
Cards accepted: Access, Visa, Diners, Amex

114 RUDSTONE WALK FARM
South Cave, Brough, North Humberside HU15 2AH Tel (01430) 422230 Fax (01430) 424552

≋≋ HIGHLY COMMENDED

A beautiful farmhouse mentioned in the Domesday Book and renowned for its hospitality and excellent table. The ambience of its surroundings, with magnificent views over the Vale of York and The Humber, entices our guests to make repeated visits to unwind and relax. Our accommodation provides exceptional quality and comfort for self-catering cottages, or bed & breakfast in luxurious en-suite rooms. Flexible arrangements all year round. Superb location, convenient for M62 and close to Beverley, York and Hull.

Bed & Breakfast per night: single occupancy from £35.00–£38.50; double room from £44.00–£65.00
Evening meal 1900 (last bookings 1600)
Bedrooms: 7 double, 7 twin

Bathrooms: 14 private, 1 private shower
Parking for 30
Cards accepted: Access, Visa, Amex, Switch/Delta

115 WENTBRIDGE HOUSE HOTEL
Wentbridge, Pontefract, West Yorkshire WF8 3JJ Tel (01977) 620444 Fax (01977) 620148

≋≋≋≋ HIGHLY COMMENDED

Dating from 1700 and situated in twenty acres of the beautiful Went Valley among century-old trees, Wentbridge House is within easy reach of the M62 and A1. A traditional open fireplace and a fine collection of Meissen porcelain welcome you to the cocktail bar. The Fleur de Lys Restaurant, with its international ambience and master sommelier, attracts cosmopolitan lovers of food and wine. Individually furnished bedrooms include the Oakroom with its Mouseman four-poster bed, antiques and persian rugs.

Bed & Breakfast per night: single room from £65.00–£85.00; double room from £75.00–£98.00
Lunch available: 1215–1400
Evening meal 1930 (last orders 2130)

Bedrooms: 1 single, 11 double, 4 twin
Bathrooms: 16 en-suite
Parking for 100
Cards accepted: Access, Visa, Diners, Amex

116 WHITLEY HALL HOTEL
Elliott Lane, Grenoside, Sheffield, South Yorkshire S30 3NR Tel (0114) 245 4444 Fax (0114) 245 5414

≋≋≋≋ HIGHLY COMMENDED

Whitley Hall dates from the 16th century and is a lovely country house standing in its own thirty acres of gardens, parkland and lakes. Privately owned as a hotel for over twenty-five years, we offer accommodation, food and service of the highest quality and in the best English tradition. This popular country hotel is ideally situated between the Yorkshire Dales and Derbyshire Peak District and only a few minutes from Sheffield's theatres, sports facilities and magnificent Meadowhall shopping complex.

Bed & Breakfast per night: single room from £45.00–£70.00; double room from £58.00–£96.00
Lunch available: 1200–1400 Not Saturday
Evening meal 1900 (last orders 2130)
Bedrooms: 2 single, 6 double, 10 twin

Bathrooms: 18 private
Parking for 100
Cards accepted: Access, Visa, Diners, Amex, Switch/Delta

117 NEW CAPERNWRAY FARM
♨♨♨ HIGHLY COMMENDED

Capernwray, Carnforth, Lancashire LA6 1AD   Tel (01524) 734284   Fax (01524) 734284

An ideal London-to-Scotland stop, three miles from Junction 35/ M6 in beautiful countryside, between the Lake District and Herriot country. High quality accommodation in an award-winning 17th-century former farmhouse, renowned for its warm hospitality, peace, comfort and excellent candle-lit dinners. Delightful, fully-equipped, no smoking bedrooms with private and en-suite facilities. Personally conducted tours to the Lake District, Herriot country and Hadrian's Wall. Brochure available. ETB's 1993 Best Bed & Breakfast in Lancashire. North West Tourism Award for Excellence: 'Bed & Breakfast of the Year' 1994.

Bed & Breakfast per night: single occupancy from £32.00–£36.00; double room from £52.00–£58.00
Half board per person: £43.50–£46.50 daily
Evening meal 1930

Bedrooms: 2 double, 1 twin
Bathrooms: 2 en-suite, 1 private
Parking for 4
Cards accepted: Access, Visa

---

118 PARROCK HEAD HOTEL
♔♔♔♔ HIGHLY COMMENDED

Woodhouse Lane, Slaidburn, Clitheroe, Lancashire BB7 3AH   Tel (01200) 446614   Fax (01200) 446313

Those appreciative of peace and tranquillity will find a perfect base for walking, touring or just relaxing at this charming converted 17th-century farmhouse nestling amongst the Bowland Fells – conveniently placed for the Lancashire coast, Cumbrian Lakes and Yorkshire Dales. Enjoy stunning views, log fires, beautiful furnishings and delicious food in the elegant candle-lit dining room. Fresh local produce is carefully prepared for the daily changing menu. Dinner, bed & breakfast only £48.50 per person.

Bed & Breakfast per night: single occupancy from £41.50–£43.50; double room from £62.00–£67.50
Bargain breaks winter and spring
Evening meal 1900 (last orders 2100)

Bedrooms: 4 double, 4 twin, 1 triple
Bathrooms: 9 en-suite
Parking for 20
Cards accepted: Access, Visa, Diners, Amex

---

119 GIBBON BRIDGE COUNTRY HOUSE HOTEL
♨♨♨♨ HIGHLY COMMENDED

Nr Chipping, Preston, Lancashire PR3 2TQ   Tel (01995) 61456   Fax (01995) 61277

Gibbon Bridge provides a well-placed retreat for exploring some of Lancashire's finest heritage, offering comfort and tranquillity and yet it is only twenty minutes away from the M6 motorway network. The restaurant offers traditional fare using fresh herbs and vegetables from the kitchen garden. While the conference facilities incorporate up-to-date audio-visual equipment, the leisure facilities feature a well-equipped gymnasium, steam room and an all-weather tennis court.

Bed & Breakfast per night: single room from £60.00–£90.00; double room from £75.00–£180.00
Half board per person: £50.00–£65.00 daily
Lunch available: 1200–1330
Evening meal 1900 (last orders 2030)

Bedrooms: 3 single, 8 double, 15 twin, 4 triple
Bathrooms: 30 private
Parking for 150
Cards accepted: Access, Visa, Diners, Amex, Switch/Delta

---

120 NORTHCOTE MANOR HOTEL

⛌⛌⛌⛌ HIGHLY COMMENDED

Northcote Road, Old Langho, Blackburn, Lancashire BB6 8BE Tel (01254) 240555 Fax (01254) 246568

Northcote Manor is a small, privately-owned and managed hotel with fourteen en-suite bedrooms. Lovingly cared for, it is situated in the Ribble Valley, one of the least known and most beautiful parts of the country. The manor is best known for its excellent restaurant which has won many awards. Gourmet One-Night Breaks are available all year round and include champagne on arrival and a five-course gourmet meal, prepared individually for each guest.

Bed & Breakfast per night: single occupancy from £64.00–£75.00; double room from £75.00–£85.00
Half board per person: £94.00–£115.00 daily
Lunch available: 1200–1330
Evening meal 1900 (last orders 2130)

Bedrooms: 10 double, 4 twin
Bathrooms: 14 en-suite
Parking for 50
Cards accepted: Access, Visa, Diners, Amex, Switch/Delta

121 REDACRE MILL

⛌⛌⛌ HIGHLY COMMENDED

Redacre, Mytholmroyd, Hebden Bridge, West Yorkshire HX7 5DQ Tel (01422) 885563

Experience true Yorkshire hospitality in our lovingly-restored waterside mill, recently featured in 'Wish You Were Here'. Relax in one-and-a-half acres of peaceful gardens, only minutes from the main routes and Mytholmroyd railway station. Visit Brontë country and the wild South Pennines of 'Summer Wine' fame. Enjoy good food, wine and personal service in the welcoming comfort of Redacre Mill. All the rooms are en-suite. Private parking. Licensed. Please ring for a brochure.

Bed & Breakfast per night: single occupancy from £30.00–£35.00; double room from £45.00–£55.00
Half board per person: £35.00–£42.00 daily;
£210.00–£265.00 weekly
Evening meal 1800 (last orders 2000)

Bedrooms: 3 double, 2 twin
Bathrooms: 5 en-suite, 1 private
Parking for 8
Cards accepted: Access, Visa

Harry Ramsden's Fish & Chips

IN 1928 a fish-fryer from Bradford set up a hut in Guiseley, from which he served fish and chips out of two pan-fryers. Business boomed, and within just three years he had opened the most luxurious fish-and-chip restaurant ever seen. His name was Harry Ramsden, and his restaurant is now famous the world over.

The success of Harry Ramsden's was due partly to its location at the terminus for all trams from Leeds and on the main route to the Lake District and the Yorkshire Dales. As the business grew, Harry hit on a winning formula. The holidaymakers liked their fish and chips, but they also wanted a meal to remember. Harry offered food that was reassuringly familiar, but in a setting to match the holiday mood – the new restaurant had ornate plaster mouldings, stained glass in the windows and silver service. People came back time and again, and they still do.

Harry Ramsden died in 1963, aged 74, but his name lives on in restaurants throughout Britain, and even abroad, all replicas of the one at Guiseley, near Leeds.

122 YORK HOUSE HOTEL ·· ·· ·· HIGHLY COMMENDED

York Place, Off Richmond Street, Ashton-under-Lyne, Lancashire OL6 7TT Tel (0161) 330 5899 Fax (0161) 343 1613

Situated in a peaceful tree lined cul-de-sac, close to the A635/A6107 junction. This very well-maintained family-run hotel has thirty four well-kept, en-suite bedrooms set around a courtyard and a garden that has won two 'Britain in Bloom' competitions. The hotel's restaurant has an excellent reputation. Keith Absolom has owned the hotel for over twenty one years and the care and attention given to his guests is to be found throughout the hotel.

Bed & Breakfast per night: single room from £46.00–£60.00; double room from £66.00–£80.00 Half board per person: £61.00–£75.00 daily Lunch available: 1200–1400 Evening meal 1900 (last orders 2130)

Bedrooms: 8 single, 19 double, 5 twin, 2 triple Bathrooms: 34 en-suite Parking for 36 Cards accepted: Access, Visa, Diners, Amex, Switch/Delta

123 OLDE DUNCOMBE HOUSE ·· ·· ·· HIGHLY COMMENDED

Garstang Road, Bilsborrow, Preston, Lancashire PR3 0RE Tel (01995) 640336

A traditional, family-run, cottage-styled bed & breakfast offering a high standard of accommodation with all the rooms en-suite, plus many extra facilities and ideal for business people and tourists. Situated alongside the tranquil Lancaster Waterway, you can enjoy the picturesque scenery on our exclusive charter boat with a full bar for a simple cruise, or a champagne buffet party (maximum of 12 people). Charter boat not included in bed & breakfast price.

Bed & Breakfast per night: single occupancy from £29.50–£39.50; double room from £39.50–£49.50 Evening meal 1800 (last orders 2030) Bedrooms: 5 double, 2 twin, 2 triple

Bathrooms: 9 private Parking for 12 Cards accepted: Access, Visa

124 STUTELEA HOTEL AND LEISURE CLUB ·· ·· ·· ·· HIGHLY COMMENDED

Alexandra Road, Southport, Merseyside PR9 0NB Tel (01704) 544220 Fax (01704) 500232

A charming hotel offering excellent cuisine and hospitality, recently refurbished to a high standard and some rooms now have balconies overlooking gardens. Extensive leisure facilities including swimming pool, jacuzzi, sauna, steam room, gymnasium, solariums, treatment room, and games room. Two licensed bars, restaurant, library, lift, gardens, and car park.

Bed & Breakfast per night: single room from £40.00–£50.00; double room from £65.00–£70.00 Half board per person: £35.00–£60.00 daily; £245.00–£390.00 weekly Evening meal 1900 (last orders 2100)

Bedrooms: 2 single, 9 double, 7 twin, 4 triple Bathrooms: 22 private, 4 private showers Parking for 16 Cards accepted: Access, Visa, Diners, Amex, Switch/Delta

125 PRESCOTT'S FARM RESTAURANT AND COUNTRY MOTEL ♕♕♕ HIGHLY COMMENDED

Lees Lane, Dalton, Wigan, Lancashire WN8 7RB Tel (01257) 464137

Originally a 16th-century farmhouse, each of our bedrooms has a separate entrance from the cobbled path opposite the restaurant that serves classical Italian and French cuisine in a delightful atmosphere. Personally supervised by the proprietors, we are ideally located in two aces of peaceful gardens and orchards, and have five luxury en-suite bedrooms. Seven minutes from Junction 27/M6.

Bed & Breakfast per night: single room from £45.00–£50.00; double room from £65.00–£70.00
Evening meal 1830 (last orders 2200)
Bedrooms: 2 single, 2 double, 1 twin

Bathrooms: 5 private
Parking for 25
Cards accepted: Access, Visa, Amex

126 LABURNUM COTTAGE GUEST HOUSE ♕♕ HIGHLY COMMENDED

Knutsford Road, Mobberley, Knutsford, Cheshire WA16 7PU Tel (01565) 872464 Fax (01565) 872464

You'll find a country home that is both luxurious and cosy, offering the very best of bed & breakfast, aiming to provide those extras not available elsewhere. We have achieved outstanding success, winning '94 B&B of the Year for both the county and north west region. The house and award-winning garden are by Tatton Park and near historic Knutsford. Explore the outstanding treasures of Cheshire and yet be within easy reach of Manchester Airport. Close to Junction 19/M6 & M56. Taxi/car hire arranged. Strictly no smoking.

Bed & Breakfast per night: single room from £28.00–£38.00; double room from £40.00–£48.00
Bedrooms: 2 single, 1 double, 2 twin

Bathrooms: 3 en-suite, 2 public
Parking for 8

127 LONGVIEW HOTEL AND RESTAURANT ♕♕♕♕ HIGHLY COMMENDED

Manchester Road, Knutsford, Cheshire WA16 0LX Tel (01565) 632119 Fax (01565) 652402

The Longview Hotel and Restaurant was once the home of a Victorian merchant and is now a family hotel of character with open log fires, an award-winning restaurant in Victorian period setting and views across the heath. Our Nimbus Room bedroom with a Victorian mahogany half-tester bed and period furniture offers something special. The other twenty two bedrooms have been decorated with care, have full en-suite facilities, tea/coffee making, television and those little extra touches.

Bed & Breakfast per night: single room from £35.00–£56.00; double room from £55.00–£80.00
Half board per person: £50.00–£71.00 daily
Dinner 1900 (last orders 2100)

Bedrooms: 6 single, 9 double, 7 twin, 1 triple
Bathrooms: 23 private
Parking for 17
Cards accepted: Access, Visa, Amex

128 BRERETON HOUSE

👑👑👑 DE LUXE

Mill Lane, Brereton, Holmes Chapel, Cheshire CW4 8AU Tel (01477) 534511

A luxurious country house with oak beams, antiques and woodburning stoves, set in an acre of gardens in open farmland, yet only five minutes from Junctions 17 & 18/M6. A high standard of comfort and service is offered and the individually decorated and furnished en-suite bedrooms have four-poster, brass or half-tester beds. Freshly cooked and imaginative dinners are served in the elegant dining room. Well situated for touring many Cheshire and National Trust attractions. Strictly no smoking.

Bed & Breakfast per night: single room from £22.50–£40.00; double room from £45.00–£60.00
Half board per person: £37.00–£54.50 daily
Evening meal 1930 (last bookings 2000)

Bedrooms: 1 single, 4 double, 1 twin
Bathrooms: 6 en-suite
Parking for 6
Cards accepted: Access, Visa

Beeston Castle and the Peckforton Hills

BOTH THE VIEW of and the view from Beeston Castle, the natural focal point of the Peckforton Hills, seem of a scale out of all proportion to the surrounding countryside. If the weather is fine, even a lengthy journey is rewarded by magnificent vistas.

The castle (now in the care of English Heritage tel. 01829 260464) was built by Ranulf de Blundeville on his return from the Crusades in 1220, and he chose his site wisely; with sheer drops on two sides, the castle is completely unassailable from the north and west. He then fortified the other two sides with a curtain wall, seven towers and a gatehouse. Surprisingly, however, Beeston had a comparatively peaceful time, and its dilapidated condition is a result of Parliamentarian revenge, known as 'slighting', for its Royalist stance in the Civil War. During the siege in 1645 the Cavaliers held out for four-and-a-half months, relying upon water from the 360ft-deep well, as as also did the unfortunate castle cats!

Beeston is the last northerly gasp of the Peckforton Hills, in reality only a short sandstone ridge about two miles long, lying ten miles south-east of Chester. They rise to 700ft at their highest point, Bulkeley Hill, and offer both glorious walking through mixed woodland, and staggering views in all directions, but most notably to the north and east. From Beeston Rock, on the proverbial clear day, the city of Liverpool is easily visible to the north-west, while it is reputed that no less than eight separate counties can be seen. Make sure that you pack your binoculars! The Sandstone Trail, a waymarked path through the best of this lovely scenery, is clearly marked from nearby main roads.

For centuries the Peckfortons were quarried for their red sandstone, and many of the surrounding farms and churches bear witness to this, although signs of the quarries, such as an old tramway, are now largely overgrown.

129 CAVENDISH HOTEL

HIGHLY COMMENDED

42–44 Hough Green, Chester, Cheshire CH4 8JQ Tel (01244) 675100 Fax (01244) 681309

A Georgian house of infinite charm with an attractive forecourt, landscaped gardens and well-lit car park, it has all the advantages of a city location whilst retaining the ambience of a country house hotel. Food is of the highest quality, prepared with a French influence and served by candle-light in an elegant dining room. Bedrooms are individually designed and equipped for your everyday comfort.
Special offer: £80 per night, half board, for two people sharing a double room.

Bed & Breakfast per night: single room from £40.00–£45.00; double room from £50.00–£65.00
Lunch available: upon request, 1200–1400
Evening meal 1900 (last orders 2100)

Bedrooms: 2 single, 11 double, 4 twin, 1 triple
Bathrooms: 18 private
Parking for 32
Cards accepted: Access, Visa, Diners, Amex

130 GREEN BOUGH HOTEL AND RESTAURANT

HIGHLY COMMENDED

60 Hoole Road, Chester, Cheshire CH2 3NL Tel (01244) 326241 Fax (01244) 326265

A family-run hotel in Victorian property, providing a personal yet professional service in a homely relaxed atmosphere; tastefully decorated with many antiques, ornaments and flower arrangements recreating a period ambience with an ornately carved oak fireplace and half-panelling. A non-smoking restaurant serves fresh produce cooked to order with mainly traditional British dishes; vegetarians are catered for at breakfast and dinner. The bedrooms are individually styled containing Victorian, Edwardian and antique brass-cast beds. Ground floor and non-smoking bedrooms available.

Bed & Breakfast per night: single room from £38.00–£43.00; double room from £48.00–£56.00
Evening meal 1900 (last orders 2030)
Bedrooms: 1 single, 13 double, 2 twin, 4 triple

Bathrooms: 20 en-suite
Parking for 21
Cards accepted: Access, Visa, Amex

KEY TO SYMBOLS

For ease of use, the key to symbols appears on the back of the cover flap and can be folded out while consulting individual entries. The symbols which appear at the end of each entry are designed to enable you to see at-a-glance what's on offer, and whether any particular requirements you have can be met. Most of the symbols are clear, simple icons and few require any further explanation, but the following points may be useful:

ALCOHOLIC DRINKS: Alcoholic drinks are available at all types of accommodation listed in the guide unless the symbol ▣ (unlicensed) appears. However, even in licensed premises there may be some restrictions on the serving of drinks, such as being available to diners only.

SMOKING: Many establishments offer facilities for non-smokers, indicated by the symbol ⌖. These may include no-smoking bedrooms and parts of communal rooms set aside for non-smokers. Some establishments prefer not to accommodate smokers at all, and if this is the case it will be made clear in the establishment description in the guide entry.

PETS: The symbol ✖ is used to show that dogs are not accepted in any circumstances. Some establishments will accept pets, but we advise you to check this at the time of booking and to enquire as to whether any additional charge will be made to accommodate them.

England's Heartland

The Cotswolds

STRETCHING FROM THE Humber Estuary in the north all the way down to the Thames Estuary and spanning the full width of England's central girth from Shrewsbury to Norwich, this large area, not surprisingly, displays much of England's renowned variety. At its heart is the Midlands, the Black Country, dominated by the vast city of Birmingham. But away from the industrial heartland, this central region of England is largely rural and agricultural. Some parts, such as the Peak District and the Cotswolds are well-known for their beauty while others, such as the Lincolnshire Wolds or North Norfolk are quiet, secret places where crowds have not yet ventured.

Birmingham is enjoying a remarkable cultural renaissance: the City of Birmingham Symphony Orchestra is one of the most renowned in the world, it is home to the D'Oyly Carte Opera Company, and its art gallery has a superb collection of Pre-Raphaelite paintings. Futhermore, the industrial heritage of the surrounding area makes for some fascinating exploration. Ironbridge Gorge marries the glorious scenery of the Severn Valley with the intriguing sites where the Industrial Revolution was born, while many of the potteries of Staffordshire are still working and may often be visited. The region is the hub of England's canal network and these waterways make for enjoyable exploration either by barge or by foot along the tow-paths.

Bradford

The Peak District, being close to the more northerly conurbations of Sheffield, Manchester and Leeds – it has been estimated that half the population of England lives within 60 miles of Buxton – attracts many visitors who appreciate both its picturesque villages and wild open spaces. This is marvellous walking country, criss-crossed with trails which are well sign-posted. The Pennine Way, the highest long-distance path in Britain, begins its journey to the Scottish border here, and the High Peak Trail also provides some excellent treks across country.

The countryside in the west of the region, in Shropshire, Hereford & Worcester and Gloucestershire, is less dramatic but has the advantage of being, for the most part, some distance from major centres of population. Here, beautiful undulating hill-country is all the more appealing for being relatively unknown, with some hidden treasures to be discovered: Hereford & Worcester has some of the most beautiful Romanesque churches in the country (Kilpeck church is especially fine), while Bridgnorth in Shropshire is a small historic town full of charm. The isolated Forest of Dean has a unique character bred of its industrial past (it also has a sculpture trail through the forest), while the nearby Wye Valley is a renowned beauty spot – Tintern Abbey and the view from Symonds Yat are high points.

Warwick Castle

The eastern side of this region is much less hilly, and in places it verges on the eerily flat. The Fen country of East Anglia captivates many with vast skyscapes that dwarf even the major landmarks such as Ely Cathedral. Much of the Fens lies just below sea level, but the high points (in terms of altitude) of this half of the region are the Lincolnshire Wolds, Dunstable Downs in Bedfordshire and Charnwood Forest in Leicestershire. For many, though, the principle attractions of England's eastern counties lie along the coast. North from the Thames estuary the area boasts some of England's finest sandy beaches which benefit from low rainfall and high sunshine. The north Norfolk coast is refreshingly windy, but it makes up for this with some of the best birdwatching terrain in the country. On the Norfolk coast, too, are the Broads, in practice best appreciated by boat, which offer some rewarding sailing opportunities. Inland, the countryside of East Anglia is pleasantly and unassumingly rolling and scenic. Parts of rural north Norfolk are especially enticing, with sleepy, forgotten villages, quiet lanes and magnificent ancient churches everywhere.

Thurne, Norfolk Broads

The greatest attraction of East Anglia, however, lies in its architecture. Cambridge, with its famous views of 'the backs' and its exquisite King's College Chapel, vies with the less well-known Stamford (the setting for the acclaimed BBC series *Middlemarch*) for the accolade of being the most picturesque East Anglian town. Elsewhere, there are some magnificent cathedrals – Ely, Peterborough and Norwich – but most appealing of all is the vernacular architecture. Here are some of the most consistently beautiful small towns and villages in England. The area experienced its boom time in the Middle Ages as a result of the wool trade, and it was then that many of its villages and towns were built. The following years brought decreased prosperity, ensuring that many beautiful timber-framed houses remained intact. For the same reason the settlements remained small, while the parish churches, built on wool money, are impressively large and rich.

Grand Union Canal

The wool trade was also responsible for creating that other famously beautiful collection of towns and villages, the Cotswolds. Here the building materials are different – warm golden local stone, rather than timber and plaster. At the northern edge of the area is some particularly pleasant unspoilt country (also famous gardens, Hidcote and Kiftsgate). Not far away is Stratford-upon-Avon which maintains its artistic integrity as the home of the respected Royal Shakespeare Company, as well as having a high density of fine medieval buildings.

The Cotswolds

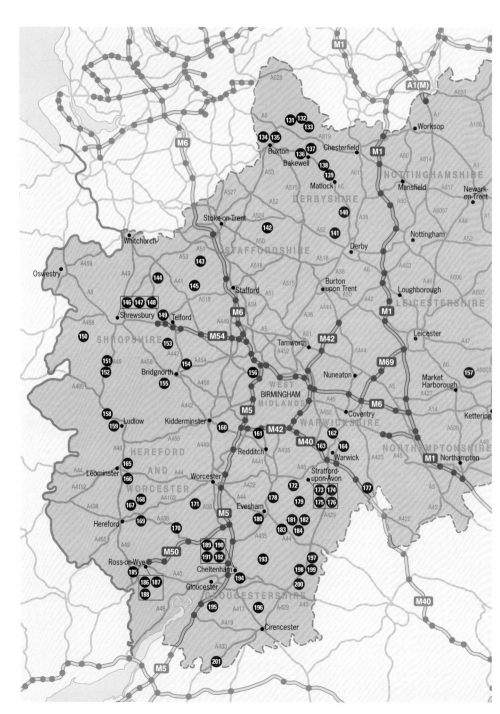

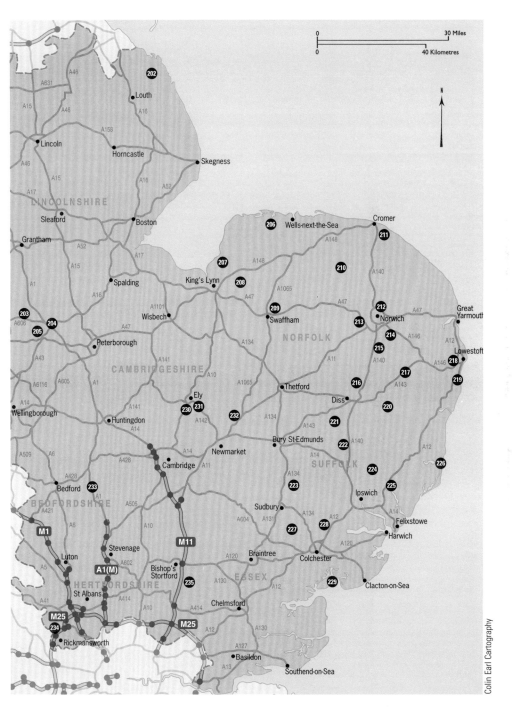

0   30 Miles

0   40 Kilometres

N

202
A46
A631
Louth
A15
A46
A16
A158
Lincoln
Horncastle
Skegness
A46
A15
A16
A52
A17
LINCOLNSHIRE
Sleaford
Boston
206 Wells-next-the-Sea
Cromer
211
Grantham
A148
A52
A17
207
A148
210
A140
A15
Spalding
King's Lynn
208
A1
203
A1101
209
212 Norwich
Great Yarmouth
A606
204
Wisbech
Swaffham
213
A47
205
A47
A134
214
Lowestoft
Peterborough
NORFOLK
215
A146
A12
A43
A141
A11
A140
A146 218
A6116 A605
A1
A1065
216
217
219
A14
Ely
Thetford
Diss
A143
Wellingborough
A141
230 231
232
220
Huntingdon
A142
A134
A143
221
A14
Bury St-Edmunds
222 A140
A12
A509 A6
A14
Newmarket
SUFFOLK
226
A428
Cambridge
A11
224
225
A428
223
Bedford
233
A505
Sudbury
Ipswich
227 228
BEDFORDSHIRE
A604 A131 A12
A14
Felixstowe
A421
A6
A10
Harwich
M1
A120
229
Clacton-on-Sea
Stevenage
M11
Braintree
Colchester
Luton
A602
A5
A1(M)
Bishop's Stortford
235
A130
ESSEX
A12
HERTFORDSHIRE
St Albans
A414
Chelmsford
A41
A10
A414
M25
234
M25
A12
A130
Rickmansworth
A127
Basildon
A13
Southend-on-Sea

Mr Straw's House

THERE ARE SOME houses which you expect the National Trust to own – and there are others where their ownership comes as a distinct surprise. No. 7 Blyth Grove, Worksop – a pleasant enough example of a semi-detached Edwardian tradesman's house – undoubtedly falls into the latter category.

By 1923 Mr William Straw, grocer and seed merchant, had prospered sufficiently to move from his home over the shop to a residential area largely reserved for professional people. With him lived his wife and his younger son Walter, who also worked in the family business. In 1932 William Straw died; his wife Florence outlived him by seven years. At her death, the older son, William, returned from London to supervise the running of No. 7, while Walter carried on the business.

Both the younger Mr Straws were unwilling to make change where change was not wholly necessary. Indeed the death of their father signalled the moment after which nothing was to change again; the calendar by the fireplace in the dining-room is for 1932, the year of Mr Straw senior's death. On the other side of the fireplace are his pipes and tobacco pouch; in the hall his hats and coats; in the 'Parents' Bedroom' his detachable collars in their special box.

But Mr Straw's House, as it has been rechristened, is much more than these individual objects. We can see what Mr Straw bought for his £767 2s 6d (the cost of the house), for No. 7 preserves the original doors, skirtings, fireplaces and cornices of a turn-of-the-century house, while also displaying exactly the decorative tastes of 1920s middle-class England (Mr Straw had the place redecorated throughout in 1923 for £70). The two brothers lived a life of routine, unchanged in 40 years. Walter would cycle every day to the shop in the Market Place, while William tended a house without central heating, telephone, television or even radio. One story seems to typify the attitude of the brothers: apparently a bulb dropped from the light fitting on to William's dinner plate one day, whereupon he declared that that wasn't going to happen again. It didn't, for the bulb has never been replaced.

Admission to Mr Straw's House is only by pre-booked, timed ticket (01909 482380).

National Trust Photographic Library

131 YE OLDE NAGS HEAD
HIGHLY COMMENDED

Castleton, Derbyshire S30 2WH Tel (01433) 620248 Fax (01433) 621604

A privately owned and personally-run 17th-century coaching house with fresh flower arrangements in abundance and antique paintings and furniture. Each bedroom is individually designed to very high standards: three are four-posters and one has a whirlpool bathroom. In the winter, log fires blaze in a bar/lounge area that serves traditional ales and an extensive menu of hot and cold food. Our elegant restaurant with first-class cuisine is open to residents and non-residents for breakfast, luncheon and dinner.

Bed & Breakfast per night: single occupancy from £42.50–£64.50; double room from £56.00–£84.00
Lunch available: 1200–1400 1200–1500 (Bar Lunch)
Evening meal 1900 (last orders 2200)
Bedrooms: 6 double, 2 twin

Bathrooms: 8 en-suite
Parking for 16
Cards accepted: Access, Visa, Diners, Amex, Switch/Delta

132 UNDERLEIGH HOUSE
HIGHLY COMMENDED

Off Edale Road, Hope, Derbyshire S30 2RF Tel (01433) 621372

A 19th-century, farmhouse-styled home with countryside views, privately situated one-and-a-half miles from the village centre. Stone-flagged floors and oak beams, along with quality furnishings, create the ambience, and each excellent en-suite room has many extras including a resident teddy bear. Renowned for hearty breakfasts and gourmet house party dinners cooked by the owner/chef, Underleigh is ideally situated for exploring the area on foot or by car. No children under 12yrs, and sorry no pets — we have our own!!

Bed & Breakfast per night: single occupancy from £30.00–£35.00; double room from £48.00–£50.00
Half board per person: £38.00–£40.00 daily; £35.00–£37.00 weekly
Evening meal 1930

Bedrooms: 3 double, 2 twin
Bathrooms: 5 en-suite
Parking for 5
Cards accepted: Access, Visa

133 STONEY RIDGE
HIGHLY COMMENDED

Granby Road, Bradwell, Derbyshire S30 2HU Tel (01433) 620538

Our lovely home is set in the heart of the Peak District National Park with good views overlooking the Hope Valley. Stoney Ridge provides the ideal base for hill-walking to visit well-dressings, country shows, sheepdog trials and more. Nearby are Castleton's caverns, Chatsworth House and Haddon Hall. Enjoy a swim in our twenty-eight by twelve foot heated indoor pool followed by breakfast on our balcony on sunny mornings.

Bed & Breakfast per night: single occupancy from £22.00; double room from £18.00–£24.00
Bedrooms: 2 double, 1 twin

Bathrooms: 2 en-suite, 1 private
Parking for 8

134 BUCKINGHAM HOTEL

🛆🛆🛆🛆 HIGHLY COMMENDED

1 Burlington Road, Buxton, Derbyshire SK17 9AS Tel (01298) 70481 Fax (01298) 72186

Set on a broad tree-lined avenue overlooking Pavilion Gardens and Serpentine Walks, the Buckingham Hotel has been owned and managed by the same couple for the past eighteen years. They have earnt an excellent reputation with the locals of Buxton for high standards of service, comfort and cuisine. It is the ideal base for that well-earned break, whether it be for peace and quiet or to explore the beautiful Peak District.

Bed & Breakfast per night: single room from £59.00–£65.00; double room from £75.00–£85.00	Bathrooms: 31 en-suite
Half board per person: £48.00 daily; £295.00 weekly	Parking for 20
Evening meal 1900 (last orders 2130)	Cards accepted: Access, Visa, Diners, Amex, Switch/Delta
Bedrooms: 2 single, 13 double, 12 twin, 4 triple	

Buxton Festival

IN 1976 TWO MUSICIANS, Malcolm Fraser and Anthony Hose, stumbled on a near derelict opera house in the beautiful Derbyshire spa town of Buxton. Determined not to see this fine building moulder away unused, the musicians began raising the funds to restore it. Three years later the opera house opened and the Buxton Festival was born. Since then every year has brought new talent and artistic enterprise to the town, and the festival, held every July, is now one of the largest in the country.

Buxton, nestling in the heart of the Peak District, is a delightful place for a festival. There was a town here in Roman times, built around the eight thermal springs which flow from the ground at a constant temperature of 82°F (28°C). In the 18th century ambitious plans by the 5th Duke of Devonshire to create a northern rival to Bath were not fully realised. Nevertheless a beautiful Georgian crescent was built and the town became a fashionable, if small, health resort and remained so into the early years of this century when the opera house was built in 1905. The opera house is very much the focus of the Buxton festival

(tel. 01298 72050). Each summer several works are staged here by any one of the great opera composers. The great appeal of the festival is that its organisers are prepared to stage lesser known works: for example, this year, Monteverdi's *The Return of Ulysses* and Britten's *The Turn of the Screw*. The festival will run between 12th and 30th July.

Traditionally proceedings begin with a well-dressing ceremony. This ancient custom probably originated in pagan thanksgivings to the water gods. In the 16th century the practice arose of creating elaborate pictures out of flower petals and other natural materials which were placed at the site of a water supply. Buxton has two main wells: Higher Buxton Well in the Market Place and St Ann's Well in the Crescent. On the first day of the festival a local clergyman leads a service of blessing at both wells.

Opera is by no means all Buxton has to offer during the festival. Several venues around the town host a wide range of different events – jazz, chamber music, poetry recitals, exhibitions, workshops and children's shows. You are also likely to encounter Morris dancers in the Pavilion Gardens or circus artists in the town centre, adding colour and fun to the artistic melting pot.

Fine examples of the art of well dressing

135 CONINGSBY
6 Macclesfield Road, Buxton, Derbyshire SK17 9AH Tel (01298) 26735

🦪🦪🦪 HIGHLY COMMENDED

We take great pleasure in welcoming guests to our Victorian house where we try to add those special touches that make all the difference when staying away from home. Our guests are assured superior accommodation, good food and impeccable cleanliness in a relaxed atmosphere where the hosts care and have time to talk. If you would like more details we would be pleased to send you our colour brochure upon request. No smoking.

Bed & Breakfast per night: single occupancy from
£32.50–£37.50; double room from £40.00–£45.00
Evening meal 1900 (last orders 1600)
Bedrooms: 3 double

Bathrooms: 3 en-suite
Parking for 6
Open: January–November

---

136 RIVERSIDE COUNTRY HOUSE HOTEL
Fennel Street, Ashford in the Water, Bakewell, Derbyshire DE4 1QF Tel (01629) 814275 Fax (01629) 812873

🦪🦪🦪🦪 HIGHLY COMMENDED

A impressive, ivy-clad Georgian manor in mature gardens with river frontage, in the centre of the Peak District with oak panelling, log-burning inglenook fireplaces, and en-suite bedrooms individually designed with every thoughtful extra. An award-winning restaurant, widely recognised as the area's best, serves home-made bread, biscuits, sweets and chocolates, with a daily menu of fresh food presented English-style on mahogany tables set with silver crystal. The Derbyshire Dales, Haddon Hall, Hardwick and Chatsworth are within a ten-minute drive.

Bed & Breakfast per night: single occupancy from
£75.00–£85.00; double room from £85.00–£130.00
Half board per person: £72.00–£75.00 daily;
£490.00–£526.00 weekly
Lunch available: 1230–1400

Evening meal 1900 (last orders 2130)
Bedrooms: 9 double, 6 twin
Bathrooms: 15 private
Parking for 25
Cards accepted: Access, Visa, Amex, Switch/Delta

---

137 THE CROFT COUNTRY HOUSE HOTEL
Great Longstone, Bakewell, Derbyshire DE45 1TF Tel (01629) 640278

🦪🦪🦪 HIGHLY COMMENDED

The Croft is in the picturesque village of Great Longstone and stands in three acres of secluded gardens and grounds. Centrally located, it provides an ideal base from which to discover the many attractions of the Peak District. The mainly Victorian house provides luxurious accommodation with nine en-suite bedrooms leading from a galleried main hall. Imaginative cuisine, an extensive wine list and personal service will all help to make your stay a memorable one.

Bed & Breakfast per night: single room from
£60.00–£65.00; double room from £85.00–£95.00
Half board per person: £81.00–£86.00 daily;
£330.00–£365.00 weekly
Evening meal 1930 (last bookings 1900)

Bedrooms: 1 single, 6 double, 2 twin
Bathrooms: 9 private
Parking for 30
Open: February–December
Cards accepted: Access, Visa

138 EAST LODGE COUNTRY HOUSE HOTEL ⬤⬤⬤⬤ HIGHLY COMMENDED

Rowsley, Matlock, Derbyshire DE4 2EF Tel (01629) 734474 Fax (01629) 733949

Set in ten acres of picturesque gardens with an ornamental pond that is home to an abundance of wild life and ducks. All the en-suite bedrooms at East Lodge Country House Hotel are individually furnished with facilities including hairdryers, trouser presses and irons. Our chef prepares a wonderful daily menu using the best locally-grown produce to create mouth-watering dishes for your enjoyment.

Bed & Breakfast per night: single room from £64.00–£68.00; double room from £76.00–£95.00
Half board per person: £60.00–£80.00 daily; £380.00–£500.00 weekly
Evening meal 1915 (last orders 2030)

Bedrooms: 3 single, 6 double, 6 twin
Bathrooms: 15 private
Parking for 30
Cards accepted: Access, Visa, Diners, Amex

139 THE RED HOUSE HOTEL ⬤⬤⬤⬤ HIGHLY COMMENDED

Old Road, Darley Dale, Matlock, Derbyshire DE4 2ER Tel (01629) 734854

A delightful country-house hotel, set in beautiful gardens, with extensive country views beyond. The Red House is a warm, intimate place in which to relax, with bedrooms individually decorated, providing all amenities. Under the personal supervision of the Adams family, the hotel is ideally situated to explore the delights of the Peak National Park, from walking, riding and golfing to visiting stately homes such as Chatsworth House, Haddon and Hardwick Halls.

Bed & Breakfast per night: single room from £50.00–£56.00; double room from £75.00–£80.00
Half board per person: £66.00–£70.00 daily; £300.00–£315.00 weekly
Lunch available: Sunday Only 1215–1400

Evening meal 1930 (last orders 2100)
Bedrooms: 1 single, 6 double, 1 twin, 1 triple
Bathrooms: 9 en-suite
Parking for 20
Cards accepted: Access, Visa, Diners, Amex

140 DANNAH FARM COUNTRY GUESTHOUSE ⬤⬤⬤ HIGHLY COMMENDED

Bowman's Lane, Shottle, Derby, Derbyshire DE56 2DR Tel (01773) 550273 Fax (01773) 550590

A lovely 18th-century farmhouse on a mixed working farm, elegantly converted and combining first-class accommodation with superb food; perfectly situated to enjoy the myriad delights of Derbyshire and wonderful walking country with many historic houses and places of interest nearby. The en-suite bedrooms (including a romantic four-poster suite) have the attention to detail that makes a stay extra special. Fully licensed. We have it all – from pot-bellied pigs to award-winning food. 'Best of Tourism' award; East Midlands Tourist Board 1994 'Bed & Breakfast of the Year' award; short-listed for 1994 ETB 'England for Excellence' award.

Bed & Breakfast per night: single room from £32.00–£55.00; double room from £54.00–£80.00
Half board per person: £42.00–£80.00 daily; £240.00–£360.00 weekly
Evening meal 1900 (last bookings 1900)

Bedrooms: 1 single, 3 double, 2 twin, 1 triple
Bathrooms: 7 private
Parking for 10
Cards accepted: Access, Visa

141 PARK VIEW FARM

HIGHLY COMMENDED

Weston Underwood, Ashbourne, Derbyshire DE6 4PA   Tel (01335) 360352

Enjoy country house hospitality in our elegant farmhouse, set in large gardens with lovely views overlooking the extensive park containing the National Trust's magnificent Kedleston Hall – hence the name of the farm. Guests have their own lounge, delightful dining room, bathroom and shower room. Beautifully furnished bedrooms with romantic antique four-poster beds. Offering superb English breakfasts, there are hotels and local inns nearby serving dinner and bar food. A non-smoking establishment.

Bed & Breakfast per night: single occupancy from £20.00–£25.00; double room from £37.00–£40.00
Bedrooms: 2 double, 1 twin

Bathrooms: 1 public, 1 shower room
Parking for 10

142 BANK HOUSE

HIGHLY COMMENDED

Farley Road, Oakamoor, Stoke-on-Trent, Staffordshire ST10 3BD   Tel (01538) 702810

A luxurious, elegant and peaceful licensed country home offering the highest standards of food and comfort, a third-of-a-mile south of the village. Each en-suite or private-bath bedroom has a beautiful view of the picturesque Churnet Valley, England's little Rhineland. Within the Staffordshire Moorlands, next to the National Park, one mile from Alton Towers, and amidst superb countryside for walking, it is also convenient for visiting the potteries, Derbyshire Dales, numerous great houses, gardens and other attractions. Heart of England Tourist Board nominee for 'England for Excellence' Award 1994.

Bed & Breakfast per night: single room from £33.00; double room from £50.00–£70.00
Half board per person: £43.00–£53.00 daily; £220.00–£297.00 weekly
Lunch available: as requested – subject to one day's notice.

Evening meal 1900 (last orders 2130)
Bedrooms: 1 single, 1 double, 1 twin
Bathrooms: 2 en-suite, 1 private
Parking for 8
Cards accepted: Access, Visa

143 THE ROUND HOUSE

HIGHLY COMMENDED

Butters Bank, Croxton, Eccleshall, Stafford, Staffordshire ST21 6NN   Tel (01630) 82631

Come and stay in this charming country home, standing in two acres and tastefully furnished with a lovely relaxed atmosphere. All the en-suite bedrooms have breath-taking views over rolling countryside. Enjoy a hearty traditional breakfast cooked on the aga. We are situated on a public footpath leading to two small lakes and within easy walking distance of a country pub. Please contact Caroline Hoggarth.

Bed & Breakfast per night: single occupancy from £20.00; double room from £34.00
Bedrooms: 2 double

Bathrooms: 1 private, 1 public
Parking for 4

144 STOKE MANOR

HIGHLY COMMENDED

Stoke on Tern, Market Drayton, Shropshire TF9 2DU Tel (01630) 685222 Fax (01630) 685666

Set in lovely peaceful countryside, yet central to Ironbridge, Wedgwood potteries, medieval Shrewsbury, Roman Chester and Hawkstone Follies, Stoke Manor offers farmhouse accommodation with that touch of luxury. The en-suite bedrooms overlook the garden and have television and hospitality trays. A two-mile walk around the farm takes you past the reservoir stocked with crayfish. Many dining places locally, and Julia & Mike provide a cellar bar for that relaxing evening drink.

Bed & Breakfast per night: single occupancy from £25.00–£27.50; double room from £40.00–£50.00
Bedrooms: 2 double, 1 twin

Bathrooms: 2 en-suite, 1 private
Parking for 20
Open: January–November

145 OULTON HOUSE FARM

HIGHLY COMMENDED

Norbury, Stafford, Staffordshire ST20 0PG Tel (01785) 284264

Situated in glorious open countryside, Oulton House is the perfect base for a peaceful rural break. Our Victorian farmhouse has warm and spacious en-suite bedrooms that are furnished with pretty fabrics and good country furniture. The dining room, where you can enjoy a tasty country breakfast, has a lovely stripped-pine floor and a very unusual carved fireplace. Relax in our comfortable sitting room or stroll around the gardens and beyond along quiet lanes and pleasant bridlepaths.

Bed & Breakfast per night: single occupancy from £25.00; double room from £37.00
Bedrooms: 2 double, 1 twin

Bathrooms: 3 en-suite
Parking for 6

146 ALBRIGHT HUSSEY HOTEL AND RESTAURANT

HIGHLY COMMENDED

Ellesmere Road, Shrewsbury, Shropshire SY4 3AF Tel (01939) 290571 or (01939) 290523 Fax (01939) 291143

This delightful 16th-century moated manor house, renowned for its culinary excellence and amongst the finest accommodation in Shropshire, is situated only two miles from Shrewsbury town centre. In a beautiful country setting, under the personal auspices of the owners Franco Vera and Paul Subbiani, it offers a high quality of service in a comfortable atmosphere.

Bed & Breakfast per night: single occupancy from £65.00–£80.00; double room from £85.00–£120.00
Half board per person: £80.00–£95.00 daily; £400.00–£500.00 weekly
Lunch available: 1200–1415

Evening meal 1900 (last orders 2200)
Bedrooms: 3 double, 2 twin
Bathrooms: 5 private
Parking for 63
Cards accepted: Access, Visa, Diners, Amex

147 ROSEVILLE
12 Berwick Road, Shrewsbury, Shropshire SY1 2LN Tel (01743) 236470

〰️〰️ HIGHLY COMMENDED

Roseville is within a ten-minute walk of the centre of medieval Shrewsbury. Close to rail and bus stations, Roseville offers comfortable, welcoming, centrally-heated accommodation, off-street parking, a varied choice breakfast menu and a professionally-prepared, select evening meal. The single, twin and double rooms have their own private facilities. Colour television is available in our guests' sitting room where tea, coffee and similar drinks are served at reasonable times. A NON-SMOKING ESTABLISHMENT.

Bed & Breakfast per night: single room from £18.00–£20.00; double room from £36.00–£40.00
Half board per person: £26.50–£29.00 daily; £160.00–£200.00 weekly
Evening meal 1900 (last bookings 1200)

Bedrooms: 1 single, 1 double, 1 twin
Bathrooms: 2 en-suite, 1 private
Parking for 3
Open: February–December

---

148 SANDFORD HOUSE HOTEL
St. Julian Friars, Shrewsbury, Shropshire SY1 1XL Tel (01743) 343829

〰️〰️ HIGHLY COMMENDED

A Grade II listed townhouse close to the fine riverside walks of the Severn, the Abbey and only a few minutes from the town centre, this small licensed hotel has been run for the last nine years by Joan & Roy Jones. Warm, friendly and informal with high standards in food and cleanliness, the mostly en-suite bedrooms have coffee/tea and colour television. Easy parking. Starting at £19 per person, discounts available for long or short stays. Please telephone for brochure.

Bed & Breakfast per night: single room from £23.00–£31.00; double room from £38.00–£43.50
Bedrooms: 2 single, 4 double, 3 twin, 1 triple, 1 family room

Bathrooms: 8 private, 1 public, 1 private shower
Parking for 3
Cards accepted: Access, Visa, Diners, Amex, Switch/Delta

---

149 BUCKATREE HALL HOTEL
The Wrekin, Wellington, Telford, Shropshire TF6 5AL Tel (01952) 641821 Fax (01952) 247540

〰️〰️〰️〰️〰️ HIGHLY COMMENDED

A country house hotel nestling at the foot of the famous Wrekin Hill, three miles from Ironbridge and one mile from Junction 7/ M54. Many of the sixty two bedrooms have balconies overlooking either an ornamental lake or gardens. Some have been specifically designed with lady travellers in mind: security spy holes, vanity mirror/hair dryer and ironing facilities. Terrace Restaurant overlooking patio and gardens. Liszt Lounge and Bar. Penthouse suite with a crown-tester bed and black and gold bathroom with whirlpool. Special weekend break: half-board from £49.50 pppn.

Bed & Breakfast per night: single room from £69.00–£75.00; double room from £79.00–£85.00
Half board per person: £86.00–£92.00 daily; £420.00–£444.00 weekly
Lunch available: 1230–1400

Evening meal 1930 (last orders 2200)
Bedrooms: 3 single, 36 double, 18 twin, 2 triple
Bathrooms: 59 private
Parking for 120
Cards accepted: Access, Visa, Diners, Amex, Switch/Delta

150 CRICKLEWOOD COTTAGE   ♛♛ HIGHLY COMMENDED

Plox Green, Minsterley, Shrewsbury, Shropshire SY5 0HT Tel (01743) 791229

A delightful 18th-century cottage at the foot of the Stiperstones Hills, retaining its original character with exposed beams, inglenook fireplace and traditional furnishings. Lovely views of the hills from all rooms, including the 'Sunroom' where breakfast is served, with an attractive blackboard menu. There is an inviting cottage garden to wander in, containing many old-fashioned and unusual plants and bordered by a trout stream. Excellent restaurants/inns nearby (one award-winning) – full details supplied. Ideal for visiting Shrewsbury and Ironbridge. No smoking. Call Debbie or Paul for a brochure.

Bed & Breakfast per night: single occupancy from £19.00–£28.50; double room from £34.00–£38.00 Half board per person: £29.00–£38.50 daily; £189.00–£248.50 weekly

Evening meal 1900 (last bookings 1000) Bedrooms: 1 double, 2 twin Bathrooms: 3 en-suite Parking for 4

---

151 JINLYE   Listed HIGHLY COMMENDED

Castle Hill, All Stretton, Church Stretton, Shropshire SY6 6JP Tel (01694) 723243

For that very special break Jinlye is a 16th-century guesthouse situated in a superb location adjoining the National Trust's six thousand acres. Open log fires and a wealth of old beams make an ideal winter retreat and a memorable summer vacation. The rooms have magnificent views and there is a large conservatory overlooking a plantswoman's garden. Find excellent home-cooking with an abundance of fresh products – desserts are a speciality! For a free colour brochure contact Jan Tory.

Bed & Breakfast per night: double room from £36.00–£48.00 Half board per person: £33.00–£37.00 daily; £214.00–£235.00 weekly

Evening meal 1900 Bedrooms: 1 double, 2 twin Bathrooms: 3 en-suite Parking for 9

---

152 MYND HOUSE HOTEL   ♛♛♛♛ HIGHLY COMMENDED

Little Stretton, Church Stretton, Shropshire SY6 6RB Tel (01694) 722212 Fax (01694) 724180

Set in an idyllic rural hamlet with thatched church, hills and walks in all directions. Ludlow, Shrewsbury and Ironbridge are within a half-hour's drive. Visit romantic monasteries, castles and churches. Interesting range of themed breaks available. Small informal hotel and restaurant, all bedrooms en-suite, two suites available, one with four-poster bed. Five-course à la carte dinners featuring cuisine of the Marches and the best of rural Italy and France. Outstanding cellar offering over three hundred wines in bottles and one hundred and seventy in halves.

Bed & Breakfast per night: single room from £35.00–£40.00; double room from £55.00–£100.00 Half board per person: £50.00–£75.00 daily Evening meal 1930 (last orders 2115) Bedrooms: 1 single, 5 double, 2 twin

Bathrooms: 8 en-suite Parking for 16 Open: February–December Cards accepted: Access, Visa, Amex, Switch/Delta

153 THE LIBRARY HOUSE

☗☗☗ HIGHLY COMMENDED

11 Severn Bank, Ironbridge, Telford, Shropshire TF8 7AN Tel (01952) 432299 Fax (01952) 433967

The Library House is a well-restored period house situated in the World Heritage site of Ironbridge Gorge, about sixty yards from the Ironbridge itself. We offer bed & breakfast accommodation in rooms which are well-heated and have colour television and complimentary tea/coffee-making facilities. All rooms have an en-suite or private bathroom. The old village library, which gives the house its name, is now a comfortable guests' lounge. Free car park passes available upon request. Strictly no smoking throughout.

Bed & Breakfast per night: single occupancy £35.00; double room from £44.00
Evening meal by prior arrangement

Bedrooms: 2 double/twin, 1 double
Bathrooms: 2 en-suite, 1 private

154 OLD VICARAGE HOTEL

☗☗☗☗ DE LUXE

Worfield, Bridgnorth, Shropshire WV15 5JZ Tel (01746) 716497 Fax (01746) 716552

An Edwardian vicarage set in two acres of grounds on the edge of a conservation village in glorious Shropshire countryside, close to Ironbridge Gorge, Severn Valley Railway and Welsh border towns. With an award-winning dining room and cellar, the Old Vicarage is personally run by Peter & Christine Iles. Two night leisure breaks available at any time of the year which include free passport tickets to the Ironbridge Gorge museums.

Bed & Breakfast per night: single occupancy from £65.00–£79.50; double room from £88.00–£110.00
Half board per person: £65.00–£80.00 daily; £416.50–£483.00 weekly
Lunch available: 1200–1400

Evening meal 1930 (last orders 2130)
Bedrooms: 8 double, 5 twin, 1 triple
Bathrooms: 14 private
Parking for 30
Cards accepted: Access, Visa, Diners, Amex

155 MIDDLETON LODGE

☗☗ HIGHLY COMMENDED

Middleton Priors, Bridgnorth, Shropshire WV16 6UR Tel (01746) 712228

An imposing stone building in a one-acre garden, with spacious bedrooms overlooking Brown Clee Hill, Middleton Lodge is within easy reach of many places of interest, including Severn Valley Railway, Ironbridge, and the historic towns of Ludlow, Shrewsbury, Much Wenlock, Bridgnorth and Church Stretton.

Bed & Breakfast per night: single occupancy from £25.00–£30.00; double room from £40.00–£50.00
Bedrooms: 2 double, 1 twin

Bathrooms: 3 private
Parking for 4

156 JONATHANS' HOTEL AND RESTAURANT 🦪🦪🦪🦪 HIGHLY COMMENDED

16–24 Wolverhampton Road, Oldbury, Warley, West Midlands B68 0LH   Tel (0121) 429 3757   Fax (0121) 434 3107

Within the intriguing maze of rooms at Jonathans', one finds an exciting country-house hotel. All the bedrooms and public areas are built for comfort and luxury and are filled with antiques and works of art related to the Victorian era. Well-known for its quality menus, the original Restaurant offers British-based cuisine whilst the Bistro provides distinctly French. Only five miles from Birmingham city centre, this elegant hotel and restaurant provides a haven of tranquillity. Park outside the door.

Bed & Breakfast per night: single room from
£69.00–£82.00; double room from £80.00–£150.00
Lunch available: 1200–1400
Evening meal 1900 (last orders 2230)
Bedrooms: 5 single, 21 double, 2 twin, 2 triple

Bathrooms: 30 en-suite
Parking for 21
Cards accepted: Access, Visa, Diners, Amex,
Switch/Delta

Garman Ryan Collection, Walsall

QUITE SIMPLY, the breadth of this collection makes it one of the most compelling – and perhaps surprising – stops on an art tour of England. Ask anyone where you could see works by Van Gogh, Turner, Picasso, Constable, Cézanne, Gainsborough, Blake, Titian, Reynolds and Gauguin outside London, and few would suggest Walsall. But here, in the Museum and Art Gallery (tel. 01922 650000), are all these artists – and many more.

The reason they are here is Kathleen Garman. She was born at Oakeswell Hall, Wednesbury, a couple of miles south-west of Walsall, and in 1955 married Sir Jacob Epstein, the renowned English sculptor. After his death in 1959 she, with the assistance of the American sculptress Sally Ryan, set about amassing the collection now on display. She originally intended to house the works of art in Oakeswell Hall, but its purchase was never realised, and in 1973 she handed 353 pictures, sculptures, antiquities and other works of art by 135 separate artists to the town.

The collection is intriguing for two distinct reasons. First is the staggering quality of all the exhibits. Degas's portrait of his sister, Marguerite, for example, is a particularly arresting work, in which light and colour have been used to tremendous effect.

The other absorbing feature is the strong influence of family, friends and the local landscape. Sir Jacob Epstein himself is understandably well represented (both by sculpture, such as the bust of TS Eliot, and by paintings, including *Autumn Landscape, Epping Forest,* with its vibrant yellows and oranges), but also on display are works by Theo Garman (son of Sir Jacob and

Lady Epstein), Michael Wishart (a nephew of Lady Epstein), Lucien Freud (former son-in-law), Augustus John and Sir Matthew Smith (both family friends) and Sally Ryan. Those who know the local area will also enjoy *A Lane at Hamstead (Staffs)* by William Ellis. This painting, in the manner of Constable or Gainsborough and dating from the 1860s, depicts a scene about three miles from Walsall. The spirit of the rural setting can still be found here in the heart of the West Midlands – as much a pleasant surprise in this location as the Garman Ryan collection itself.

Mother and Child by Sally Ryan from the Garman Ryan Collection

157 HOMESTEAD HOUSE

~~~ ~~~ HIGHLY COMMENDED

5 Ashley Road, Medbourne, Market Harborough, Leicestershire LE16 8DL Tel (01858) 565724 Fax (01858) 565324

Homestead House is situated in an elevated position overlooking the Welland Valley on the edge of the picturesque village of Medbourne, which dates back to Roman times. The village has a brook running through the centre and is surrounded by open countryside. There is a wealth of local places of interest to visit. We provide home cooking with local and seasonal produce from our own garden. Our varied menu includes locally-caught trout. A warm welcome awaits you.

Bed & Breakfast per night: single occupancy from £20.00–£22.00; double room from £35.00–£40.00
Half board per person: £25.50–£30.00 daily
Evening meal 1800 (last orders 2000)

Bedrooms: 3 twin
Bathrooms: 3 en-suite
Parking for 6
Cards accepted: Access, Visa

---

158 FAIRVIEW

~~~ ~~~ HIGHLY COMMENDED

Green Lane, Onibury, Craven Arms, Shropshire SY7 9BL Tel (01584) 77505

A three-hundred-year-old cottage smallholding set amidst the beautiful south Shropshire Hills on a quiet country lane, one-and-a-half miles from the main road. Fairview has panoramic views of the Clee Hills, Wenlock Edge and Ludlow. Old-fashioned care and courtesy go hand-in-hand with good home cooking using our own and, whenever possible, local produce. Although only a small establishment, we endeavour to ensure that your stay with us will be relaxed, friendly and enjoyable in our no smoking household.

Bed & Breakfast per night: single occupancy from £15.50–£17.00; double room from £31.00–£34.00
Half board per person: £26.00–£27.00 daily
Evening meal 1930 (last bookings 1930)

Bedrooms: 2 double, 1 twin
Bathrooms: 1 public, 1 en-suite shower
Parking for 8
Open: April–October

---

159 THE FEATHERS AT LUDLOW

~~~ ~~~ ~~~ HIGHLY COMMENDED

Bull Ring, Ludlow, Shropshire SY8 1AA Tel (01584) 875261 Fax (01584) 876030

Ludlow has been described as the most beautiful and historic small town in England, enjoying the beauty of the Teme, Severn and Wye valleys which comprise part of the incomparable Welsh Marches. An outstanding landmark, this lovely Jacobean building is a hotel with an excellent reputation for fine traditional food and comfort, offering as it does luxury rooms as well as eight four-posters. Its situation in the centre makes it possible to explore the town on foot.

Bed & Breakfast per night: single room from £60.00–£85.00; double room from £98.00–£140.00
Half board per person: £70.00–£110.00 daily;
£400.00–£600.00 weekly
Lunch available: 1130–1400

Evening meal 1900 (last orders 2100)
Bedrooms: 11 single, 15 double, 12 twin, 2 triple
Bathrooms: 40 en-suite
Parking for 40
Cards accepted: Access, Visa, Diners, Amex, Switch/Delta

160 BROCKENCOTE HALL
✦✦✦✦ DE LUXE

Chaddesley Corbett, Kidderminster, Worcestershire DY10 4PY Tel (01562) 777876 Fax (01562) 777872

Nestling in the heart of the Worcestershire countryside, Brockencote Hall is set in seventy acres of private parkland with its own lake. It is the perfect place for relaxation. Proprietors Alison and Joseph Petitjean have created a charming Gallic oasis in the heart of England, combining traditional French comfort and friendliness with superb French cuisine. The hotel offers a choice of seventeen superb en-suite bedrooms, including one that has been especially designed to provide comfort for disabled guests.

Bed & Breakfast per night: single occupancy from
£80.00–£80.00; double room from £110.00–£135.00
Half board per person: £65.00 daily
Lunch available: 1230–1345
Evening meal 1930 (last orders 2130)

Bedrooms: 13 double, 3 twin, 1 triple
Bathrooms: 17 private
Parking for 50
Cards accepted: Access, Visa, Diners, Amex

161 ALCOTT FARM
✦✦ HIGHLY COMMENDED

Weatheroak, Alvechurch, Worcestershire B48 7EH Tel (01564) 824051 or Mobile 0734 163253

Alcott Farm is situated in the middle of beautiful grounds and rolling countryside, yet is only a twenty minute drive from Birmingham Airport, the Conference Centre, the National Exhibition Centre, Solihull, Stratford and Redditch. It is only five minutes from Junction 3/M42. This beautiful country home has luxurious en-suite bedrooms with all the facilities, and unlimited safe parking and stabling available. Good pubs and restaurants are nearby. John and Jane Poole offer a warm welcome.

Bed & Breakfast per night: single occupancy from
£20.00–£25.00; double room from £40.00–£40.00
Bedrooms: 2 twin

Bathrooms: 2 en-suite
Parking for 20

162 VICTORIA LODGE HOTEL
✦✦✦ HIGHLY COMMENDED

180 Warwick Road, Kenilworth, Warwickshire CV8 1HU Tel (01926) 512020 Fax (01926) 58703

Victoria Lodge is a family-run hotel providing genuinely luxurious accommodation for those who appreciate the finer things in life and enjoy being looked after with care and courtesy. All the highly appointed bedrooms are en-suite. We have our own car park and a Victorian walled garden for guests' use. From its central Kenilworth location, the hotel is ideally situated for touring Shakespeare country and the Cotswolds. Victoria Lodge is a non-smoking establishment.

Bed & Breakfast per night: single room from
£29.50–£32.00; double room from £39.50–£47.00
Evening meal 1700 (last orders 1930)
Bedrooms: 1 single, 4 double, 2 twin

Bathrooms: 7 en-suite
Parking for 10
Cards accepted: Access, Visa, Amex, Switch/Delta

163 NORTHLEIGH HOUSE

HIGHLY COMMENDED

Five Ways Road, Hatton, Warwick, Warwickshire CV35 7HZ Tel (01926) 484203 or Mobile 0374 101894

A personal welcome, the individually designed rooms with colour co-ordinated furnishings, en-suite bathrooms, television, fridge, kettle and many thoughtful extras make this the perfect hide-away in rural Warwickshire. A full English breakfast is freshly cooked to suit guests' individual tastes. Evening meals can be arranged, although there are excellent country pubs nearby, as well as the historic towns of Stratford-upon-Avon and Warwick, and the exhibition centres. Please call Sylvia Fenwick for brochures. No smoking.

Bed & Breakfast per night: single room from £28.00–£38.00; double room from £38.00–£55.00
Bedrooms: 1 single, 5 double, 1 twin
Bathrooms: 7 private

Parking for 8
Open: February–November
Cards accepted: Access, Visa

164 LANSDOWNE HOTEL

HIGHLY COMMENDED

87 Clarendon Street, Leamington Spa, Warwickshire CV32 4PF Tel (01926) 450505 Fax (01926) 421313

One of many elegant Regency properties centrally situated in this attractive spa town, the Lansdowne affords a relaxed tranquil atmosphere. The comprehensive menus are changed daily, providing guests with a choice of freshly prepared dishes that always include seasonal produce. David and Gillian Allen's personal selection of good quality wines underline the Lansdowne's overall policy of excellent value and perfectly complement the high standard of cuisine which is recognised by most major discerning guides.

Bed & Breakfast per night: single room from £28.95–£49.95; double room from £51.95–£59.90
Evening meal 1830 (last orders 2030)
Bedrooms: 5 single, 5 double, 5 twin

Bathrooms: 12 en-suite, 3 public
Parking for 10
Cards accepted: Access, Visa

165 LOWER BACHE

HIGHLY COMMENDED

Kimbolton, Leominster, Herefordshire HR6 0ER Tel (01568) 750304

A sympathetically restored 17th-century farmhouse set in fourteen acres within a tiny tranquil valley, Lower Bache provides an annex with self-contained suites, each with its own bath/shower room and private sitting room. Peace, privacy and fine food are the hallmarks of this charming country retreat. Rich in wildlife, the surrounding countryside provides unsurpassed opportunities for walking, riding and the enjoyment of rural England at its very best.

Bed & Breakfast per night: single occupancy from £29.50; double room from £49.00
Half board per person: £35.50–£47.00 daily; £273.00–£329.00 weekly

Evening meal 1950 (last bookings 1230)
Bedrooms: 2 double, 1 twin
Bathrooms: 3 en-suite
Parking for 10

166 HEATH HOUSE
HIGHLY COMMENDED

Humber, Stoke Prior, Leominster, Herefordshire HR6 0NF Tel (01568) 760385

Set in peaceful countryside between Hereford and Ludlow and about four miles east of Leominster, this old stone farmhouse is full of character. The bedrooms and the lounge are spacious. Margaret and Peter Neal are both here to help you relax and enjoy your stay. For those who wish to walk and explore, there is a wealth of history in the unspoilt countryside of the Marches.

Bed & Breakfast per night: single occupancy from £16.00–£21.50; double room from £37.00–£40.00 Half board per person: £28.00–£38.50 daily; £175.00–£238.00 weekly Evening meal 1900 (last orders 2000)

Bedrooms: 1 double, 1 twin, 1 triple
Bathrooms: 3 private
Parking for 6
Open: March–November

167 FELTON HOUSE
HIGHLY COMMENDED

Felton, Hereford, Hereford and Worcester HR1 3PH Tel (01432) 820366

Marjory and Brian Roby extend a warm welcome to their romantic and homely old stone former rectory. With three acres of beautiful gardens, you can enjoy the tranquil setting and period atmosphere of four-poster, half-tester and brass beds, a well-stocked library, drawing and garden rooms, all centrally heated. In the superb dining room, select from a full English or vegetarian breakfast menu; excellent evening meals available at local inns. Just off the A417, eight miles from Hereford, Leominster and Bromyard.

Bed & Breakfast per night: single room from £16.00–£18.00; double room from £32.00–£36.00 Bedrooms: 1 single, 2 double, 1 twin

Bathrooms: 1 private, 1 public, 2 en-suite
Parking for 6
Open: January–November

168 THE STEPPES
HIGHLY COMMENDED

Ullingswick, Hereford, Hereford and Worcester HR1 3JG Tel (01432) 820424 Fax (01432) 820042

This award-winning country-house hotel with an intimate atmosphere, abounds in antique furniture, inglenook fireplaces, oak beams and flag-stoned floors. The old dairy now houses a magnificent cobbled bar with Dickensian atmosphere, and a restored timber-framed barn and converted stable accommodate six large luxury en-suite bedrooms. Outstanding cordon bleu cuisine is served by candle-light, and highly-praised breakfasts come with an imaginative selection.

Bed & Breakfast per night: single occupancy from £40.00–£45.00; double room from £75.00–£80.00 Half board per person: £46.00–£55.00 daily; £308.00–£375.00 weekly Evening meal 1930 (last orders 2100)

Bedrooms: 4 double, 2 twin
Bathrooms: 6 private
Parking for 8
Cards accepted: Access, Visa

169 DORMINGTON COURT COUNTRY HOUSE HOTEL & RESTAURANT   HIGHLY COMMENDED
Dormington, Hereford, Hereford and Worcester HR1 4DA Tel (01432) 850370 Fax (01432) 850370

Listed as one of Herefordshire's finest farm manor houses, part Georgian and part Elizabethan, converted into a country house hotel. The elegant public rooms and bedrooms have country views and all the facilities. Two acres of gardens with a wealth of trees are surrounded by apple orchards and hop fields, so quiet and relaxing, yet only five miles from the busy city centre. The food and wines are of the highest standard. Owned and operated by a family with a lifetime's experience.

Bed & Breakfast per night: single occupancy from £32.00–£36.00; double room from £58.00–£60.00
Half board per person: £46.00–£49.00 daily; £294.00–£308.00 weekly
Evening meal 1900 (last orders 2045)

Bedrooms: 3 double, 2 twin, 1 triple
Bathrooms: 6 en-suite
Parking for 20
Cards accepted: Access, Visa

170 THE BARN HOUSE   HIGHLY COMMENDED
New Street, Ledbury, Herefordshire HR8 2DX Tel (01531) 632825

This spacious 17th-century house, of great atmosphere and character, was once the home of the Ledbury Mineral Water Company and has a large, mature, walled garden and secure parking. Situated in the centre of the old market town of Ledbury, close to the foothills of the Malverns and the Wye valley, it is easily accessible from the cities of Hereford, Worcester and Gloucester. No smoking.

Bed & Breakfast per night: double room from £44.00–£54.00
Bedrooms: 2 double, 1 twin

Bathrooms: 1 private, 1 private shower
Parking for 4
Cards accepted: Access, Visa

171 WYCHE KEEP COUNTRY HOUSE   HIGHLY COMMENDED
22 Wyche Road, Malvern, Worcestershire WR14 4EG Tel (01684) 567018 Fax (01684) 561676

Wyche Keep is a mock castle perched high on the Malvern Hills. Built by the family of Prime Minister Sir Stanley Baldwin, it has a long history of entertaining house guests. All luxury suites enjoy spectacular sixty-mile views, and magical rhododendron gardens lead to hill ridge walks. Guests are treated to personal attention and can savour memorable English four-course candle-lit dinners. We specialise in unique and privileged tour holidays with the resident historian host, through Wales and the Cotswolds. A non-smoking establishment. Fully licensed.

Bed & Breakfast per night: single occupancy from £30.00–£40.00; double room from £40.00–£60.00
Half board per person: £35.00–£45.00 daily; £245.00–£315.00 weekly

Evening meal 1930 (last orders 2000)
Bedrooms: 1 double, 2 twin
Bathrooms: 2 en-suite, 1 private
Parking for 6

172 GRAVELSIDE BARN

HIGHLY COMMENDED

Binton, Stratford-upon-Avon, Warwickshire CV37 9TU Tel (01789) 750502 or (01789) 297000 Fax (01789) 298056

Serenely situated on a hilltop in the middle of rolling Warwickshire farmland, with magnificent views of the surrounding countryside and Cotswold Hills, Gravelside Barn offers the discerning traveller all of today's modern conveniences and comforts in a stunning and tranquil setting. A great base for exploring Shakespeare country and the Heart of England, or simply a place to relax. Three-and-a-half miles from Stratford and ten minutes from Junction 15/M40. Please ring for a brochure. Totally non-smoking.

Bed & Breakfast per night: single occupancy from £30.00–£35.00; double room from £40.00–£50.00
Bedrooms: 2 double, 1 twin

Bathrooms: 3 private
Parking for 6
Cards accepted: Access, Visa

173 PAYTON HOTEL

HIGHLY COMMENDED

6 John Street, Stratford-upon-Avon, Warwickshire CV37 6UB Tel (01789) 266442 Fax (01789) 266442

Situated in the centre of Stratford-upon-Avon in a quiet exclusive location, yet only three minutes' walk to both the theatre and Shakespeare's birthplace. Experience the delights of a stay in this charming listed Georgian house where the caring proprietors – John & June Rickett – will warmly welcome you. Tasteful, individually-furnished, cosy en-suite bedrooms include a Victorian room with an antique brass bed and a four-poster room. An excellent four-course breakfast is served until 0945 at weekends.

Bed & Breakfast per night: single occupancy from £38.00–£39.75; double room from £26.00–£28.00
Bedrooms: 3 double, 2 twin

Bathrooms: 4 en-suite, 1 en-suite shower
Parking for 3
Cards accepted: Access, Visa, Amex

174 VICTORIA SPA LODGE

HIGHLY COMMENDED

Bishopton Lane, Stratford-upon-Avon, Warwickshire CV37 9QY Tel (01789) 267985 or (01789) 204728 Fax (01789) 204728

An elegant Grade II Listed spa lodge in a country setting close to the town centre, with seven beautifully-appointed en-suite bedrooms. Built in 1837 and the former home of cartoonist Bruce Bairnsfather (Old Bill) and Sir Barry Jackson (Founder, Birmingham Repertory Theatre), this is the first hotel Queen Victoria gave her name to – the Royal Coat of Arms is built into the gables. Full fire certificate. Paul & Dreen Tozer are your hosts and look forward to welcoming you. Totally non-smoking.

Bed & Breakfast per night: single occupancy from £35.00–£38.00; double room from £22.50–£25.00
Bedrooms: 3 double, 1 twin, 3 family rooms

Bathrooms: 7 private
Parking for 12
Cards accepted: Access, Visa

175 WELCOMBE HOTEL AND GOLF COURSE 🥄🥄🥄🥄🥄 HIGHLY COMMENDED

Warwick Road, Stratford-upon-Avon, Warwickshire CV37 0NR Tel (01789) 295252 Fax (01789) 414666 Telex 31347

Just one-and-a-half miles from Stratford-upon-Avon, the Welcombe is a Jacobean-style mansion set within a one-hundred-and-fifty-seven acre parkland estate with its own 18-hole/par 70 golf course. Extensive formal gardens and flood-lit tennis courts combined with fine oak panelling, paintings and antique furniture to make the Welcombe one of England's leading country-house hotels. Excellent award-winning cuisine and fine wines. Country weekends, theatre and golf breaks available. There is a minimum half board two-night booking for weekend breaks.

Bed & Breakfast per night: single room from £95.00–£115.00; double room from £125.00–£210.00
Half board per person: £82.50–£150.00 daily; £577.00–£1050.00 weekly
Lunch available: 1200–1400

Evening meal 1900 (last orders 2130)
Bedrooms: 2 single, 36 double, 38 twin
Bathrooms: 76 private
Parking for 120
Cards accepted: Access, Visa, Diners, Amex

176 PEARTREE COTTAGE 🥄🥄 HIGHLY COMMENDED

7 Church Road, Wilmcote, Stratford-upon-Avon, Warwickshire CV37 9UX Tel (01789) 205889 Fax (01789) 262862

Situated in the Shakespearean village of Wilmcote, this Elizabethan Grade II listed building is set in nearly an acre of shady garden, overlooking Mary Arden's house. The cottage, and its later extension, is furnished throughout with country antiques. Breakfast is served in the stone-flagged and beamed dining room. Dinners are available at two good pub/restaurants within walking distance. The cottage provides a convenient centre for Shakespeare country, the Cotswolds and the NEC.

Bed & Breakfast per night: single occupancy from £28.00–£32.00; double room from £40.00–£46.00
Bedrooms: 4 double, 2 twin, 1 triple

Bathrooms: 7 private
Parking for 8

177 CRANDON HOUSE 🥄🥄 HIGHLY COMMENDED

Avon Dassett, Leamington Spa, Warwickshire CV33 0AA Tel (01295) 770652

This lovely country house set in twenty acres with beautiful views over unspoilt countryside, offers affordable luxury and an especially warm welcome. Attractive bedrooms with colour television, tea tray, hairdryer and many extras to make your stay enjoyable. Guests' dining room and sitting rooms with full central heating and log fires in chilly weather. Delicious breakfasts from extensive menu. Peaceful and quiet, yet within easy reach of Stratford, Warwick, Oxford and the Cotswolds. Located between Junctions 11 & 12/M40.

Bed & Breakfast per night: single occupancy from £22.00–£30.00; double room from £36.00–£43.00
Half board per person: £31.00–£34.00 daily; £210.00–£245.00 weekly
Evening meal 1900

Bedrooms: 1 double, 2 twin
Bathrooms: 2 en-suite, 1 private
Parking for 22
Cards accepted: Access, Visa

178 SALFORD HALL HOTEL

🛏️🛏️🛏️🛏️ HIGHLY COMMENDED

Abbots Salford, Evesham, Worcestershire WR11 5UT Tel (01386) 871300 Fax (01386) 871301

A romantic Grade I listed Tudor manor situated at the gateway to Shakespeare country and the Cotswolds. With every modern comfort combined with old world charm and quaint black and white passageways, our superb food in the Stanford Room completes the picture for a special memorable visit.

Bed & Breakfast per night: single room from £75.00–£105.00; double room from £95.00–£120.00
Half board per person: £59.50–£125.00 daily;
£357.00–£521.50 weekly
Evening meal 1930 (last orders 2130)

Bedrooms: 2 single, 23 double, 8 twin
Bathrooms: 33 private
Parking for 50
Cards accepted: Access, Visa, Diners, Amex, Switch/Delta

179 WINTON HOUSE

🛏️🛏️ HIGHLY COMMENDED

The Green, Upper Quinton, Stratford-upon-Avon, Warwickshire CV37 8SX Tel (01789) 720500 or Mobile 0831 485483

Situated in an area of outstanding natural beauty, six miles from Stratford, this historic Victorian farmhouse makes an ideal base for touring, walking and cycling. Antique beds, old lace and hand-made quilts decorate the spacious en-suite bedrooms. Heartbeat award-winning breakfasts are served with home-made jams and fruit from our orchard. Two village pubs serve local fare. Cycles are available for use on the disused railway track to Stratford.

Bed & Breakfast per night: single occupancy from £30.00–£30.00; double room from £42.00–£42.00
Bedrooms: 1 double, 1 twin, 1 family room

Bathrooms: 3 private
Parking for 5

180 THE EVESHAM HOTEL

🛏️🛏️🛏️🛏️ HIGHLY COMMENDED

Cooper's Lane, Off Waterside, Evesham, Worcestershire WR11 6DA Tel (01386) 765566 / Reservations (0800) 716969 Fax (01386) 765443

An excellent centre for Stratford, the Cotswolds and the Wye Valley. Fully modernised, the hotel is of Tudor/Georgian origins. The integral indoor pool nestles into the relaxing two-and-a-half acre garden. Consistent guide entries for food guarantee efficiently-served and satisfying meals and the widest range of wines and spirits in the country. National awards for idiosyncrasy suggest that a visit is relaxingly memorable – our style is un-Britishly informal. There is a minimum booking of two nights for half board accommodation.

Bed & Breakfast per night: single room from £53.00–£61.00; double room from £82.00–£84.00
Half board per person: £43.00–£57.00 daily;
£317.00–£350.00 weekly
Lunch available: 1230–1400, seven days a week

Evening meal 1900 (last orders 2130)
Bedrooms: 6 single, 22 double, 11 twin, 1 triple
Bathrooms: 40 private
Parking for 45
Cards accepted: Access, Visa, Diners, Amex, Switch/Delta

181 CHARINGWORTH MANOR   🏆🏆🏆🏆 DE LUXE

Charingworth, Chipping Campden, Gloucestershire GL55 6NS Tel (01386) 593555 Fax (01386) 593353

The manor of Charingworth dates back to the 14th C and is set in lovely gardens amidst the gently rolling Cotswold countryside where peace and tranquillity are found. The emphasis is on a warm welcome and a relaxed atmosphere. Staff at Charingworth are friendly and attentive, and the restaurant offers food prepared and served with care. Guests can relax in the leisure spa or discover the villages and famous gardens and houses of the Cotswolds.

Bed & Breakfast per night: single occupancy from £90.00–£120.00; double room from £110.00–£185.00
Half board per person: £74.00–£117.00 daily
Lunch available: 1230–1400
Evening meal 1900 (last orders 2230)

Bedrooms: 13 double, 8 twin, 3 triple
Bathrooms: 24 private
Parking for 30
Cards accepted: Access, Visa, Diners, Amex

182 COTSWOLD HOUSE HOTEL AND RESTAURANT 🏆🏆🏆🏆 HIGHLY COMMENDED

The Square, Chipping Campden, Gloucestershire GL55 6AN Tel (01386) 840330 Fax (01386) 840310

Situated in pride of place on Chipping Camden's historic high street, the Cotswold House is a must for independent travellers in search of high standards of hospitality, comfort, discreet attentive service and an informal and friendly atmosphere. Bedrooms are charmingly individual with well-appointed bathrooms, and public rooms have a quietly understated elegance. The restaurant, arguably the most beautiful dining room in the Cotswolds, enjoys delightful views of the gardens and offers interesting and delicious seasonal menus featuring fresh local produce and specialities.

Bed & Breakfast per night: single room from £69.50–£80.00; double room from £99.50–£132.50
Lunch available: 1200–1500
Evening meal 1915 (last orders 2130)

Bedrooms: 3 single, 6 double, 5 twin, 1 four-poster
Bathrooms: 15 private
Parking for 12
Cards accepted: Access, Visa, Amex

183 DORMY HOUSE   🏆🏆🏆🏆 HIGHLY COMMENDED

Willersey Hill, Broadway, Worcestershire WR12 7LF Tel (01386) 852711 Fax (01386) 858636

The 17th-century Dormy House is ideally located for visiting the picturesque villages of the Cotswolds as well as Shakespeare's Stratford-upon-Avon. Enjoy the beautifully appointed rooms, superb restaurant and high standard of cuisine and service. Our croquet lawn, putting green, sauna/steam room, gym, games room and nature trail offer the chance to combine leisure with pleasure. Pamper yourself with a Champagne Weekend or a carefree mid-week break in the Heart of England.

Bed & Breakfast per night: single room from £58.00–£70.00; double room from £116.00–£140.00
Half board per person: £80.00–£98.50 daily
Lunch available: 1230–1400
Evening meal 1900 (last orders 2130)

Bedrooms: 7 single, 15 double, 24 twin, 3 suites
Bathrooms: 49 en-suite
Parking for 90
Cards accepted: Access, Visa, Diners, Amex, Switch/Delta

184 ORCHARD HILL HOUSE
Listed HIGHLY COMMENDED

Broad Campden, Chipping Campden, Gloucestershire GL55 6UU Tel (01386) 841473

Situated in one of the most picturesque villages in the Cotswolds, Orchard Hill House dates back to 1646 and has been beautifully restored to provide comfort and style with old original charm. The rooms are beautifully furnished. Two are in the main house and, for something more private, a converted hayloft offers total individuality. Breakfast at our ten-foot elm refectory table in our flagstone-floored dining hall. The friendliest atmosphere you could wish to find. Orchard Hill House is a totally non-smoking establishment.

Bed & Breakfast per night: single occupancy from £35.00–£40.00; double room from £40.00–£55.00
Bedrooms: 2 double, 1 twin, 1 triple

Bathrooms: 3 en-suite, 1 private
Parking for 6

185 GLEWSTONE COURT HOTEL
HIGHLY COMMENDED

Glewstone, Ross-on-Wye, Herefordshire HR9 6AW Tel (01989) 770367 Fax (01989) 770282

Located in the heart of the Wye Valley, an area of outstanding natural beauty, Glewstone Court is a unique hotel where the priority is placed on making guests feel totally welcome. The style is relaxed country-house, with comfortable furnishings, period decor, open log fires and a warm, friendly ambience. Food is always prepared to a high standard using local produce – Hereford beef, Wye salmon and Welsh lamb are constantly on the menu.

Bed & Breakfast per night: single room from £40.00–£60.00; double room from £60.00–£90.00
Half board per person: £60.00–£66.00 daily; £350.00–£400.00 weekly
Lunch available: 1200–1400

Evening meal 1900 (last orders 2200)
Bedrooms: 1 single, 4 double, 1 twin, 1 family room
Bathrooms: 7 private
Parking for 20
Cards accepted: Access, Visa

186 EDDE CROSS HOUSE
HIGHLY COMMENDED

Edde Cross Street, Ross-on-Wye, Herefordshire HR9 7BZ Tel (01989) 565088

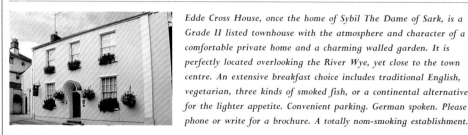

Edde Cross House, once the home of Sybil The Dame of Sark, is a Grade II listed townhouse with the atmosphere and character of a comfortable private home and a charming walled garden. It is perfectly located overlooking the River Wye, yet close to the town centre. An extensive breakfast choice includes traditional English, vegetarian, three kinds of smoked fish, or a continental alternative for the lighter appetite. Convenient parking. German spoken. Please phone or write for a brochure. A totally nom-smoking establishment.

Bed & Breakfast per night: single occupancy from £20.00–£23.00
Bedrooms: 3 double, 1 twin

Bathrooms: 3 en-suite, 1 private
Open: February–November

187 PENGETHLEY MANOR

⚛⚛⚛⚛ HIGHLY COMMENDED

Ross-on-Wye, Herefordshire HR9 6LL Tel (01989) 730211 Fax (01989) 730238

Set in its own fifteen acres of landscaped gardens and surrounded by glorious parkland, Pengethley Manor is a true country manor house. A 9-hole golf improvement course, outdoor summer heated pool, croquet and giant chess are some of the facilities available for your enjoyment. Four-poster bedrooms and spa baths are available for the special occasion and the superb cuisine and attentive staff make your stay a memorable occasion.

Bed & Breakfast per night: single room from £70.00–£115.00; double room from £100.00–£160.00
Half board per person: £67.00–£95.00 daily; £402.00–£570.00 weekly
Lunch available: 1200–1400

Evening meal 1900 (last orders 2130)
Bedrooms: 2 single, 11 double, 10 twin, 1 triple
Bathrooms: 24 private
Parking for 70
Cards accepted: Access, Visa, Diners, Amex, Switch/Delta

188 RUDHALL FARM

⚛⚛ HIGHLY COMMENDED

Ross-on-Wye, Herefordshire HR9 7TL Tel (01989) 780240

This elegant early-Georgian farmhouse offers something special: the best hospitality where our guests' comfort is of prime importance. The welcome starts with a tea tray in either the sitting room or the attractive terraced garden and moves on to luxury accommodation with a breakfast catering to all diets. With panoramic views across the tranquil valley and a peaceful millstream path that guests can stroll along to Ross-On-Wye. This is a perfect base for discovering the beautiful Wye valley and beyond. Guests frequently return!

Bed & Breakfast per night: single room from £18.50–£20.00; double room from £33.00–£36.00
Bedrooms: 1 single, 2 double

Bathrooms: 1 private
Parking for 10

189 BEECHWORTH LAWN HOTEL

⚛⚛⚛ HIGHLY COMMENDED

133 Hales Road, Cheltenham, Gloucestershire GL52 6ST Tel (01242) 522583

Near to the town centre and conveniently located for shopping and leisure activities, Beechworth Lawn offers a period hotel carefully restored. Decorated and furnished with the highest quality beds, linen and soft-furnishings for your complete comfort and pleasure. There is high-quality accommodation and food with discreet friendly service. With our all-year low rates, twenty-four hour access and off-street parking, we will make your stay in Cheltenham a memorable and happy one.

Bed & Breakfast per night: single room from £24.00–£34.00; double room from £40.00–£50.00
Half board per person: £35.00–£45.00 daily; £220.50–£283.50 weekly

Evening meal 1800
Bedrooms: 2 single, 2 double, 3 twin, 2 triple
Bathrooms: 5 en-suite, 1 private shower
Parking for 12

190 HOTEL ON THE PARK

👑👑👑👑 DE LUXE

Evesham Road, Cheltenham, Gloucestershire GL52 2AH Tel (01242) 518898 Fax (01242) 511526

This exclusive townhouse hotel is set within a classic example of a Regency villa and successfully combines the highest standards of traditional hotel-keeping with the charm and character of a period house. The twelve individually-designed bedrooms and suites and the elegant, candle-lit public rooms complement a restaurant serving some of the best modern British cooking on offer today. Situated opposite Pittville Park and five minutes from the race-course and town centre. Weekly rates available upon application.

Bed & Breakfast per night: single occupancy from
£74.50–£114.50; double room from £94.00–£134.00
Half board per person: £64.50–£84.50 daily
Lunch available: 1230–1415
Evening meal 1930 (last orders 2130)

Bedrooms: 8 double, 4 twin
Bathrooms: 12 private
Parking for 10
Cards accepted: Access, Visa, Diners, Amex

191 REGENCY HOUSE HOTEL

👑👑👑 HIGHLY COMMENDED

50 Clarence Square, Pittville, Cheltenham, Gloucestershire GL50 4JR Tel (01242) 582718 Fax (01242) 262697

This restored gentleman's residence, situated in one of Cheltenham's beautiful squares, combines regency elegance with 20th-century facilities. Regency House is within easy walking distance of the town's many amenities. The famous Pittville Pumproom and park, the sports centre and race-course are to the north, whilst the elegant town-centre shopping, theatres and museums are to the south. Our visitors' book repeatedly reveals appreciation of the high standards achieved. Call us for a brochure.

Bed & Breakfast per night: single occupancy from
£29.50–£36.00; double room from £40.00–£48.00
Half board per person: £37.00–£47.00 daily;
£224.00–£323.00 weekly
Evening meal 1800 (last orders 1930)

Bedrooms: 5 double, 3 triple
Bathrooms: 8 private
Parking for 5
Cards accepted: Access, Visa, Amex

Cheese-rolling at Cooper's Hill

ENGLAND, IT SEEMS, has its fair share of eccentric customs. One such custom is the cheese rolling at Cooper's Hill, a mile from Brockworth, near Gloucester. Every Spring Bank Holiday a man in a white coat and top hat, standing by the maypole at the top of the hill, begins proceedings by hurling a round cheese down the precipitous slope, claimed to be one-in-one but probably closer to one-in-two. After a certain interval, he gives the signal for the assembled local youth to hurtle down in hot pursuit of the speeding cheese. The competitors' primary aim should be to catch the Double Gloucester before it reaches the foot of the slope, but as this race between mature cheese and youthful athleticism is invariably won by the former, their main aim is to be the second object to the bottom of the hill. Such prowess is rewarded with the Double Gloucester itself. Runners invariably fall headlong down the course, and history rather sadly relates that one year in the 19th century the jubilant victor, a young girl, dropped dead at the foot of the hill.

Gloucester Museum

192 STRETTON LODGE
🛏️🛏️🛏️ HIGHLY COMMENDED

Western Road, Cheltenham, Gloucestershire GL50 3RN Tel (01242) 528724 or (01242) 570771 Fax (01242) 570771

Think of the desirable essentials of good hospitality and trust us to have thought of them too. Our townhouse, thoughtfully restored to a high standard of comfort yet retaining its period ambience, stands in a central yet quiet road providing a convenient base, whatever the purpose of your visit. Many of our guests return to sample the blend of informal yet discreet service, spacious rooms and generous breakfast choice. Ring Kath or Eric Price for brochure.

Bed & Breakfast per night: single room from £40.00–£52.50; double room from £55.00–£67.50
Half board per person: £42.50–£67.50 daily
Evening meal 1830

Bedrooms: 1 single, 1 double, 1 twin, 1 triple
Bathrooms: 4 en-suite
Parking for 6
Cards accepted: Access, Visa, Amex

---

193 SUDELEY HILL FARM
🛏️🛏️ HIGHLY COMMENDED

Winchcombe, Cheltenham, Gloucestershire GL54 5JB Tel (01242) 602344

A friendly welcome awaits you on our eight-hundred-acre sheep and arable farm. The 15th-century listed farmhouse is situated above Sudeley Castle, with a large garden and panoramic views across the valley. A comfortable lounge, log fires, separate dining room, non-smoking en-suite bedrooms with television and facilities for hot drinks. Central for exploring the Cotswolds. Good pub food in Winchcombe, half a mile away.

Bed & Breakfast per night: single occupancy from £22.00–£28.00; double room from £40.00–£40.00
Bedrooms: 1 double, 1 twin, 1 triple

Bathrooms: 3 en-suite
Parking for 10

---

194 CHARLTON HOUSE
🛏️🛏️ HIGHLY COMMENDED

18 Greenhills Road, Charlton Kings, Cheltenham, Gloucestershire GL53 9EB Tel (01242) 238997 Fax (01242) 238997

Charlton House is a small friendly family-run guesthouse located in a good residential area of Cheltenham with views of the Cotswold Hills. Our comfortable home is fully double glazed and centrally heated with a high standard of fitments and furnishings throughout. Good home cooking with your special dietary requirements provided by a trained nutritionist. Tariff on application. Weekly terms and optional evening meal. Ample off-road parking. Sorry, no pets. Entirely non-smoking.

Bed & Breakfast per night: single room from £20.00–£30.00; double room from £40.00–£50.00
Half board per person: £30.00–£40.00 daily; £180.00–£240.00 weekly
Evening meal 1800 (last orders 1930)

Bedrooms: 1 single, 1 double, 1 twin
Bathrooms: 1 private, 1 en-suite shower
Parking for 5
Cards accepted: Access, Visa, Switch/Delta

195 GILBERT'S

▬▬ HIGHLY COMMENDED

Gilbert's Lane, Brookthorpe, Gloucester, Gloucestershire GL4 0UH Tel (01452) 812364 Fax (01452) 812364

This beautiful listed building has been tastefully brought up to date with modern comforts and conveniences whilst retaining the dignity and atmosphere of the past. It is set in organically-run grounds in open countryside beneath the Cotswolds, with easy access to Gloucestershire, many interests and an excellent village pub. Personal touches bring guests back time and again, be they on business or on holiday – they revel in the respect shown for individual needs for privacy and pampering.

Bed & Breakfast per night: single room from £21.00–£26.00; double room from £42.00–£49.00
Bedrooms: 1 single, 2 double, 1 twin

Bathrooms: 4 private
Parking for 6

196 SHAWSWELL COUNTRY HOUSE

▬▬ DE LUXE

Rendcomb, Cirencester, Gloucestershire GL7 7HD Tel (01285) 831779

'Far from the Madding Crowd.' Centrally located, our 17th-century Cotswold stone house is approached via a no-through road and set in twenty-five acres with spectacular views over the Churn Valley. It has a wealth of beams and inglenooks and has been lovingly restored and furnished with great care. Shawswell offers total peace and tranquillity, the ideal base for touring, walking or cycling. We aim to provide high standards with personal service in a relaxed atmosphere. Your hosts: Muriel and David Gomm.

Bed & Breakfast per night: single room from £30.00–£35.00; double room from £45.00–£60.00
Evening meal 1900–1930
Bedrooms: 1 single, 3 double, 1 twin

Bathrooms: 5 en-suite
Parking for 8
Open: February–November

197 COLLEGE HOUSE

▬▬ HIGHLY COMMENDED

Chapel Street, Broadwell, Moreton-in-Marsh, Gloucestershire GL56 0TW Tel (01451) 832351

College House is a 17th-century residence of great character located in a quiet and enchanting Cotswold village. It has superb bedrooms and luxurious bathrooms, of which two are en-suite, and a sitting room with a large inglenook fireplace for exclusive guest use. Breakfast and, if desired, three-course dinners are served in the beamed dining-room. Broadwell is just two miles from Stow-on-the-Wold and Oxford; Cheltenham and Stratford-upon-Avon are all easily accessible.

Half board per person: £19.50–£25.00 daily
Evening meal 1800 (last bookings 1200)
Bedrooms: 3 double

Bathrooms: 2 en-suite, 1 private
Parking for 6

198 GRAPEVINE HOTEL

🍷🍷🍷🍷 HIGHLY COMMENDED

Sheep Street, Stow-on-the-Wold, Cheltenham, Gloucestershire GL54 1AU Tel (01451) 830344 Fax (01451) 832278

An award-winning 17th-century market town hotel in the antiques centre of the Cotswolds. Romantic conservatory restaurant crowned by a magnificent historic vine and a finely furnished garden and vine rooms. The outstanding personal service provided by a loyal team of staff is perhaps the secret of the hotel's success. This, along with the exceptionally high standard of overall comfort, hospitality and fine food, has earned the Grapevine its many accolades.

Bed & Breakfast per night: single room from £74.00–£94.00; double room from £108.00–£148.00 Half board per person: £47.00–£109.00 daily; £331.55 weekly
Lunch available: 1200–1400

Evening meal 1900 (last orders 2130) Bedrooms: 1 single, 10 double, 10 twin, 1 triple, 1 family room
Bathrooms: 23 private
Parking for 23

Cards accepted: Access, Visa, Diners, Amex, Switch/Delta

199 STOW LODGE HOTEL

🍷🍷🍷🍷 HIGHLY COMMENDED

The Square, Stow-on-the-Wold, Cheltenham, Gloucestershire GL54 1AB Tel (01451) 830485

Privately owned and family-run Cotswold Manor House Hotel, set back in its own gardens in a secluded corner of the market square. Bedrooms are comfortably furnished with a private bathroom, and the non-smoking restaurant offers excellent home cooking and an interesting extensive wine list. There are open log fires for those cooler days in both the bar and residents' lounge. The hotel is an ideal base for touring the Cotswolds and Shakespeare country and for those requiring a relaxing holiday.

Bed & Breakfast per night: single room from £39.00–£65.00; double room from £58.00–£95.00 Half board per person: £45.00–£62.00 daily; £265.00–£389.00 weekly
Lunch available: 1200 –1400

Evening meal 1900 (last orders 2100) Bedrooms: 1 single, 11 double, 8 twin, 2 triple Bathrooms: 20 private, 1 private shower
Parking for 30
Open: February–December

Cards accepted: Diners, Amex

200 COOMBE HOUSE

🍷🍷 HIGHLY COMMENDED

Rissington Road, Bourton-on-the-Water, Cheltenham, Gloucestershire GL54 2DT Tel (01451) 821966 Fax (01451) 810477

Quietly located just a river-side walk from the centre of this beautiful Cotswold village, this delightful home provides a haven for guests who appreciate high levels of cleanliness, comfort and attention. Fresh thoughtfully appointed bedrooms, charming reception rooms, and an interesting garden for the enthusiast. Ideally located for discovering the superb Cotswold countryside, houses, gardens and castles. London is seventy-five miles, Oxford and Stratford twenty-six. Local knowledge available to assist with routes, ideas and restaurants. No smoking.

Bed & Breakfast per night: single occupancy from £36.00–£42.00; double room from £50.00–£65.00 Bedrooms: 3 double, 2 twin, 2 triple

Bathrooms: 7 private
Parking for 10
Cards accepted: Access, Visa, Amex

201 TAVERN HOUSE

♨♨ DE LUXE

Willesley, Tetbury, Gloucestershire GL8 8QU Tel (01666) 880444 Fax (01666) 880254

A delightfully situated 17th-century Grade II listed former staging-post, this elegant Cotswold-stone country house is only one mile from Westonbirt Arboretum which has one of Europe's largest collections of trees, plants and shrubs. The four en-suite bedrooms have direct-dial telephone, television, hairdryer and much more. A charming secluded garden offers peace and tranquillity, far from the madding crowd. Convenient for Bath, Gloucester, Cheltenham and Stow. A country house atmosphere with attention to detail being our keynote.

Bed & Breakfast per night: single occupancy from £45.00–£50.00; double room from £55.00–£63.00
Bedrooms: 3 double, 1 twin

Bathrooms: 4 en-suite
Parking for 4
Cards accepted: Access, Visa

The Lincolnshire Wolds

IF YOUR TASTE is for soaring peaks and fast-flowing rivers, you may be disappointed in the Wolds, but this 40-mile ridge of chalk uplands between the Wash and the Humber Estuary has much to offer. First is the sense of space: whenever you are here, you will never find crowds, for this is a sparsely populated corner of our land, with hamlets and villages in preference to towns and cities. Second is the sense of history, both in archaeological and architectural remains and in place-names. The Romans chose Caister as their main settlement in the area (*castrum* is Latin for camp), and a small section of their wall survives. The Anglo-Saxons' presence is clear from the element '–ing' in many names, while the Scandinavian influence is particularly pronounced through '–thorpes' and '–bys'. The Dutch, too, have clearly left their mark on the vernacular architecture.

Above all, though, the Wolds are to be meandered through. Old Bolingbroke at the Wolds' southern end is one of the prettiest villages (it gave its name to Henry IV) while Alfred, Lord Tennyson grew up in the old rectory (private) at Somersby ('in which it seemed always afternoon'). There are fine views to be had from much of the ridge, which reaches a height of 552ft near Normanby-le-Wold. Similarly, the town of Louth is best explored on foot, with Westgate particularly noteworthy for fine Georgian architecture.

A view across the Lincolnshire Wolds

202 WICKHAM HOUSE
≋≋ HIGHLY COMMENDED

Church Lane, Conisholme, Louth, Lincolnshire LN11 7LX Tel (01507) 358 465

We are pleased to offer bed & breakfast in our 18th-century cottage. Wickham House is situated in a quiet lane off the A1031. The comfortable bedrooms, one on the ground floor, are all en-suite, with colour television and tea/coffee tray. Beamed ceilings in lounge and dining room (separate tables). Cosy library with local maps and information. Central heating throughout. No smoking in cottage, please.

Bed & Breakfast per night: double room from £36.00
Bedrooms: 1 single, 1 double, 1 twin

Bathrooms: 3 en-suite
Parking for 4

203 BARNSDALE LODGE HOTEL
≋≋≋≋ HIGHLY COMMENDED

The Avenue, Exton, Oakham, Leicestershire LE15 8AH Tel (01572) 724678 Fax (01572) 724961

Set in the heart of Rutland's beautiful countryside overlooking Rutland water, this 17th-century farmhouse welcomes you with luxury and warmth. Traditional English fayre is served in an Edwardian dining room using fresh, locally grown produce. International wines complement the menus. Afternoon tea, elevenses and buttery menus are always available in our conservatory. Our seventeen en-suite bedrooms are filled with antique furniture (with twelve additional bedrooms available from April). The ideal retreat from everyday life. Come and discover the tranquillity of Rutland.

Bed & Breakfast per night: single room from £49.50–£55.00; double room from £55.00–£79.50
Lunch available: 1200–1430
Evening meal 1900 (last orders 2145)

Bedrooms: 4 single, 17 double, 6 twin, 2 triple
Bathrooms: 29 en-suite
Parking for 107
Cards accepted: Access, Visa, Switch/Delta

204 GEORGE OF STAMFORD
≋≋≋≋ HIGHLY COMMENDED

71 St. Martins, Stamford, Lincolnshire PE9 2LB Tel (01780) 55171 Fax (01780) 57070

Situated in the heart of the finest stone-built town in England, this ancient hotel has cared for the every need of tourists and businessmen for over nine hundred years. The atmosphere of the George contributes splendidly to any sojourn here, however fleeting. Whether feasting in the panelled dining room, the flower-laden garden lounge, or the wonderful courtyard, or reposing in the delightful individually decorated bedrooms, the staff excel at their duty to make your visit truly memorable.

Bed & Breakfast per night: single room from £72.00–£95.00; double room from £85.00–£160.00
Lunch available: 1230–1430 (Garden Lounge menu all day)
Evening meal 1800 (last orders 2230)
Bedrooms: 12 single, 24 double, 11 twin

Bathrooms: 47 en-suite
Parking for 120
Cards accepted: Access, Visa, Diners, Amex, Switch/Delta

205 THE PRIORY ☙☙☙ HIGHLY COMMENDED

Church Road, Ketton, Stamford, Lincolnshire PE9 3RD Tel (01780) 720215 Fax (01780) 721881

An historic Grade II listed country house in a quiet village setting near Stamford, England's finest stone town and the setting for 'Middlemarch'. Spacious luxury en-suite bedrooms with high ceilings, panelled walls and shuttered windows. Imaginatively decorated and, of course, with colour television, hospitality trays, phones and teddy bears. Views over delightful lawns and gardens down to river frontage. Eat in the large conservatory or feature dining room. Near Rutland Water, Burghley House and forest walks. Colour brochure available.

Bed & Breakfast per night: single occupancy from £28.00–£35.00; double room from £38.00–£55.00 Half board per person: £31.50–£40.00 daily; £207.00–£260.00 weekly Evening meal from 1900 (last orders 1930)

Bedrooms: 2 double, 1 twin Bathrooms: 2 en-suite, 1 private Parking for 10 Cards accepted: Access, Visa

206 THE HOSTE ARMS ☙☙☙ HIGHLY COMMENDED

The Green, Burnham Market, King's Lynn, Norfolk PE31 8HD Tel (01328) 738257 Fax (01328) 730103

Situated in the idyllic and precious village of Burnham Market with fifteen beautiful bedrooms, all elegantly furnished. Excellent à la carte and blackboard menus are available, both utilising the local fresh fish and produce available from the North Norfolk coastline. Local real ales are served straight from the barrel and an extensive wine list offers over seventy wines. Every Monday and Friday features jazz and rhythm & blues nights, and the year-round art gallery displays all tastes of art. Amazing value off-season offer: two nights for the price of one, Sunday–Thursday, 1.11.94–31.3.95, excluding Christmas and New Year.

Bed & Breakfast per night: single room from £48.00; double room from £76.00–£84.00 Half board per person: £50.00–£57.75 daily; £278.00–£280.00 weekly Lunch available: 1200–1430

Evening meal 1900 (last orders 2130) Bedrooms: 2 single, 15 double, 5 twin Bathrooms: 22 private Parking for 35 Cards accepted: Access, Visa

207 THE OLD RECTORY Listed DE LUXE

Wolferton, Sandringham, Norfolk PE31 6HF Tel (01485) 540496

The Old Rectory was short-listed for the 1994 'England for Excellence' Award for Bed & Breakfast of the Year. A quiet country house with a warm, friendly atmosphere in four-and-a-half acres of wooded grounds on the Royal Sandringham estate. Built in the mid-19th-century in attractive Norfolk carrstone and featuring an elegant drawing room, sitting room with television, hard tennis court and croquet lawn. Excellent for walks and birdwatching at Wolferton Marsh. Delicious evening meals available, prepared by the proprietor.

Bed & Breakfast per night: single occupancy from £35.00–£40.00; double room from £55.00–£60.00 Half board per person: £47.50–£50.00 daily Evening meal 1900 (last orders 2100)

Bedrooms: 1 double, 2 twin Bathrooms: 2 en-suite, 1 private Parking for 10

208 CONGHAM HALL COUNTRY HOUSE HOTEL   〰〰〰〰 HIGHLY COMMENDED

Grimston, King's Lynn, Norfolk PE32 1AH Tel (01485) 600250 Fax (01485) 601191

Welcome to peaceful west Norfolk and Congham Hall, set in forty acres of parkland, with a cricket pitch and herb gardens. Whether you visit for a quiet weekend break or business meetings, you will find your needs are understood and gently catered for. A Georgian manor house, it was converted into a hotel in 1982. Christine and Trevor Forecast and staff have retained the family-home atmosphere and welcoming warmth that is evident in all they do for you. Non-smoking restaurant.

Bed & Breakfast per night: single room from £75.00–£80.00; double room from £99.00–£180.00
Lunch available: 1230–1400
Evening meal 1930 (last orders 2130)

Bedrooms: 1 single, 4 double, 9 twin
Bathrooms: 14 en-suite
Parking for 50
Cards accepted: Access, Visa, Diners, Amex

---

209 CORFIELD HOUSE   〰〰〰 HIGHLY COMMENDED

Sporle, Swaffham, Norfolk PE32 2EA Tel (01760) 723636

Corfield House is an attractive brick-built house standing in half an acre of lawned gardens in the peaceful village of Sporle near Swaffham, an ideal base for touring Norfolk. Some of the comfortable en-suite bedrooms (one ground floor) have fine views across open fields and all have television, clock radio and a fact-file on places to visit. Good home-cooked food using excellent local produce. No smoking throughout.

Bed & Breakfast per night: single room £23.00; double room from £37.00–£43.00
Half board per person: from £30.50–£35.00 daily; £205.00–£220.00 weekly
Evening meal 1900 (last bookings 1730)

Bedrooms: 1 single, 2 double, 2 twin
Bathrooms: 5 en-suite
Parking for 5
Open: April–December
Cards accepted: Access, Visa

---

210 WESTWOOD BARN   〰〰 HIGHLY COMMENDED

Wood Dalling, Norwich, Norfolk NR11 6SW Tel (01263) 584108

Westwood Barn is an exclusive 15th-century building converted to provide three double and one twin en-suite, ground-floor bedrooms, including a four-poster bedroom. A magnificent sitting room with many original beams and an enormous inglenook fireplace. Idyllic rural location for discovering the charms and tranquillity of North Norfolk: two miles from the picturesque village of Heydon, with National Trust properties, Norwich, the coast and broads all within a twelve mile radius. Illustrated brochure available.

Bed & Breakfast per night: single room from £28.00–£28.00; double room from £42.00–£48.00
Evening meal 1900 by arrangement
Bedrooms: 2 double, 1 twin

Bathrooms: 3 en-suite
Parking for 10

---

211 SHRUBLANDS FARM

Northrepps, Cromer, Norfolk NR27 0AA Tel (01263) 579297 Fax (01263) 579297

HIGHLY COMMENDED

We are situated one-and-a-half miles from the sea on the beautiful north Norfolk coast with its sandy beaches and bird sanctuaries. Ideal for those wishing to explore by car, cycle or on foot. The house dates back to the 18th century and is set in a large garden with lawns and mature trees. We offer a warm welcome and excellent farmhouse cooking. Evening meals are available upon request. No smoking.

Bed & Breakfast per night: single occupancy from £22.00; double or twin room from £38.00–£40.00
Half board per person: £27.50–£30.50 daily
Evening meal 1900 (last orders 2000)

Bedrooms: 1 double, 2 twin
Bathrooms: 1 en-suite, 2 private
Parking for 4

Bird Reserves of the North Norfolk Coast

THE NORTH NORFOLK coast is a paradise for birds – and for bird watchers. The 20 or so miles between Holme and Salthouse provide some of the best bird watching sites in Britain. This strip of coast contains a remarkable variety of habitats – heathland, pine forest, saltmarsh, shallow lagoons, tidal mud flats and sand dunes – attracting a phenomenal range of different species, many of them rare. In addition, the coast's prominent easterly position, jutting out into the North Sea, makes it a landing stage for thousands of migrants.

Most of this coast is now protected by conservation organisations. The main reserves are:

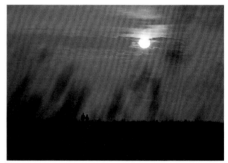

Cley-next-the-Sea coastline

Holme
A good mix of habitat attracts a variety of birds to the Holme Bird Observatory Reserve (run by the Norfolk Naturalists Trust). The observatory has a good natural history display.

Titchwell
This reserve, run by the Royal Society for the Protection of Birds, is very accessible to the public: the path runs through woods and along a raised bank to a hide on the beach, making it possible to get excellent views of the bird-thronged reedbeds, mudflats and shoreline. An excellent information centre provides details of everything likely to be seen.

Holkham
Holkham itself is in the heart of a vast National Nature Reserve stretching from Burnham Overy Staithe to Blakeney. The pine woods behind the dunes at Holkham are home to a host of small birds,

while the wild saltmarshes attract winter flocks of white-fronted, pink-footed and brent geese.

Cley-next-the-Sea
This is the jewel in the ornithological crown of north Norfolk. It was the first ever bird reserve, founded in 1926 by the Norfolk Naturalists' Trust. An astonishing total of 325 different species have been recorded here, some of which may be spotted from perimeter paths and public hides.

Blakeney Point
This still-growing spit of land sticking out into the North Sea is owned by the National Trust and may be reached on foot from Cley or by boat from Blakeney or Morston. The area is famous for its large tern colonies and is also a landing point for small migrants. The birds may be viewed from a hide on the point. Common and grey seals may also be seen.

212 CATTON OLD HALL　　　　🏵🏵🏵 HIGHLY COMMENDED

Lodge Lane, Old Catton, Norwich, Norfolk NR6 7HG Tel (01603) 419379 Fax (01603) 400339

Built during the English civil war in 1632 and restored to a high standard, providing luxury bed & breakfast accommodation for business or pleasure. The oak-beamed rooms are tastefully decorated and well-appointed, providing guests with little extras to make a stay memorable, such as romantic candle-light dinners and winter log fires. Ideal for visiting the Cathedral city or exploring the Norfolk countryside. Guests will enjoy the relaxed atmosphere and a chance to be pampered in this impressive family home.

Bed & Breakfast per night: single occupancy from £37.50–£45.00; double room from £55.00–£65.00
Half board per person: £53.50–£61.00 daily
Evening meal 1800 (last orders 2100)

Bedrooms: 2 double, 2 twin
Bathrooms: 4 en-suite
Parking for 20
Cards accepted: Access, Visa, Diners, Amex

213 THE OLD RECTORY　　　　🏵🏵 DE LUXE

Watton Road, Little Melton, Norwich, Norfolk NR9 3PB Tel (01603) 812121 or (01603) 810279 Fax (01603) 812521

Beautiful Victorian country house set in three-and-a-half acres, furnished with antiques, offering open log fires, books, magazines, games, sun-terraces, croquet lawn. Three double bedrooms, elegantly decorated with en-suite/private bathrooms, television and beverage-making facilities. Grand luxurious Victorian four-poster suite for special occasions. Situated only five miles from Norwich city centre with its Norman castle, cathedral, medieval churches and narrow cobbled streets. Conveniently placed for exploring the Broads, stately homes, traditional fishing villages and seaside.

Bed & Breakfast per night: single occupancy from £32.00–£39.00; double room from £44.00–£58.00
Bedrooms: 3 double

Bathrooms: 2 en-suite, 1 private
Parking for 10
Cards accepted: Diners

214 OAKFIELD　　　　🏵🏵 HIGHLY COMMENDED

Yelverton Road, Framingham Earl, Norwich, Norfolk NR14 7SD Tel (01508) 492605

You can be assured of a warm welcome, a relaxed atmosphere, every comfort and excellent breakfasts at Oakfield which is situated in a beautiful quiet location, yet only five miles from the centre of the fine city of Norwich. Oakfield is ideally positioned for visiting the Broads, the lovely heritage coastlines of North Norfolk and Suffolk, Minsmere and many other bird sanctuaries. Local pubs and restaurants serve good evening meals. Ample car parking space. Four acres of adjacent meadowland.

Bed & Breakfast per night: single room from £16.00–£20.00; double room from £32.00–£40.00
Bedrooms: 1 single, 1 double, 1 twin

Bathrooms: 1 private, 1 private shower
Parking for 6

215 THE LODGE

🦪🦪 HIGHLY COMMENDED

Cargate Lane, Saxlingham Thorpe, Norwich, Norfolk NR15 1TU Tel (01508) 471422

A listed Regency house in three acres of secluded grounds, conveniently situated close to the A140 south of Norwich. All the rooms are elegantly furnished in the best country house tradition and give a warm, friendly ambience. Guests are welcome to relax in two spacious sitting rooms, or enjoy cocktails in the restored conservatory. Imaginative, candle-lit dinners are prepared using fresh produce and herbs from the garden. Guests may invite friends to join them for dinner. Licensed.

Bed & Breakfast per night: single room from £28.00; double room from £48.00
Half board per person: £41.00–£45.00 daily; £258.30–£283.50 weekly

Evening meal 1930 (last orders 2000)
Bedrooms: 1 single, 1 double, 1 twin
Bathrooms: 2 en-suite, 1 private
Parking for 12

216 THE OLD RECTORY

🦪🦪 HIGHLY COMMENDED

Gissing, Diss, Norfolk IP22 3XB Tel (01379) 677575 Fax (01379) 674427

This handsome and exuberantly furnished Victorian house stands in grounds of mature garden and woodland, and is a haven of peace, comfort and elegance. Bedrooms are spacious with private or en-suite bathrooms. Every effort has been made to ensure a memorable stay: tea/coffee making facilities, colour television, note paper, fresh flowers and an extensive range of toiletries. Breakfast is copious and beautifully presented. Candle-lit dinners are available by prior arrangement. Croquet, large indoor pool. No smoking.

Bed & Breakfast per night: single occupancy from £36.00–£42.00; double room from £48.00–£58.00
Half board per person: £43.50–£48.50 daily
Lunch available: Packed lunches by arrangement
Evening meal 1945 (last bookings 1945)

Bedrooms: 1 double, 2 twin
Bathrooms: 3 private
Parking for 6

217 EARSHAM PARK FARM

🦪🦪 HIGHLY COMMENDED

Harleston Road, Earsham, Bungay, Suffolk NR35 2AQ Tel (01986) 892180 Fax (01986) 892180

Park Farm has historic links with the 14th century and the Duke of Norfolk. The beautiful Victorian farmhouse, set on a hill overlooking the Waveney Valley, is secluded with superb views. All the en-suite rooms are spacious, centrally heated, well-fitted and include television and beverage facilities. Enjoy our large gardens, farm walks and superb farmhouse breakfasts using the best local produce. We care for all your comforts in this non-smoking home-from-home.

Bed & Breakfast per night: single occupancy from £22.00–£26.00; double room from £35.00–£39.00
Evening meal 1800 (last orders 2000)
Bedrooms: 2 double, 1 twin

Bathrooms: 3 private
Parking for 11
Cards accepted: Diners

218 IVY HOUSE FARM

☰☰ HIGHLY COMMENDED

Ivy Lane, Oulton Broad, Lowestoft, Suffolk NR33 8HY Tel (01502) 501353 Fax (01502) 501539

Tucked away down a leafy drive in a quiet broadside location adjacent to a nature reserve, the farmhouse stands in a large country garden bordered by ponds and meadows. All the rooms have views of the garden and surrounding countryside. Log fires. From Easter the conversion of farm buildings and a thatched barn will provide ten spacious en-suite rooms with two suitable for the disabled, and a restaurant.

Bed & Breakfast per night: single occupancy from
£30.00–£35.00; double room from £43.00–£52.00
Bedrooms: 1 double, 1 twin, 1 triple

Bathrooms: 3 private
Parking for 12
Cards accepted: Access, Visa, Diners

219 THE OLD RECTORY

☰☰ HIGHLY COMMENDED

157 Church Road, Kessingland, Lowestoft, Suffolk NR33 7SQ Tel (01502) 740020

Set in two acres of beautiful gardens, enjoying peace and tranquillity well away from the road, with no worries about parking, our house is a very attractive former rectory built around 1830. Delightfully furnished with many antiques, all the bedrooms face south, overlooking the garden, and are light, spacious and comfortable. During your stay with us we want our home to be your home and on leaving, a lovely memory.

Bed & Breakfast per night: single occupancy from
£22.00–£24.00; double room from £40.00–£44.00
Bedrooms: 2 double, 1 twin

Bathrooms: 3 en-suite, 1 public
Parking for 6
Open: May–September

220 CHIPPENHALL HALL

☰☰☰ HIGHLY COMMENDED

Fressingfield, Eye, Suffolk IP21 5TD Tel (01379) 586733 or (01379) 588180 Fax (01379) 586272

A listed Tudor manor of Saxon origin, recorded in Domesday book, enjoying total rural seclusion in seven acres of gardens with ponds, and a heated outdoor pool set in a rose-covered courtyard. The manor is heavily beamed with inglenook log fireplaces. For that special anniversary with friends, arrange for pre-dinner drinks served in the bar and fine food and wines served by candle-light. Chippenhall is one of the very few country houses with an award for excellence. Located one mile south of Fressingfield, B1116.

Bed & Breakfast per night: single occupancy from
£48.00–£54.00; double room from £54.00–£60.00
Half board per person: £50.00–£53.00 daily;
£341.00–£361.00 weekly
Lunch available: sandwiches etc only 1230–1400

Evening meal 1930 (last bookings 1800)
Bedrooms: 3 double
Bathrooms: 3 en-suite
Parking for 12
Cards accepted: Access, Visa

221 THE OLD GUILDHALL
≋≋≋ HIGHLY COMMENDED

Mill Street, Gislingham, Eye, Suffolk IP23 8JT Tel (01379) 783361

This 15th-century guildhall has three en-suite bedrooms and is a fine example of timbered architecture with attractive grounds, central heating, television and tea/coffee-making facilities. The proprietor specialises in traditional English cooking. Parking. Golf within five miles. Bargain breaks.

Bed & Breakfast per night: single occupancy £35.00; double room £50.00	Bedrooms: 1 double, 2 twin	
Half board per person: £35.00 daily; £200.00 weekly	Bathrooms: 3 en-suite	
Evening meal 1900 (last bookings 1600)	Parking for 5	
	Open: February–December	

222 CHERRY TREE FARM
≋≋ HIGHLY COMMENDED

Mendlesham Green, Stowmarket, Suffolk IP14 5RQ Tel (01449) 766376

Martin and Diana Ridsdale invite guests to enjoy their hospitality in this timber-framed farmhouse. Situated in the very heart of rural Suffolk, it makes an ideal base for exploring this and neighbouring counties. Great care is taken in the preparation and cooking of all meals which are served around a refectory table. Bread is home baked and seasonal vegetables garden-fresh. The wine list includes an extensive range of East Anglian-produced wines.

Bed & Breakfast per night: single occupancy from £30.00–£30.00; double room from £40.00–£46.00	Bedrooms: 3 double	
Half board per person: £33.00–£36.00 daily	Bathrooms: 3 en-suite	
Evening meal 1900 (last bookings 1400)	Parking for 3	
	Open: February–December	

223 ANGEL HOTEL
≋≋≋ HIGHLY COMMENDED

Market Place, Lavenham, Sudbury, Suffolk CO10 9QZ Tel (01787) 247388 Fax (01787) 247057

Situated in the centre of England's finest medieval town, the Angel is family-run and offers quiet relaxation and fine food in a warm and happy atmosphere. We use only the best local fresh ingredients for a menu that changes daily and is complemented by a good wine list with a well-kept range of Suffolk real-ales. An ideal base from which to explore Suffolk's heritage towns and countryside.

Bed & Breakfast per night: single occupancy from £37.50–£50.00; double room from £50.00–£60.00	Evening meal 1845 (last orders 2115)	
Half board per person: £40.00–£45.00 daily; £280.00 weekly	Bedrooms: 6 double, 1 twin, 1 triple	
Lunch available: 1200–1415	Bathrooms: 8 private	
	Parking for 5	
	Cards accepted: Access, Visa, Switch/Delta	

224 OTLEY HOUSE
Helmingham Road, Otley, Ipswich, Suffolk IP6 9NR Tel (01473) 890 253 Fax (01473) 890 009

🏵🏵 HIGHLY COMMENDED

A 17th-century manor house in peaceful mature grounds with a small lake, just six miles from Woodbridge, offering a very high standard of accommodation with four luxuriously furnished bedrooms with en-suite bathrooms, a billiard room, continental lounge, Regency dining room, and open fires. Our continental cooking and fine wines will spoil you. An ideal base for touring historic East Anglia and capturing the bracing sea air on the nearby coast. A paradise for golfers.

Bed & Breakfast per night: single occupancy from £40.00–£48.00; double room from £48.00–£62.00
Half board per person: £40.50–£47.50 daily; £283.50–£332.50 weekly
Evening meal 1930 (last bookings 1600)

Bedrooms: 2 double, 2 twin
Bathrooms: 4 en-suite
Parking for 8
Open: March–October (other months by demand)

Timber frames and pargeting

SUFFOLK'S ANCIENT VILLAGES are full of old, beautiful buildings and rich in a variety of architectural styles. A striking feature of the county is the remarkable legacy of timber-framed houses, mostly dating from the Middle Ages, a time when Suffolk grew rich as a result of the wool trade. Places such as Lavenham and Kersey became important and wealthy cloth-manufacturing centres. Civic buildings and homes for prosperous merchants and farmers were constructed in the fashion of the day, from a solid framework of oak with wattle and daub between the timbers. The guildhall at Lavenham, a particularly splendid example, is open to the public, providing a

complete view of the exterior and interior makeup of this 16th-century building. The decline of the wool trade meant that few had the money to modernise and 'improve' their dwellings in subsequent centuries, so these villages remain remarkably unaltered, containing some of the most picturesque streets of timber-framed houses and shops to be found anywhere in England.

Pargeting, another charming architectural feature of Suffolk, surprisingly came about as a cost-cutting measure, rather than the extravagant display of craftsmanship it now seems. Timber-framed buildings required enormous amounts of wood – a fairly substantial farmhouse might require as many as 300 mature oaks in its construction. Inevitably, timber became scarce and therefore even more expensive, but in an age before the widespread use of bricks, there were no local alternatives to wood. Instead builders resorted to using poor quality timber frames which they disguised by means of plaster. Making a virtue out of a necessity, however, they began to create elaborate decorations in the plasterwork, 'combing' it into swirling designs or modelling it into flowers and tendrils or geometric patterns. The term for this was 'parget' or 'pargeting' from the old French word 'pargeter' – to throw over – because the plaster was thrown over the timber frame. A glance upwards in many Suffolk villages reveals how widespread this decorative style became. Some of the most extravagant examples of the technique may be seen at the Ancient House in Ipswich and in Nethergate Street, Clare.

The ornate Ancient House in Ipswich

225 SECKFORD HALL HOTEL
 HIGHLY COMMENDED

Woodbridge, Suffolk IP13 6NU Tel (01394) 385678 Fax (01394) 380610

A romantic Elizabethan mansion set in picturesque Suffolk country gardens. With oak panelling, beamed ceilings, inglenook fireplaces and antique furniture, Seckford Hall is a haven of seclusion and tranquillity with a terrace, lake, four-poster bedrooms, suites, two restaurants, leisure club with indoor pool, gym and spa bath, and 18-hole golf course.

Bed & Breakfast per night: single room from £79.00–£99.00; double room from £99.00–£140.00
Lunch available: 1230–1345
Evening meal 1915 (last orders 2130)

Bedrooms: 3 single, 14 double, 10 twin, 1 triple, 4 family rooms
Bathrooms: 32 private
Parking for 102
Cards accepted: Access, Visa, Diners, Amex

226 WENTWORTH HOTEL
 HIGHLY COMMENDED

Wentworth Road, Aldeburgh, Suffolk IP15 5BD Tel (01728) 452312 Fax (01728) 454343

With the comfort and style of a country hotel, Wentworth Hotel sits facing the sea on the Suffolk coast. Two comfortable lounges with antique furniture and open fires provide ample space to relax. Each bedroom has colour television, telephone, radio, hairdryer, tea-making and many have sea views. The restaurant serves a variety of fresh produce, including local seafood. Choose a light lunch from the bar menu and, weather permitting, eat outside in the sunken terrace garden. Year-round bargain get-aways available.

Bed & Breakfast per night: single room from £53.00–£59.00; double room from £86.00–£107.00
Half board per person: £50.50–£67.00 daily
Lunch available: 1200–1400
Evening meal 1900 (last orders 2100)

Bedrooms: 7 single, 11 double, 20 twin
Bathrooms: 37 private
Parking for 30
Cards accepted: Access, Visa, Diners, Amex, Switch/Delta

227 BUTLERS FARM
 HIGHLY COMMENDED

Colne Road, Bures, Suffolk CO8 5DN Tel (01787) 227243

Away from the bustle of modern life, this 17th-century timber-framed house offers peace and tranquillity. Set in its own ninety acres, guests keep returning to the warmth and comfort offered within the two en-suite rooms and one room with adjacent bathroom. Meals are offered willingly with twenty-four hours notice. This is a special base from which to explore Suffolk and Constable country. Quick and easy access from London's Liverpool Street (one hour): we'll collect guests from local station.

Bed & Breakfast per night: single occupancy from £19.00–£35.00; double room from £38.00–£55.00
Half board per person: £30.00–£50.00 daily; £205.00–£330.00 weekly
Lunch available: 1200–1400

Evening meal 1930 (last orders 2100)
Bedrooms: 1 double, 2 twin
Bathrooms: 2 en-suite
Parking for 6

228 THE BAUBLE

⚜⚜ HIGHLY COMMENDED

Higham, Colchester, Essex CO7 6LA Tel (01206) 337254 Fax (01206) 337263

The Bauble is an old property, carefully restored and ideally placed in the picturesque hamlet of Higham for touring East Anglia. With one-and-a-half acres of mature gardens overlooking water meadows in the heart of Constable country, Dedham, Flatford, Lavenham and Beth Chatto's garden are close by and Cambridge, Norwich, Aldeburgh and the coast are all within an hour's drive. Find us on the B1068 from the A12, through the village, immediately over the River Brett, on the left towards Stoke-by-Nayland.

Bed & Breakfast per night: single room from £20.00–£25.00; double room from £38.00–£45.00
Bedrooms: 1 single, 2 twin

Bathrooms: 1 private, 1 en-suite shower
Parking for 5

Constable Country

THE GREAT ENGLISH landscape painter John Constable (1776–1837) was born in the Suffolk village of East Bergholt. Although he later travelled widely in Britain, painting scenes as diverse as the Lake District, Stonehenge and Salisbury Cathedral, his chief inspiration was the landscape in which he spent his happy childhood. He loved the quiet Suffolk landscape: the flat meadows with the River Stour winding lazily under willow trees, cows grazing peacefully, a church spire or a windmill glimpsed in the distance, and the incandescent East Anglian sky towering over everything. 'These things made me a painter,' he said, 'and I am grateful.'

In Constable's day the River Stour would have been an important and busy waterway, full of boats and barges, with the lock gates never still and the mill-wheels always turning. Today the river is quiet and peaceful, but in other respects the landscape is virtually unchanged. It is quite possible to stand in the places where Constable stood and sketched around 200 years ago. Many of the buildings are still there: Flatford Mill, Willie Lott's Cottage, the churches at East Bergholt, Dedham and Stoke-by-Nayland. The pond at Flatford Mill is where Constable painted his most famous picture of all, *The Haywain* (now in the possession of the National Gallery in London). The mill is owned by the National Trust and has now become a field study centre for arts-based courses. Bridge Cottage, just upstream from Flatford Mill and also owned by the National Trust, was depicted in a number of Constable's paintings and now houses a display about the life and career of the artist.

Suffolk's famous Flatford Mill

229 BROMANS FARM

Listed HIGHLY COMMENDED

Mersea Island, East Mersea, Colchester, Essex CO5 8UE Tel (01206) 383235

Bromans Farm is peacefully situated in the country a few minutes walk from the sea and a nature reserve. Dating from the 14th century, it has been carefully restored to offer every modern comfort. The house is centrally heated and visitors are invited to unwind in the delightfully furnished sitting and dining rooms. Nine miles from Colchester, Mersea Island has excellent road and intercity rail connections with London and the ferry ports of Harwich and Felixstowe.

Bed & Breakfast per night: single occupancy from
£20.00–£25.00; double room from £30.00–£40.00
Bedrooms: 3 twin

Bathrooms: 2 private
Cards accepted: Access, Visa

230 SPRINGFIELDS

Listed DE LUXE

Ely Road, Little Thetford, Ely, Cambridgeshire CB6 3HJ Tel (01353) 663637 Fax (01353) 663130

Springfields, the lovely, spacious home of Mr and Mrs Derek Bailey, is furnished with taste and charm and set in one acre of the most beautiful gardens, displaying year-round colour, and situated in a quiet location one-and-a-half miles from Ely Cathedral and eleven miles from Cambridge's city centre. Relax in three elegant and delightful bedrooms, all overlooking gardens and offering superior modern amenities. A perfect base from which to explore the changeless beauty of the Fens. Stay a while and smell the roses! A non-smoking establishment.

Bed & Breakfast per night: single occupancy from
£25.00–£25.00; double room from £40.00–£40.00
Bedrooms: 1 double, 2 twin

Bathrooms: 1 en-suite, 1 public
Parking for 10
Open: January–November

231 FORGE COTTAGE

HIGHLY COMMENDED

Lower Road, Stuntney, Ely, Cambridgeshire CB7 5TN Tel (01353) 663275 or Mobile 0831 833932 Fax (01353) 662260

Located in the small village of Stuntney, one mile from Ely, this 17th-century farmhouse sits in a peaceful part of the village within two-and-a-half acres of landscaped gardens. With stunning views of Ely Cathedral, it is elegantly furnished with antiques and features oak beams and inglenook fireplaces. The accommodation consists of two comfortable en-suite rooms decorated in superior chintz-style soft furnishings, with colour television and tea/coffee making facilities.

Bed & Breakfast per night: single occupancy from
£30.00–£30.00; double room from £45.00–£45.00
Bedrooms: 1 double, 1 twin

Bathrooms: 2 en-suite
Parking for 4

232 BRAMBLES
⚊⚊ HIGHLY COMMENDED

Mildenhall Road, Worlington, Bury St Edmunds, Suffolk IP28 8RY Tel & Fax (01638) 713121

Set in three acres of lovely grounds, Brambles is ideally placed for visits to Cambridge, Bury St. Edmunds and Ely. Our individually-tailored Newmarket tours for horse-racing enthusiasts are a must. As a private house, guests are welcomed as part of the family and enjoy the comfort of personal service. Breakfast and dinner are served in our elegant dining room where fresh produce and creative and imaginative cooking combine to give you a stay to remember.

Bed & Breakfast per night: double room £50.00; single occupancy of double room £30.00; (10% discount for 3 days or more)
Evening meal 2000 (£18.00)

Bedrooms: 1 double, 2 twin
Bathrooms: 3 private
Parking for 6

---

233 HIGHFIELD FARM
⚊⚊ HIGHLY COMMENDED

Great North Road, Sandy, Bedfordshire SG19 2AQ Tel (01767) 682332

A tranquil and welcoming house with a warm and friendly atmosphere, set in its own grounds on an attractive arable farm, to which most guests return. Some rooms are on the ground floor and in delightfully converted stables. Highfield is set well back from the A1, giving quiet and peaceful seclusion, yet easily accessible and convenient for Cambridge, the RSPB, the Shuttleworth Aircraft Museum, London and much more. Ample safe parking. Closed Christmas. A no-smoking house. Contact Mrs Margaret Codd.

Bed & Breakfast per night: single occupancy from £19.00–£25.00; double room from £32.00–£38.00
Bedrooms: 2 double, 3 twin, 1 triple

Bathrooms: 4 en-suite, 1 private
Parking for 8

---

234 BEDFORD ARMS AT CHENIES
⚊⚊⚊⚊ HIGHLY COMMENDED

(A Thistle Country House Hotel), Chenies, Rickmansworth, Hertfordshire WD3 6EQ Tel (01923) 283301 Fax (01923) 284825

The Bedford Arms, a Thistle Country House Hotel and Restaurant, is just minutes from Junction 18/M25 and twenty miles from central London, on the edge of the Chiltern Hills. This delightful ten-bedroom hotel offers luxurious comfort in its beautifully furnished rooms (one a four-poster), every modern facility, en-suite marble tiled bathrooms, and satellite television. Excellent classical French and English food is served in the oak-panelled restaurant and the pub serves traditional light meals and real ales.

Bed & Breakfast per night: single room from £95.00–£125.00; double room from £105.00–£125.00
Lunch available: 1200–1415
Evening meal 1930 (last orders 2200)

Bedrooms: 3 single, 6 double, 1 twin
Bathrooms: 10 en-suite
Parking for 120
Cards accepted: Access, Visa, Diners, Amex

235 DOWN HALL COUNTRY HOUSE HOTEL ♛♛♛♛♛ HIGHLY COMMENDED

Hatfield Heath, Bishop's Stortford, Hertfordshire CM22 7AS Tel (01279) 731441 Fax (01279) 730416

Down Hall is a majestic Victorian mansion set in over one hundred acres of beautiful woodland, park-land and landscaped gardens in the Hertfordshire countryside. From the luxurious bedrooms and splendour of the restaurants to the extensive indoor and outdoor leisure facilities, Down Hall combines the elegance of centuries with the excellence of today. The perfect venue for a carefree stay, with time to enjoy those finer things in life.

Bed & Breakfast per night: single room from £95.25; double room from £133.50
Half board per person: £77.50 daily (weekends only)
Lunch available: 1230–1400
Evening meal 1900 (last orders 2130)

Bedrooms: 16 single, 76 double, 11 twin
Bathrooms: 103 en-suite
Parking for 130
Cards accepted: Access, Visa, Diners, Amex, Switch/Delta

The Dunmow Flitch

THIS STRANGE CUSTOM is thought to date back to 1244, when the practice may have been brought over from Brittany by the Fitzwalters, a local Dunmow family. To win the flitch (or side) of bacon, a couple must prove that in the first twelve months and a day of their marriage they have not exchanged a single word of anger, and never repented the day they wed. The winners are also awarded the right to sit in a special chair in the Little Dunmow church.

The ceremony fell into abeyance and was revived by Harrison Ainsworth, a historical novelist. It is now held every four years in Great Dunmow with a bewigged judge who conducts a trial with the utmost (mock) seriousness. The once-common phrase 'to eat Dunmow bacon' means to live in married bliss but apparently few actually managed to do so as between 1244 and 1773, only eight couples won the flitch!

Mary Evans Picture Library

England's West Country

Brixham

ENGLAND TAPERS RATHER SLOWLY but inexorably, towards its western conclusion at Land's End. Rugged cliffs fending off the Atlantic represent the western extreme of England's mainland, and symbolise for many the essence of Cornwall. This is the county with more coastline than any other, indeed where the sea is never more than half an hour's drive away. The beautiful coastline, allied with a benign climate, has combined to make this one of England's most popular holiday destinations. Although the Cornish language has now died in everything but place names the spirit of a land apart lives on. Indeed, before the Tamar railway bridge was opened in the 19th century, Cornwall was the remotest county in England. Now the Cornish are well served by rail and road and a journey there is nothing like the daunting prospect of years ago – even though Penzance is further from London than Carlisle.

Walkers are well served both in the largely gentle interior – Bodmin Moor is the wild and bleak exception – and especially on the scenically spectacular coastal path. This is almost always the best way to explore the coastline, as roads tend to hold back from the creeks, coves, bays and drowned valleys which give Cornwall its majesty – a majesty set off to perfection by such villages as Polperro, Port Isaac and Mevagissey.

Torquay

Devon's variety is one of its greatest assets: once again the coast is superb, with highpoints at Exmoor in the north, where verdant oak and birch woods plummet into the Bristol Channel, and at the equally dramatic coast of the South Hams around Salcombe and Dartmouth. Devon has two national parks in Dartmoor and Exmoor – the former a surprising wilderness, whilst Exmoor is smaller, but has the glory of the sea. Both rise to impressive heights, Exmoor reaching 1,704ft at Dunkery Beacon and Dartmoor just over 2,000ft at Higher Willhays. Devon's population is fairly scattered, with large urban centres only at Plymouth, Torbay and Exeter. The last of these boasts one of England's most beautiful cathedrals, in which you can see the longest span of Gothic vaulting in England.

Looe

Somerset, too, has a magnificent cathedral, though this is in England's smallest city. Containing no less than 356 separate statues of various worthies, the beauty of Wells Cathedral's 13th-century west front is staggering, and the buildings of the town as a whole, and the Vicar's close in particular, give admirable support. Glastonbury and Cheddar are towns in the Mendips with well-known historical and geological attractions, making this range of hills a fine base for family holidays. The other hills in the county – Brendon Hills on the edge of Exmoor, Black Down Hills south-west of Taunton, the peaceful Quantocks near Bridgwater – all dwarf the final range, the Poldens. These wouldn't even count, were they not on the edge of the Somerset Levels, the lowest-lying part of England's West Country, beside which they seem every bit as large as their bigger cousins.

Avon has some fine limestone scenery in its share of
the Mendips, two established seaside resorts in
Weston-super-Mare and Clevedon, and a small bite of
the Cotwolds on its northern border. Its two cities,
Bristol and Bath both reward exploration, with the
suburb of Clifton being Bristol's rather impressive imitation of neighbouring Bath's Georgian splendour.

Dorset is thoroughly pleasing, without ever over-
stating its case, though as so often in the West
Country its coastline is upon occasion sublime, as at
the undercliff at Lyme Regis. The downs, inland, have
become less heath and more fields since Hardy's day,
but the gentle pace of life – there are no large towns –
and the picturesque villages with thatch almost as common as tile, make
this an excellent English touring and walking county.

For much of this century Wiltshire was overlooked in its own right,
more often passed through on the way to its more illustrious neigh-
bours. Now, though, its open downland, its relatively small population,
its exquisite small towns and villages (Bradford on Avon, Castle Combe,
Malmesbury and Ramsbury, for example), its canals and its prehistoric
sites make it increasingly popular. It's also a county of superlatives, with
the largest series of canal locks in England to be found just outside
Devizes, the tallest medieval spire on Salisbury cathedral (404ft), and the
highest concentration of tumuli, barrows, standing stones, hillforts and
ancient paths.

This sense of our long-dead ancestors walking these counties – from
the Arthurian connections of Cornwall, and the mythical stories of
Joseph of Arimathea at Glastonbury to the builders of Stonehenge and
Avebury – is perhaps the enduring and unifying theme to England's
West Country.

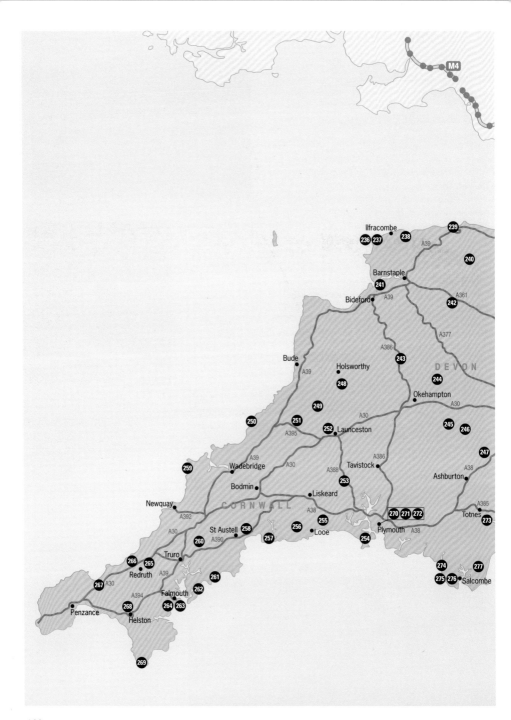

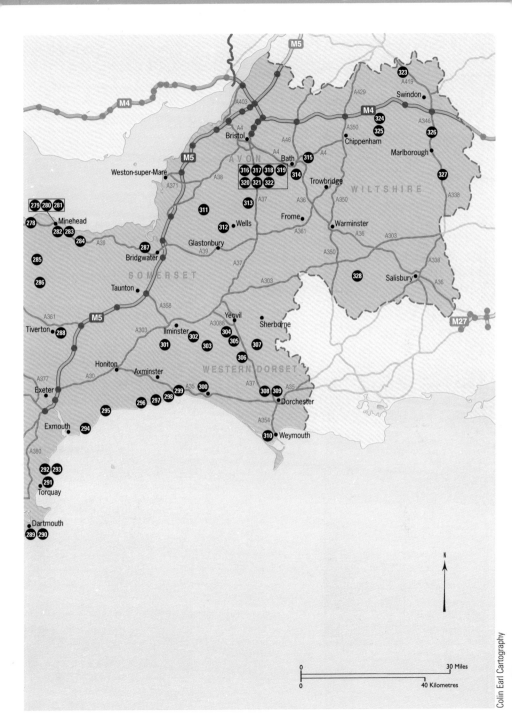

England's West Country map showing locations:

M5, M4, A419, 323, Swindon, A429, A403, M4, 324, A346, A350, 325, 326, A4, Bristol, A46, Chippenham, Marlborough, M5, A4, Bath, 315, A4, 316 317 318 319, 314, 327, Weston-super-Mare, A38, 320 321 322, Trowbridge, WILTSHIRE, A371, A338, 279 280 281, 313, A37, A36, A350, 278, 311, Frome, Warminster, Minehead, 312, Wells, A361, A36, A303, 282 283, 284, A39, 287, Glastonbury, A350, A338, 285, Bridgwater, A39, A37, 286, SOMERSET, 328, Salisbury, A36, Taunton, A303, A358, A361, M5, Yeovil, M27, Tiverton, 288, A303, Ilminster, A3088, Sherborne, 304, 301, 302, 305, 306, 307, 303, 306, Honiton, Axminster, WESTERN DORSET, A377, A30, A37, Exeter, 296 297 298 299, 300, 308 309, A35, 295, Dorchester, Exmouth, 294, A354, A380, 310, Weymouth, 292 293, 291, Torquay, Dartmouth, 289 290

N

0   30 Miles
0   40 Kilometres

121

236 WATERSMEET HOTEL
HIGHLY COMMENDED

Mortehoe, Woolacombe, Devon EX34 7EB Tel (01271) 870333 Fax (01271) 870890

Set on the National Trust Atlantic coastline with panoramic views of Hartland Point and Lundy Island, the three acres of garden enclose a lawn tennis court, an open air swimming pool and steps to the beach below. The resident owners ensure the Watersmeet offers the comfort and peace of a country house, and all the main bedrooms, lounges and the octagonal restaurant overlook the sea. The Watersmeet offers a wine list to complement its national award-winning cuisine and service.

Half board per person: £50.00–£85.00 daily; £350.00–£540.00 weekly
Lunch available: 1230–1400
Evening meal 1900 (last orders 2030)
Bedrooms: 4 single, 9 double, 7 twin, 3 triple

Bathrooms: 23 private
Parking for 50
Open: February–November
Cards accepted: Access, Visa, Diners, Amex

237 THE CLEEVE HOUSE
HIGHLY COMMENDED

Mortehoe, Woolacombe, Devon EX34 7ED Tel (01271) 870719

The Cleeve offers a holiday to remember and our friendly hotel is renowned for its top-quality cuisine, using fresh local produce, with lobster a speciality. Excellent accommodation with en-suite rooms individually designed for your every comfort. We also have ample private parking. There are plenty of activities for everyone: golf, fishing, surfing, riding, walks, and boat trips as well as National Trust properties, gardens and smugglers coves to explore. Brochure with pleasure from Marian & Richard Ashfold.

Bed & Breakfast per night: single occupancy from £29.00–£38.00; double room from £38.00–£54.00
Half board per person: £29.00–£37.00 daily; £223.00–£244.00 weekly
Lunch available: Summer Only 1200 1430

Evening meal 1930 (last bookings 1800)
Bedrooms: 5 double, 1 twin
Bathrooms: 6 private
Parking for 9
Open: March–October

Cards accepted: Access, Visa

238 BESSEMER THATCH HOTEL AND RESTAURANT
HIGHLY COMMENDED

Berrynarbor, Devon EX34 9SE Tel (01271) 882296

Situated in one of Devon's prettiest villages and only ten miles from the Exmoor border, Bessemer Thatch is the perfect retreat from life's stresses and strains. Four-poster bedrooms with a charming decor and furnishings compliment this lovely old 13th-century building that offers peace and quiet with more than a little comfort. In the dining room with its cosy inglenook fireplace enjoy the very best of traditional English menus which are always carefully prepared and presented. Truly somewhere special.

Half board per person: £41.00–£56.00 daily; £287.00–£342.00 weekly
Evening meal 1930 (last orders 2130)

Bedrooms: 3 double
Bathrooms: 1 en-suite, 2 private
Cards accepted: Access, Visa

239 VICTORIA LODGE ≋≋≋ HIGHLY COMMENDED

31 Lee Road, Lynton, Devon EX35 6BS Tel (01598) 753203

An elegant Victorian, family-run hotel with top awards for its comfort, hospitality and outstanding cuisine. All bedrooms are centrally heated, en-suite and beautifully decorated, with colour television and beverage-making facilities, and some are de luxe four-poster rooms. Dine by candle-light in our elegant dining room and enjoy our four-course dinner that combines an imaginative blend of English and continental cuisine. Private car park. Special rates for weekly and short breaks. No smoking.

Bed & Breakfast per night: single occupancy from £18.00–£30.00; double room from £36.00–£60.00
Half board per person: £32.00–£44.00 daily;
£210.00–£283.00 weekly
Evening meal 1900 (last bookings 1630)

Bedrooms: 8 double, 1 twin, 1 family room
Bathrooms: 10 en-suite, 1 public
Parking for 8
Open: February–November
Cards accepted: Access, Visa

240 SIMONSBATH HOUSE HOTEL ≋≋≋≋ HIGHLY COMMENDED

Simonsbath, Minehead, Somerset TA24 7SH Tel (0164) 383259

The first house to be built within the Royal Forest of Exmoor in 1654, Simonsbath House is now a small and friendly family-run country house hotel situated in an ideal position for exploring the Exmoor National Park and the north Devon coastline, on foot or by car. Receive peace and quiet, unstinting comfort, generous and deliciously interesting home-cooked food, rooms with log fires and panelling and some with four-poster beds.

Bed & Breakfast per night: single room from £44.00–£60.00; double room from £78.00–£90.00
Half board per person: £63.00–£78.00 daily;
£399.00–£504.00 weekly
Evening meal 1900 (last orders 2030)

Bedrooms: 4 double, 3 twin
Bathrooms: 7 en-suite
Parking for 30
Open: February–November
Cards accepted: Access, Visa, Diners, Amex

241 THE COMMODORE HOTEL ≋≋≋≋ HIGHLY COMMENDED

Marine Parade, Instow, Devon EX39 4JN Tel (01271) 860347 Fax (01271) 861233

Situated in the waterside village of Instow, one of the prettiest locations on the North Devon coast and the ideal touring centre for golf, walking and sailing. Our spacious and inviting restaurant is noted for its fresh cuisine and friendly attentive service in an atmosphere of style and comfort. The individually designed rooms are spacious and tastefully decorated to a high standard. The hotel is now enjoying its twenty-fifth year, personally owned and managed by the Woolaway family.

Bed & Breakfast per night: single room from £40.00–£50.00; double room from £60.00–£90.00
Half board per person: £40.00–£50.00 daily
Evening meal 1900 (last orders 2115)

Bedrooms: 1 single, 12 double, 7 twin
Bathrooms: 20 private
Parking for 150
Cards accepted: Access, Visa, Amex, Switch/Delta

242 MARSH HALL Country House Hotel
≈≈≈≈ HIGHLY COMMENDED

Marsh Hall, South Molton, Devon EX36 3HQ Tel (01769) 572666 Fax (01769) 574230

Marsh Hall is a lovely Victorian country house with stained-glass windows, chandeliers and tessellated tiled floors, set in three acres of lawns and woodland. With its spacious lounges, gallery and bedrooms, it is the ideal place in which to relax and enjoy the comforts of life. The lovely pink and green award-winning restaurant serves a four-course dinner with mouth-watering dishes devised from local fare and fresh produce grown in the hotel's herb, vegetable and fruit gardens.

Bed & Breakfast per night: single room from £40.00–£47.00; double room from £65.00–£85.00
Half board per person: £50.00–£65.00 daily; £295.00–£350.00 weekly
Evening meal 1900 (last orders 2030)

Bedrooms: 1 single, 4 double, 2 twin
Bathrooms: 7 en-suite
Parking for 20
Cards accepted: Access, Visa, Diners, Amex

243 GIFFORDS HELE
≈≈≈ HIGHLY COMMENDED

Meeth, Okehampton, Devon EX20 3QN Tel (01837) 810009 Fax (01837) 810009

Blissful indoor pool, sauna and wildflower walks to relax you. Food fit for a gourmet and staff that care about your comfort. Our Domesday Farmstead is set deep in the Devonshire countryside where tradition and courtesy are a natural ingredient of your stay. Lying north of Dartmoor in the Torridge valley, we are near Rosemoor RHS Gardens and make an ideal touring base. Two longhouse cottages are also available for the independent minded.

Bed & Breakfast per night: single occupancy from £31.00–£37.00; double room from £46.00–£58.00
Half board per person: £38.00–£52.00 daily
Evening meal 1900 (last orders 2130)

Bedrooms: 1 double, 1 twin, 1 triple
Bathrooms: 3 en-suite
Parking for 8

244 LOWER NICHOLS NYMET FARM
≈≈ HIGHLY COMMENDED

Lower Nichols Nymet, North Tawton, Devon EX20 2BW Tel (01363) 82510

We offer a haven of comfort and rest on our farm that is set in rolling countryside in the centre of Devon. On holiday, food becomes important – we serve hearty and healthy breakfasts and candle-lit dinners using local produce. Our elegantly furnished en-suite bedrooms have glorious views. There are many National Trust properties and other attractions to visit. This is a perfect base for exploring the beauties of the West Country. A non-smoking establishment. Brochure available.

Bed & Breakfast per night: single occupancy from £17.00–£18.50; double room from £34.00–£37.00
Half board per person: £27.50–£29.00 daily
Bedrooms: 1 double, 1 family

Bathrooms: 2 en-suite
Parking for 4
Open: March–October

245 MILL END HOTEL
☸☸☸☸ HIGHLY COMMENDED

Sandypark, Chagford, Newton Abbot, Devon TQ13 8JN   Tel (01647) 432282   Fax (01647) 433106

Converted from a working mill, Mill End has retained all its rural charm. The mill wheel still turns in the courtyard and the Teign, which runs by the door, is one of the ten best sea-trout rivers in the country, with fishing available to guests. The gardens and walks are delightful and the hotel is ideal as a touring centre for the West. Then again, you could just sleep!

Bed & Breakfast per night: single room from £45.00–£55.00; double room from £70.00–£90.00	Bedrooms: 1 single, 5 double, 8 twin, 2 triple
Half board per person: £55.00–£70.00 daily	Bathrooms: 16 private
Lunch available: 1230–1400 by appointment	Parking for 17
Evening meal 1930 (last orders 2100)	Cards accepted: Access, Visa, Diners, Amex, Switch/Delta

Walking the Letterboxes of Dartmoor

IN 1854 JAMES PERROTT, a guide based in Chagford, left a small receptacle at Cranmere Pool, scarcely more than an isolated puddle in the depths of wildest Dartmoor. Partly because it was a remote and difficult place to find, those who managed to track it down were keen then to leave some record of their minor achievement. Successful walkers would sign a visitors' book and then place their own visiting cards besides those accumulating at Cranmere Pool.

Later, after the introduction of postcards, the custom metamorphosed into the practice of placing stamped, self-addressed postcards at Cranmere Pool. The next visitor would place his or her own card in the box and remove the one left by the previous visitor. The intrigue lay in the time it took for the postcard to be reunited with its writer. The visitors' book was still signed, however, and in 1908 the number of signatures totalled a huge 1,741.

From the humble beginnings of just a single letterbox, the idea has taken off in recent decades and at any one time there may be over 1000 'letterboxes' scattered over this wildest, least-populated tract of southern England. These contain a visitors' book, a rubber stamp and an ink pad, the latter two items being an innovation allowing the walker to 'collect' letterbox stamps on a piece of paper or the postcard itself (provided it doesn't cover the postage stamp). The 1:25,000 large-scale Ordnance Survey map for Dartmoor still clearly marks

'Cranmere Pool Letter Box' beside a minute body of water in the midst of a sea of featureless moorland. For those interested in signing their name in the visitors' book of the original letterbox, the grid reference is: SX603858.

A few of the many personal stamps used by letterbox hunters

246 WOOSTON FARM

≋≋≋ HIGHLY COMMENDED

Moretonhampstead, Newton Abbot, Devon TQ13 8QA Tel (01647) 440367

Wooston Farm is situated above the Teign Valley in the Dartmoor National Park, with views over open moorland. The farmhouse is surrounded by a delightful garden. There are plenty of walks to take on the moor and in the wooded Teign Valley. Good home cooking and cosy log fires await you at Wooston with two double en-suite rooms (one four-poster), and one twin room. Mountain bikes available. Open all year except Christmas.

Bed & Breakfast per night: double room from
£17.00–£20.00
Half board per person: £27.00–£30.00 daily
Evening meal 1800 (last orders 1830)

Bedrooms: 2 double, 1 twin
Bathrooms: 2 private, 1 private shower
Parking for 3

247 EDGEMOOR HOTEL

≋≋≋≋ HIGHLY COMMENDED

Haytor Road, Bovey Tracey, Devon TQ13 9LE Tel (01626) 832466 Fax (01626) 834760

'Loaded with charm', this wistaria-clad country house hotel is personally run by resident proprietors Rod and Pat Day. With its beautiful gardens and lovely en-suite bedrooms (including some four-posters) the Edgemoor provides the ideal setting in which to unwind from the cares of modern life. Friendly attentive staff, good food, fine wines and beautiful countryside combine to help make your stay memorable and enjoyable.

Bed & Breakfast per night: single room from
£37.95–£44.75; double room from £65.00–£89.50
Half board per person: £47.00–£61.25 daily;
£280.00–£346.50 weekly
Lunch available: 1215–1400

Evening meal 1930 (last orders 2100)
Bedrooms: 3 single, 6 double, 2 twin, 1 triple
Bathrooms: 12 en-suite
Parking for 50
Cards accepted: Access, Visa, Diners, Amex

248 COURT BARN COUNTRY HOUSE HOTEL

≋≋≋≋ HIGHLY COMMENDED

Clawton, Holsworthy, Devon EX22 6PS Tel (01409) 271219 Fax (01409) 271309

Situated in quiet Devon countryside, this is one of the South West's great small touring hotels in five acres of gardens. Quiet country roads and clean safe beaches are just a few miles away on the Heritage coast, nature walks, cycle trails, National Trust houses and gardens are close. Enjoy the best of hospitality, good food and wines in a peaceful setting with an outdoor croquet lawn, badminton and lawn tennis courts. Court Barn is a place to remember.

Bed & Breakfast per night: single room from
£28.00–£35.00; double room from £56.00–£80.00
Half board per person: £48.00–£55.00 daily;
£280.00–£350.00 weekly
Lunch available: 1200–1400

Evening meal 1930 (last orders 2130)
Bedrooms: 1 single, 3 double, 2 twin, 2 triple
Bathrooms: 8 private, 1 private shower
Parking for 17
Cards accepted: Access, Visa, Diners, Amex

249 WHEATLEY FARM

☰☰☰ HIGHLY COMMENDED

Maxworthy, Launceston, Cornwall PL15 8LY Tel (01566) 781232 Fax (01566) 781232

Escape and unwind at Wheatley, where personal attention and a friendly atmosphere are a priority, as is our traditional and imaginative farmhouse cuisine. This is a lovely old farmhouse set in landscaped gardens on a family working farm in the peace of the Cornish countryside. Delightful pretty bedrooms, all with en-suite facilities, one with a romantic four-poster bed. Beautifully situated just a few miles from the spectacular rugged north coast and sandy coves.

Bed & Breakfast per night: double room from £38.00–£40.00
Half board per person: £30.00–£32.00 daily
Evening meal 1830 (last bookings 1400)

Bedrooms: 2 double, 2 family rooms
Bathrooms: 4 en-suite
Parking for 4
Open: April–September

250 POLKERR GUEST HOUSE

☰☰☰ HIGHLY COMMENDED

Tintagel, Cornwall PL34 0BY Tel (01840) 770382

Somewhere special was what we envisaged when we planned the decor of our en-suite rooms, dining room and the recently-constructed large and restful sun lounge that overlooks the garden: guests visiting Polkerr Guest House enjoy accommodation of the highest standard. Situated within a few minutes' walk of Tintagel village, the historic castle and cliffs that offer superb views of the coast, we are also ideally located for exploring the beauty of the country.

Bed & Breakfast per night: single room from £14.00–£17.00; double room from £30.00–£40.00
Half board per person: £23.00–£28.00 daily;
£161.00–£196.00 weekly

Evening meal 1830–1900
Bedrooms: 1 single, 3 double, 1 twin, 2 triple
Bathrooms: 6 en-suite, 1 private shower
Parking for 9

251 THE OLD VICARAGE

☰☰ HIGHLY COMMENDED

Treneglos, Launceston, Cornwall PL15 8UQ Tel (01566) 781351

An elegant Grade II listed Georgian vicarage set within its own grounds in peaceful seclusion near the spectacular north Cornwall coast. We pride ourselves on our hospitality and personal service which, together with high standards of furnishings, assure your absolute comfort. The en-suite bedrooms are fully-equipped, together with fresh flowers and personal touches expected of The Old Vicarage. Superb food is served with imaginative cuisine using produce from our own kitchen gardens. No smoking.

Bed & Breakfast per night: single occupancy from £19.50; double room £39.00
Bed & Breakfast per week: single occupancy from £129.50
Half board per person: £31.50 daily; £213.50 weekly
Evening meal 1800 (last orders 2130)

Bedrooms: 2 double
Bathrooms: 2 private
Parking for 10
Open: Easter–November

252 HURDON FARM

 HIGHLY COMMENDED

Launceston, Cornwall PL15 9LS Tel (01566) 772955

The elegant 18th-century stone farmhouse is superbly situated amidst the picturesque surroundings of a four-hundred acre working farm. The house has a comfortably relaxed and informal atmosphere. Exquisitely prepared food is a speciality and a typical dinner might comprise of a Stilton-stuffed pear or prawn roulade, steak & kidney pie or lamb en croûte, fruit-filled brandy baskets or steamed sticky toffee pudding, always served with lashings of clotted cream, followed by cheese and freshly ground coffee! Central heating throughout. Totally non-smoking.

Bed & Breakfast per night: single occupancy from £15.00–£18.00; double room from £30.00–£36.00
Half board per person: £24.50–£27.50 daily; £144.50–£165.50 weekly
Evening meal 1830 (last bookings 1630)

Bedrooms: 3 double, 1 twin, 1 triple, 1 family room
Bathrooms: 4 private, 1 private shower
Parking for 6
Open: May–October

253 EAST CORNWALL FARMHOUSE

HIGHLY COMMENDED

Fullaford Road, Callington, Cornwall PL17 8AN Tel (01579) 50018

Beautifully situated, former silver-mine Captain's home. Sympathetically restored in the style of a farmhouse. Close to National Trust's Cotehele House, the Rivers Tamar and Lynher and St. Mellion Golf Club. Ideal for exploring Dartmoor and Bodmin Moor, and within easy reach of both the north and south coasts. A warm friendly welcome with service above and beyond expectations. Evening meals of home grown and local produce by arrangement.

Bed & Breakfast per night: single room from £15.00–£19.00; double room from £30.00–£38.00
Half board per person: £22.50–£29.00 daily; £144.50–£204.00 weekly
Evening meal 1830

Bedrooms: 1 single, 2 double, 1 twin
Bathrooms: 1 en-suite, 1 public, 1 en-suite shower
Parking for 6
Open: March–November

254 HALFWAY HOUSE INN

HIGHLY COMMENDED

Fore Street, Kingsand, Torpoint, Cornwall PL10 1NA Tel (01752) 822279

Situated on the Cornwall coastal path, just thirty yards from the beach. At the heart of the historical colour-washed villages of Kingsand and Cawsand, adjacent to Mount Edgcumbe Park and a ferry ride away from the great naval city of Plymouth. The intimate restaurant specialises in locally-caught sea food, complemented by a selection of fine wines and real ales. A haven of peace and tranquillity, your stay here will be a truly unforgettable experience.

Bed & Breakfast per night: single room from £19.50; double room from £39.00
Half board per person: £30.00–£38.00 daily; £190.00–£245.00 weekly
Lunch available: 1200–1400

Evening meal 1900 (last orders 2200)
Bedrooms: 1 single, 3 double, 1 family room
Bathrooms: 5 en-suite
Cards accepted: Access, Visa, Diners, Amex

255 COOMBE FARM

HIGHLY COMMENDED

Widegates, Looe, Cornwall PL13 1QN Tel (01503) 240223

A lovely country house surrounded by lawns, meadows, woods and streams with superb views to the sea, and with log fires, delicious home cooking, and candle-light dining (licensed). All bedrooms are en-suite and have colour television, radio, tea/coffee making facilities and direct dial telephone. In the grounds are many animals and flowers, a swimming pool, and a stone barn with snooker and table tennis. Nearby are golf, fishing, tennis, horse riding and glorious walks and beaches.

Bed & Breakfast per night: single occupancy from £18.00–£24.00; double room from £36.00–£48.00
Half board per person: £30.00–£36.00 daily; £200.00–£245.00 weekly
Evening meal 1900 (last bookings 1900)

Bedrooms: 3 double, 3 twin, 4 family rooms
Bathrooms: 10 private
Parking for 12
Open: March–October

256 TRENDERWAY FARM

HIGHLY COMMENDED

Pelynt, Looe, Cornwall PL13 2LY Tel (01503) 72214

Built in the late 16th century, this mixed working farm is set in peaceful, beautiful countryside at the head of the Polperro Valley. Bedrooms here are truly superb – with bathrooms as big as some hotel bedrooms – and are decorated with the flair of a professional interior designer. A hearty farmhouse breakfast is served in the sunny conservatory, using local produce. Although an evening meal is not provided, an excellent range of nearby restaurants can be recommended. Totally non-smoking.

Bed & Breakfast per night: double room from £44.00–£56.00
Bedrooms: 3 double, 1 twin

Bathrooms: 4 en-suite
Parking for 4
Open: January–November

257 MARINA HOTEL

HIGHLY COMMENDED

Esplanade, Fowey, Cornwall PL23 1HY Tel (01726) 833315 Fax (01726) 833315

This Georgian hotel was originally built as the summer residence of the Bishop of Truro and is situated on the waterside with its own quay and moorings. The hotel faces south and most rooms (four have balconies) overlook the estuary. The private walled garden provides a quiet sunny spot from which to observe the waterside traffic. The restaurant overlooks the water and the talented chef, Dean Rodgers, provides a feast of local fish, shell fish, meat and game.

Bed & Breakfast per night: single occupancy from £40.00 winter–£51.00 high season; double room per person from £26.00 winter–£40.00 high season
Half board per person (based on 2 people sharing): daily, from £42.00 winter –£56.00 high season; weekly, from

£266.00 winter–£364.00 high season
Bedrooms: 6 double, 5 twin
Bathrooms: 11 private
Open: March–January
Cards accepted: Access, Visa, Amex, Switch/Delta

258 BOSCUNDLE MANOR HIGHLY COMMENDED

Tregrehan, St Austell, Cornwall PL25 3RL Tel (01726) 813557 Fax (01726) 814997

A lovely house in over ten acres of secluded grounds with a practice golf area. The rooms are very attractively furnished with antiques, pictures and family possessions. The bedrooms are extremely comfortable and most have spa baths and power showers. There is an outstanding wine list and beautifully prepared fresh food is served. Andrew and Mary Flint have been here for over fifteen years and their personal involvement and enthusiasm create a relaxed and happy atmosphere.

Bed & Breakfast per night: single room from
£55.00–£65.00; double room from £90.00–£110.00
Half board per person: £65.00–£85.00 daily;
£385.00–£525.00 weekly
Evening meal 1930 (last orders 2030)

Bedrooms: 2 single, 3 double, 5 twin
Bathrooms: 10 private
Parking for 15
Open: April–October
Cards accepted: Access, Visa, Amex

259 TREGLOS HOTEL HIGHLY COMMENDED

Constantine Bay, Padstow, Cornwall PL28 8JH Tel (01841) 520727 Fax (01841) 521163

Situated in an area of outstanding natural beauty, this delightful country-house hotel is perhaps the finest on this coast. The restaurant has recently been completely refurbished and our extensive table d' hôte menu is renowned for featuring locally-caught fish. The hotel is ideally placed to play many leading golf courses, enjoy spectacular coastal walks and to explore our historic National Trust properties and gardens.

Bed & Breakfast per night: single room from
£35.00–£64.50; double room from £62.00–£120.00
Half board per person: £42.50–£69.00 daily;
£296.00–£420.00 weekly
Lunch available: 1245–1400

Evening meal 1930 (last orders 2145)
Bedrooms: 8 single, 3 double, 29 twin, 4 suites
Bathrooms: 44 private
Parking for 58
Open: March–November

Cards accepted: Access, Visa

Trerice

THE NATIONAL TRUST, which owns Trerice, has made use of the stables to house a collection of lawnmowers. This bizarre display charts 250 years of the machines development . The idea of using a cylindrical cutter was inspired by a process in the cloth industry for trimming the nap. Later saw the introduction of mowers pulled by horses, equipped with leather slippers to prevent turf damage. This, plus steam-driven, chain-driven, side-wheel and of course, petrol-driven variations may all be seen at Trerice (tel. 01637 874404).

The house itself, built in 1573, is of weathered golden stone with four unusual curled and scrolled gables. The great chamber has a spectacular barrel ceiling, as well as a splendid fireplace with the date ANNO DOMINI MCCCCCLXX3, the final 3 added as the plasterer realised he hadn't left enough room for the correct form, III. The hall is lit by a magnificent double-storey mullioned window containing 576 individual panes of glass, many of them 16th-century.

Mary Evans Picture Library

260 BISSICK OLD MILL

🌊🌊🌊 HIGHLY COMMENDED

Ladock, Truro, Cornwall TR2 4PG   Tel (01726) 882557

Bissick Old Mill is known to be three hundred years old and continued as a flour mill until the mid-1960s. Its conversion has been sympathetically conceived to provide modern conveniences whilst maintaining its former character, including slate floors, natural stone walls and beamed ceilings. Our aim is to provide you with the perfect environment in which to relax and enjoy the beauty of Cornwall, all areas of which are readily accessible from our central location.

Bed & Breakfast per night: single room from £25.00–£32.00; double room from £50.00–£54.00
Half board per person: £36.00–£46.00 daily; £227.00–£290.00 weekly
Lunch available: 1200–1400

Evening meal 1900 (last bookings 1700)
Bedrooms: 1 single, 2 double, 1 twin
Bathrooms: 3 en-suite, 1 public
Parking for 9
Cards accepted: Access, Visa

261 LUGGER HOTEL

🌊🌊🌊🌊 HIGHLY COMMENDED

Portloe, Truro, Cornwall TR2 5RD   Tel (01872) 501322   Fax (01872) 501691

Dating from the 17th century and originally an inn frequented by smugglers, The Lugger is situated at the very waters-edge of a picturesque cove on the beautiful and unspoilt Cornish Roseland Peninsular. Internationally renowned for its first-class accommodation, superb food and wide selection of wines, the hotel has been in the ownership of the welcoming Powell family for three generations. It is the perfect place for lovers of nature and those in search of peace and seclusion.

Half board per person: £60.00–£65.00 daily; £350.00–£420.00 weekly
Lunch available: 1200–1400 Bar Lunches
Evening meal 1900 (last orders 2100)
Bedrooms: 3 single, 8 double, 8 twin

Bathrooms: 19 en-suite
Parking for 25
Open: February–November
Cards accepted: Access, Visa, Diners, Amex, Switch/Delta

262 ROSEVINE HOTEL

🌊🌊🌊🌊 HIGHLY COMMENDED

Porthcurnick Beach, Portscatho, Truro, Cornwall TR2 5EW   Tel (01872) 580230 or (01872) 580206   Fax (01872) 580230

Located immediately above an attractive sandy beach, this quiet country house hotel is set in large pleasant gardens and enjoys superb sea views across Gerans Bay and the unspoilt fishing village of Portscatho. Family-run with friendly staff, its top-class chefs provide excellent international cuisine in a spacious dining room with sea views. The hotel is situated within easy reach of many National Trust properties and gardens and numerous delightful coastal walks.

Bed & Breakfast per night: single room from £26.00–£38.00; double room from £52.00–£76.00
Half board per person: £39.00–£72.00 daily; £275.00–£480.00 weekly
Lunch available: 1200–1400

Evening meal 1915 (last orders 2030)
Bedrooms: 1 single, 4 double, 8 twin, 2 triple
Bathrooms: 14 en-suite, 1 private
Parking for 40
Open: March–October

Cards accepted: Access, Visa

263 PENMERE MANOR HOTEL

🍤🍤🍤🍤 HIGHLY COMMENDED

Mongleath Road, Falmouth, Cornwall TR11 4PN Tel (01326) 211411 Fax (01326) 371588 Telex 45608 PMHTL

A Georgian country house set in five acres of garden and woodland, Penmere Manor is a resort in itself. Bolitho's Restaurant offers extensive cuisine, whilst Fountains Bar is an alternative choice for informal dining and drinking. Penmere's leisure facilities have much for all ages – with indoor and outdoor pools, spa, sauna, mini gym, croquet and lots more games and activities – and it is within easy reach of beaches, walks and famous gardens.

Bed & Breakfast per night: single room from £55.00–£57.00; double room from £83.00–£112.00. Half board per person: £54.50–£74.00 daily; £359.00–£499.00 weekly. Evening meal 1900 (last orders 2100)

Bedrooms: 10 single, 8 double, 6 twin, 15 triple
Bathrooms: 39 private
Parking for 50
Cards accepted: Access, Visa, Diners, Amex

264 GREEN LAWNS HOTEL

🍤🍤🍤🍤 HIGHLY COMMENDED

Western Terrace, Falmouth, Cornwall TR11 4QJ Tel (01326) 312734 Fax (01326) 211427

Where can you relax in an elegant, centrally positioned, chateau-style hotel with views across the beautiful bay? The Green Lawns Hotel and the famous Garras Restaurant! If you are looking for a holiday where high standards and personal attention are paramount, you will enjoy an excellent choice of imaginative cuisine from a table d' hôte or à la carte menu. All our guests enjoy free membership to the Garras Leisure Club with its magnificent indoor swimming pool. 'Britain in Bloom' winners 1994.

Bed & Breakfast per night: single room from £44.00–£70.00; double room from £70.00–£104.00. Half board per person: £49.00–£84.00 daily; £324.00–£530.00 weekly. Lunch available: 1200–1345

Evening meal 1845 (last orders 2200)
Bedrooms: 6 single, 17 double, 9 twin, 2 triple, 6 family rooms
Bathrooms: 40 en-suite
Parking for 60
Cards accepted: Access, Visa, Diners, Amex, Switch/Delta

265 CROSSROADS HOTEL

🍤🍤🍤🍤 HIGHLY COMMENDED

Scorrier, Redruth, Cornwall TR16 5BP Tel (01209) 820551 Fax (01209) 820392

Crossroads Hotel is a purpose-built hotel with modern facilities, situated at the Scorrier exit of the A30, near Redruth. It makes an ideal venue for visiting all parts of Cornwall. We have a fine reputation for our service and food, and endeavour to meet the special requirements of our guests. There are ground floor bedrooms available and a lift. We hope to have the pleasure of welcoming you to Crossroads Hotel.

Bed & Breakfast per night: single room from £29.00–£38.00; double room from £40.00–£51.00. Half board per person: £29.00–£48.00 daily; £210.00–£280.00 weekly. Evening meal 1900 (last orders 2130)

Bedrooms: 6 single, 12 double, 15 twin, 3 triple
Bathrooms: 36 private
Parking for 140
Cards accepted: Access, Visa, Diners, Amex, Switch/Delta

266 AVIARY COURT HOTEL
♨♨♨♨ HIGHLY COMMENDED

Marys Well, Illogan, Redruth, Cornwall TR16 4QZ Tel (01209) 842256 Fax (01209) 843744

A charming three-hundred-year-old Cornish country house set in its own grounds on the edge of Illogan Woods, ideal for touring the South West peninsular and its many local attractions. Six well-equipped individual bedrooms with tea/coffee making facilities, biscuits, mineral water, fresh fruit, direct-dial telephone, remote control television and a view of the gardens. The resident family proprietors ensure personal service, offering well-cooked varied food that uses as much Cornish produce as possible.

Bed & Breakfast per night: single occupancy from £40.00; double room from £56.00
Half board per person: £52.00 daily; £480.00 weekly (two persons)
Lunch available: 1230–1330 Sunday Only

Evening meal 1900 (last orders 2030)
Bedrooms: 4 double, 1 twin, 1 triple
Bathrooms: 6 private
Parking for 25
Cards accepted: Access, Visa, Diners, Amex

The Tate at St Ives

CORNWALL, and St Ives in particular, has long attracted artists, drawn by its picturesque shoreline and dramatic seascapes – among its early visitors were Turner, Whistler and Sickert. But the 'St Ives School', as it later became known, did not become truly established until the middle of the 20th century.

It all began in 1928 when the painter Ben Nicholson and his fellow artist Christopher Wood visited St Ives on a painting expedition.

Through an open cottage door, they happened to glimpse the retired mariner and rag-and-bone merchant Alfred Wallis whiling away the lonely hours since his wife's death, painting pictures on cardboard using left-over marine paint. Wallis's naive paintings (mostly of ships) in flat colour with little attempt at perspective appealed to the modernist aesthetic which had no interest in realism, and Nicholson was inspired to return to St Ives at the outbreak of war in 1939, bringing his wife, the sculptress Barbara Hepworth. They met with the potters Bernard Leach and Shoji Hamada, who had already been working there since the 1920s, and, after the war, were joined by a growing band of modernist artists.

In 1975 Barbara Hepworth was killed in a fire at her studio and her death marked the end of the great period of St Ives's artistic influence. Her studio was later given to the Tate Gallery in London and is now open as a museum where her serene workspace and sculpture garden can be appreciated. Other work by St Ives artists was also bequeathed, but lack of space meant that it languished unseen in the basement for many years, until in 1993 the Tate opened another gallery at St Ives (tel. 01726 796226), specifically devoted to the work of artists connected with the locality. The site chosen was a derelict gasworks in the midst of town, overlooking Porthmeor beach. Here a dramatically modern construction was built, its white walls, slate roofs and small windows deliberately echoing those of the huddled terraces of fishermen's cottages near by.

The focus of the building, its round entrance lobby, is a witty reference to the vanished gasometers, while inside all is gracefully curving, smooth white walls, ash balustrades and cool stone floors. The marvellous views of sea and shore from the gallery's balcony and restaurant are reflected in many of the paintings on the walls, while the influence of the sea has also had a more unexpected impact on the interior design of the building – it actually has a special closet to accommodate visitors' surfboards!

267 TREGLISSON ⬳⬳ HIGHLY COMMENDED

11 Wheal Alfred Road, Hayle, Cornwall TR27 5JT Tel (01736) 753141

Treglisson, a listed Grade II 18th-century farmhouse, is set in peaceful rural surroundings, yet only one mile from the A30. A hearty breakfast is served in our elegant dining room or new conservatory. We also have an indoor heated swimming pool. Personal service and attention to detail ensure our guests enjoy a comfortable and relaxing stay. The area abounds with charming fishing villages, galleries, historic tin-mines, breath-taking coastal walks and golden sandy beaches.

Bed & Breakfast per night: single occupancy from £23.50; double room from £35.25
Bedrooms: 2 double, 1 twin, 2 family rooms

Bathrooms: 5 en-suite
Parking for 20
Open: January–October and December

268 NANSLOE MANOR ⬳⬳⬳ HIGHLY COMMENDED

Meneage Road, Helston, Cornwall TR13 0SB Tel (01326) 574691 Fax (01326) 564680

Nansloe, a Georgian manor, is set in the lovely wooded Loe Valley near Helston and is well placed for exploring Cornwall. It is owned and managed by John and Wendy Pyatt who take every care for your comfort and well-being. The food is delicious and imaginatively prepared, using as much local produce as possible. Log fires in the winter and lovely fresh flowers in the summer add to the welcoming atmosphere of the house. The dining room is non-smoking.

Bed & Breakfast per night: single room from £45.00; double room from £70.00–£116.00
Half board per person: £45.00–£73.00 daily
Evening meal 1900 (last orders 2030)

Bedrooms: 1 single, 2 double, 4 twin
Bathrooms: 7 private
Parking for 30
Cards accepted: Access, Visa

269 HOUSEL BAY HOTEL ⬳⬳⬳ HIGHLY COMMENDED

Housel Cove, The Lizard, Helston, Cornwall TR12 7PG Tel (01326) 290417 Fax (01326) 290359

An elegant Victorian hotel on Britain's most southerly coast, the views across the ocean are spectacular and a secluded sandy beach nestles below the hotel. The Cornish coastal path, which runs through the hotel gardens, leads east towards Cadgwith and Coverack and west towards Kynance Cove. Fully licensed with a stylish restaurant and a bar with panoramic views. All bedrooms are en-suite with satellite television and there is a passenger lift.

Bed & Breakfast per night: single room from £28.00–£45.00; double room from £56.00–£90.00
Half board per person: £43.00–£60.00 daily; £249.00–£348.00 weekly
Lunch available: 1200–1400

Evening meal 1930 (last orders 2100)
Bedrooms: 4 single, 12 double, 7 twin
Bathrooms: 23 private
Parking for 34
Cards accepted: Access, Visa, Amex

270 ATHENAEUM LODGE
Listed HIGHLY COMMENDED

4 Athenaeum Street, The Hoe, Plymouth, Devon PL1 2RH Tel (01752) 665005

An elegantly decorated Grade II listed Victorian guest house furnished to a very high standard under the personal supervision of resident owners, Margaret and Tony Rowe. Close to the sea front, historic Barbican, shopping centre, theatre and the Plymouth Pavilion. There are well-appointed bedrooms with colour satellite television, central heating, hair dryer, clocks, and tea/coffee making facilities; access with own key at all times, and a private car park. Brochure available upon request. Non-smoking dining room.

Bed & Breakfast per night: single room from £20.00–£30.00; double room from £30.00–£36.00
Bedrooms: 1 single, 3 double, 6 triple

Bathrooms: 5 private, 2 private showers, 1 public
Parking for 5

271 BOWLING GREEN HOTEL
HIGHLY COMMENDED

9–10 Osborne Place, Lockyer Street, Plymouth, Devon PL1 2PU Tel (01752) 667485 Fax (01752) 255150

Situated in the historic naval city of Plymouth opposite the world famous 'Drakes Bowling Green', this elegant Georgian hotel has superbly appointed bedrooms offering all the modern facilities the traveller requires. With a full breakfast menu and friendly and efficient family staff, you can be sure of a memorable visit to Plymouth. The Bowling Green Hotel is centrally situated for the Barbican, Theatre Royal, leisure/conference centre and ferry port, with Dartmoor only a few miles away.

Bed & Breakfast per night: single room from £28.00–£34.00; double room from £36.00–£46.00
Bedrooms: 1 single, 6 double, 2 twin, 3 triple
Bathrooms: 8 private, 4 public

Parking for 4
Cards accepted: Access, Visa, Diners, Amex, Switch/Delta

272 PLYMOUTH MOAT HOUSE
HIGHLY COMMENDED

Armada Way, Plymouth, Devon PL1 2HJ Tel (01752) 662866 or (01752) 665923 Fax (01752) 673816 Telex 45637

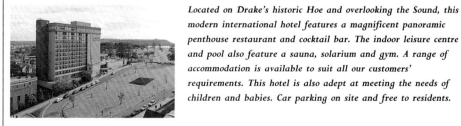

Located on Drake's historic Hoe and overlooking the Sound, this modern international hotel features a magnificent panoramic penthouse restaurant and cocktail bar. The indoor leisure centre and pool also feature a sauna, solarium and gym. A range of accommodation is available to suit all our customers' requirements. This hotel is also adept at meeting the needs of children and babies. Car parking on site and free to residents.

Bed & Breakfast per night: single occupancy from £50.00–£90.00; double room from £50.00–£90.00
Half board per person: £35.00–£65.00 daily;
£175.00–£375.00 weekly
Lunch available: 1230–1430 excluding Saturdays

Evening meal 1830 (last orders 2230)
Bedrooms: 110 double, 102 twin
Bathrooms: 212 private
Parking for 175
Cards accepted: Access, Visa, Diners, Amex

273 THE WATERMANS ARMS
❦❦❦ HIGHLY COMMENDED
Bow Bridge, Ashprington, Totnes, Devon TQ9 7EG Tel (01803) 732214 Fax (01803) 732214

This ancient hostelry has the most enviable riverside setting imaginable, nestling in a sheltered valley at the head of Bow Creek on the River Dart. Riverside tables, ten award-winning en-suite bedrooms, sumptuous food to satisfy all tastes, real ales and cider, log fires, candle-lit restaurant, caring staff and a world of character in this famous historic inn, only two-and-a-half miles from Totnes. An ideal place to relax, central for exploring the South Hams. Children and pets welcome. Nominated by the West Country Tourist Board for 'England for Excellence' B&B Award 1994.

Bed & Breakfast per night: single occupancy from £34.50–£42.50; double room from £59.00–£65.00
Half board per person: £44.50–£48.50 daily;
£290.50–£305.00 weekly
Lunch available: 1200 1430

Evening meal 1830 (last orders 2130)
Bedrooms: 7 double, 3 twin
Bathrooms: 10 en-suite
Parking for 60
Cards accepted: Access, Visa, Switch/Delta

274 THURLESTONE HOTEL
❦❦❦❦❦ HIGHLY COMMENDED
Thurlestone, Kingsbridge, Devon TQ7 3NN Tel (01548) 560382 Fax (01548) 561069

An intimate atmosphere, characteristic of grand establishments, distinguishes us from others due to our location on the Devon coast, in an area of outstanding natural beauty. Sixty-eight en-suite bedrooms, well-furnished with every facility, including video in some rooms. A restaurant with a reputation for fine food, superb wine and long-serving staff. Leisure activities include indoor swimming pool, spa bath, sauna, solarium, 9-hole championship golf course and tennis, squash and badminton courts as well as opportunities for walks and fishing. Please telephone for brochure.

Bed & Breakfast per night: single room from £50.00
Half board per person: £50.00–£95.00 daily
Lunch available: 1230–1400
Evening meal 1930 (last orders 2100)

Bedrooms: 7 single, 16 double, 32 twin, 13 triple
Bathrooms: 68 private
Parking for 119
Cards accepted: Access, Visa

275 OLD WALLS
Listed HIGHLY COMMENDED
Combe, Salcombe, South Devon TQ7 3DN Tel (01548) 844440

Old Walls is a 17th-century thatched cottage nestling in a peaceful valley by the sea, where the aroma of newly-baked bread and freshly-brewed coffee will waft up to your room, enticing you down to the breakfast table. Home-made preserves, muesli and freshly-squeezed juice will be the preamble to Salcombe Smokies or Ham & Eggs with potato farls. Just the ticket for a day of walking, sailing or lazing on the beach.

Bed & Breakfast per night: single occupancy from £18.00–£40.00; double room from £36.00–£44.00
Half board per person: £28.00–£50.00 daily;
£196.00–£350.00 weekly

Evening meal 1800 (last orders 2000)
Bedrooms: 2 double, 1 twin
Bathrooms: 2 private, 1 private shower
Parking for 5

276 TIDES REACH HOTEL
☙☙☙☙☙ HIGHLY COMMENDED

South Sands, Salcombe, Devon TQ8 8LJ Tel (01548) 843466 Fax (01548) 843954

Located in a tree-fringed sandy cove where country meets the sea, with a glorious view across the Salcombe Estuary, you can relax in style in this beautifully furnished and decorated hotel. Pamper yourself in the superb leisure complex, extensively-equipped and with a sunny tropical atmosphere. Award-winning creative cuisine served with courtesy and care in our garden-room restaurant.

Bed & Breakfast per night: single occupancy from £57.00–£72.00; double room from £94.00–£162.00
Half board per person: £66.00–£96.00 daily; £343.00–£560.00 weekly
Evening meal 1900 (last orders 2130)

Bedrooms: 18 double, 17 twin, 3 family rooms
Bathrooms: 38 en-suite
Parking for 100
Open: March–November
Cards accepted: Access, Visa, Diners, Amex, Switch/Delta

277 WHITE HOUSE HOTEL
☙☙☙ HIGHLY COMMENDED

Chillington, Kingsbridge, Devon TQ7 2JX Tel (01548) 580580 Fax (01548) 581124

The White House is a lovely Grade II listed building of great aesthetic and architectural appeal. Set in an acre of lawned and terraced gardens in one of the most beautiful corners of coastal England, the house has a unique atmosphere reminiscent of a quieter and less hurried age. An elegant restaurant and cosy bar, comfortable lounges with log fires, interesting wines and home cooking from the kitchen range are all here for your delight.

Half board per person: £44.00–£54.00 daily; £287.00–£336.00 weekly
Evening meal 1900 (last orders 2005)
Bedrooms: 3 double, 3 twin, 1 triple

Bathrooms: 4 en-suite, 1 public, 3 en-suite showers
Parking for 8
Open: April–December
Cards accepted: Access, Visa

278 THE OAKS HOTEL
☙☙☙☙ HIGHLY COMMENDED

Porlock, Somerset TA24 8ES Tel (01643) 862265 Fax (01643) 862265

Commanding superb views of sea, village and Exmoor countryside, the hotel is surrounded by the majestic trees from which it takes its name. The Edwardian atmosphere of the hotel is reflected throughout, with quality period furnishings – not, however, at the expense of all the modern comforts one would expect of a hotel of this calibre. The owners are totally hands-on in their commitment to the best possible service, food and value.

Bed & Breakfast per night: single occupancy £50.00; double room £80.00
Half board per person: £55.00–£65.00 daily; £350.00–£420.00 weekly
Evening meal 1900 (last orders 2030)

Bedrooms: 6 double, 3 twin
Bathrooms: 9 private
Parking for 11
Open: March–December
Cards accepted: Access, Visa, Amex

279 BENARES HOTEL

☙ ☙ ☙ ☙ HIGHLY COMMENDED

Northfield Road, Minehead, Somerset TA24 5PT Tel (01643) 704911 Fax (01643) 706373 Telex 57515

Minehead is an ideal centre for touring Exmoor, and Benares is ideally situated within Minehead. The town centre is a five-minute stroll through the park and the sea-front is just one-hundred yards away and yet the hotel is extremely peaceful at any time of the year. Our five-course dinner includes local dishes and as many as twenty puddings to choose from. The service we offer is quietly efficient and relaxingly friendly.

Bed & Breakfast per night: single occupancy from £43.50; double room from £81.00
Half board per person: £45.50–£60.00 daily; £304.50–£350.00 weekly
Evening meal 1900 (last orders 2030)

Bedrooms: 4 single, 6 double, 6 twin, 3 triple
Bathrooms: 19 private
Parking for 22
Open: March–October and December
Cards accepted: Access, Visa, Diners, Amex

280 CHANNEL HOUSE HOTEL

☙ ☙ ☙ ☙ HIGHLY COMMENDED

Church Path, Off Northfield Road, Minehead, Somerset TA24 5QG Tel (01643) 703229

An elegant Edwardian country house perfectly located for exploring the beauty of Exmoor and situated on the lower slopes of Minehead's picturesque North Hill where it nestles in two acres of award-winning gardens. The high standards of cuisine and accommodation will best suit those seeking superior quality and comfort. If you would like to experience smiling service in the tranquil elegance of this lovely hotel we will be delighted to send you our brochure and sample menu.

Half board per person: £54.50 daily; £304.00–£322.00 weekly
Evening meal 1900 (last orders 2030)
Bedrooms: 2 double, 5 twin, 1 triple
Bathrooms: 8 en-suite

Parking for 10
Open: March–November and Christmas
Cards accepted: Access, Visa, Diners

281 MARSTON LODGE HOTEL

☙ ☙ ☙ HIGHLY COMMENDED

St. Michaels Road, North Hill, Minehead, Somerset TA24 5JP Tel (01643) 702510

Built as an Edwardian gentleman's residence, Marston Lodge is in an acre of beautiful gardens with all the elegance and style of that age retained, and every comfort and luxury added to make a perfect holiday venue. You will never tire of the panoramic sea and moorland views from your lovely bedroom, and you can indulge yourself in our tempting food prepared with produce from the garden. You will find relaxation, comfort, good food and personal service. A hotel for non-smokers.

Bed & Breakfast per night: single room from £26.00–£28.00; double room from £52.00–£56.00
Half board per person: £38.00–£40.00 daily; £225.00–£244.00 weekly
Lunch available: 1230–1400 lunch snacks

Evening meal 1900 (last orders 1930)
Bedrooms: 2 single, 6 double, 2 twin, 2 triple
Bathrooms: 12 en-suite
Parking for 10
Open: March–October

282 DOLLONS HOUSE
⚌⚌ HIGHLY COMMENDED
10 Church Street, Dunster, Minehead, Somerset TA24 6SH   Tel (01643) 821880

A 16th-century listed building, Dollons is a delightful house in the centre of the village with castle views and a small walled garden. Years ago Dollons was the village pharmacy and also supplied marmalade to the Houses of Parliament. The shop now sells good local crafts. All the rooms are en-suite, well-furnished and decorated with their own theme. There is a well-appointed guests' sitting room with access to the verandah and garden. Totally non-smoking.

Bed & Breakfast per night: double from £42–£47
Bedrooms: 2 double, 1 twin

Bathrooms: 3 en-suite
Cards accepted: Access, Visa, Diners, Amex

283 EXMOOR HOUSE HOTEL
⚌⚌⚌ HIGHLY COMMENDED
12 West Street, Dunster, Minehead, Somerset TA24 6SN   Tel (01643) 821268

Situated in this delightful Medieval village close to Dunster Castle and two miles from the coast, we can accommodate just fourteen guests, thus enabling us to provide a friendly, personal but professional service in exclusive premises. Quality farm-fresh food, incorporated into varied menus (including vegetarian), is served in our licensed and candle-lit dining room. You can relax in our south-facing rear garden or enjoy walks on Exmoor, horse riding, shooting golf and more. No smoking.

Bed & Breakfast per night: single occupancy from £25.50–£26.50; double room from £51.00–£57.00
Half board per person: £40.00–£43.00 daily; £245.00–£262.50 weekly
Evening meal 1930 (last bookings 1900)

Bedrooms: 4 double, 3 twin
Bathrooms: 7 en-suite
Open: February–November
Cards accepted: Access, Visa, Diners, Amex

284 LANGTRY COUNTRY HOUSE HOTEL
⚌⚌⚌ HIGHLY COMMENDED
Washford, Watchet, Somerset TA23 0NT   Tel (01984) 40484

A delightful, Victorian country house standing in picturesque gardens surrounded by paddocks and tall pine trees. Situated on the fringe of Exmoor and within easy reach of the coast, Dunster and Minehead, all the bedrooms are spacious and elegantly furnished, with en-suite bathrooms, beverage facilities and colour televisions. Some rooms have four-poster beds. We also have a beautifully furnished licensed dining room and bar-lounge, offering a varied menu complemented by an extensive wine list at reasonable prices. A no-smoking hotel.

Bed & Breakfast per night: double room from £40.00–£46.00
Half board per person: £33.00–£36.00 daily; £225.00–£238.00 weekly
Evening meal 1900 (last orders 2000)

Bedrooms: 4 double, 2 twin
Bathrooms: 6 private
Parking for 12
Open: March–October

285 ROYAL OAK INN, WINSFORD

HIGHLY COMMENDED

Exmoor National Park, Somerset TA24 7JE Tel (01643) 85455 Fax (01643) 85388

Our beautiful 12th-century inn, looking immaculate beneath a toupée of thatch in one of England's prettiest villages, has been lovingly decorated and furnished. In this setting we provide a very high standard of cuisine, two cheerful bars, a good cellar and comfortable rooms. And – perhaps the most important of all – efficient and friendly service. We bid you welcome! We hope that you will always be pleased to come and regret having to go.

Bed & Breakfast per night: single occupancy from £57.50–£70.00; double room from £65.00–£90.00
Half board per person: £55.00–£65.00 daily; £350.00–£420.00 weekly
Evening meal 1930 (last orders 2130)

Bedrooms: 11 double, 2 twin, 1 triple
Bathrooms: 14 private
Parking for 25
Cards accepted: Access, Visa, Diners, Amex

286 ASHWICK HOUSE HOTEL

HIGHLY COMMENDED

Dulverton, Somerset TA22 9QD Tel (01398) 23868 Fax (01398) 23868

A small, luxury country-house hotel twelve hundred feet above the wooded hills of Exmoor and completely surrounded by some of the most beautiful, unspoilt countryside in the South West. Inside, the hotel offers personal service with log fires, antiques and fine fresh food. A world of utter peace and relaxation!

Half board per person: £51.00–£65.00 daily
Lunch available: 1230–1345 Sunday Only
Evening meal 1915 (last orders 2030)

Bedrooms: 4 double, 2 twin
Bathrooms: 6 en-suite
Parking for 20

287 BLACKMORE FARM

HIGHLY COMMENDED

Cannington, Bridgwater, Somerset TA5 2NE Tel (01278) 653442 Fax (01278) 653442

A unique Grade I listed 14th-century manor house retaining many period features including oak beams, stone archways, log fires and its own private chapel. A traditional farmhouse breakfast is served in the Great Hall. All the bedrooms are en-suite, one with a four-poster bed. You can be assured of a warm welcome to this family home situated in a quiet, rural location, with views of the Quantock Hills. An ideal base for touring Bath, Somerset and Exmoor.

Bed & Breakfast per night: single occupancy from £18.00–£30.00; double room from £34.00–£45.00
Bedrooms: 2 double, 1 triple

Bathrooms: 3 private
Parking for 6

288 LOWER COLLIPRIEST FARM

Tiverton, Devon EX16 4PT Tel (01884) 252321

≋≋≋ HIGHLY COMMENDED

The thatched farmhouse, built around a courtyard garden, is tucked down a quiet lane a mile from Tiverton. The bedrooms and en-suite bathrooms are spacious and thoughtful extras with well-provisioned tea trays adding to your comfort. After a dinner of freshly cooked local produce, stroll to the river and pond across the meadow or relax by the inglenook fire on cooler evenings. During the day unwind by exploring the farm and its natural beauty.

Bed & Breakfast per night: single room from £20.00–£22.50; double room from £40.00–£45.00
Half board per person: £27.00–£29.00 daily; £186.00–£190.00 weekly
Evening meal 1900 (last bookings 1200)

Bedrooms: 3 single, 2 twin
Bathrooms: 5 en-suite
Parking for 4
Open: February–November

289 THE CAPTAINS HOUSE

18 Clarence Street, Dartmouth, Devon TQ6 9NW Tel (01803) 832133

≋≋ HIGHLY COMMENDED

A charming small Grade II listed house built c1730 and containing the original staircase and Adam-style fire surroundings. It is conveniently situated in a quiet street just off the River Dart, and a three-minute walk from the harbour and historic town centre. Each bedroom is individually furnished and decorated but with every modern facility. Full English breakfast with a choice, served with home-made breads and preserves, can be taken either downstairs or upstairs.

Bed & Breakfast per night: single room from £24.00–£28.00; double room from £34.00–£48.00
Bedrooms: 1 single, 3 double, 1 twin

Bathrooms: 4 en-suite, 1 private
Cards accepted: Amex

290 ROYAL CASTLE HOTEL

The Quay, Dartmouth, Devon TQ6 9PS Tel (01803) 833033 Fax (01803) 835445

≋≋≋ HIGHLY COMMENDED

Open all year

This unique 17th-century coaching hostelry in the heart of the historic port of Dartmouth has an unrivalled location that is ideal for short-breaks at any time of the year. Twenty-five luxuriously-appointed, en-suite bedrooms are individually decorated and furnished, some with four-poster or brass beds and jacuzzi. The elegant restaurant on the first floor overlooks the estuary and specialises in select regional produce and locally-caught sea food. Two bars serve delicious food, traditional ales and a good choice of wines. We look forward to welcoming you.

Bed & Breakfast per night: single room from £40.00–£60.00; double room from £70.00–£110.00
Half board per person: £45.00–£65.00 daily; £270.00–£295.00 weekly
Lunch available: 1200–1430 Bar Food

Evening meal 1845 (last orders 2200)
Bedrooms: 4 single, 10 double, 7 twin, 4 triple
Bathrooms: 25 private
Garage parking for 4
Cards accepted: Access, Visa, Switch/Delta

291 FAIRMOUNT HOUSE HOTEL   〰〰〰 HIGHLY COMMENDED
Herbert Road, Chelston, Torquay, Devon TQ2 6RW Tel (01803) 605446 Fax (01803) 605446

Enjoy the best of both worlds – coast and country. Only a few minutes from the sea, Fairmount is an award-winning small hotel with a country house atmosphere, peacefully situated on a south-facing sheltered hillside, about a mile from Torquay Harbour and close to Cockington Country Park. There are beautifully appointed bedrooms, a cosy conservatory bar, log fires, lamp-lit dinners with good food and fine international wines, all with the best hospitality and informal service. Dogs welcome too.

Bed & Breakfast per night: single room from £26.50–£29.00; double room from £53.00–£58.00
Half board per person: £37.50–£40.00 daily; £245.00–£262.50 weekly
Bar-snack lunches available: 1200–1330

Evening meal 1830 (last orders 1930)
Bedrooms: 2 single, 4 double, 2 triple/twin
Bathrooms: 8 private
Parking for 8
Open: March–October

Cards accepted: Access, Visa, Amex

292 BARN HAYES COUNTRY HOTEL   〰〰〰 HIGHLY COMMENDED
Brim Hill, Maidencombe, Torquay, Devon TQ1 4TR Tel (01803) 327980

A warm, friendly and comfortable country hotel in an area of outstanding natural beauty, overlooking the countryside and sea in a peaceful South Devon valley. Your relaxation and well-being are guaranteed. In these lovely surroundings, you will receive our personal attention and genuine hospitality with excellent traditional cuisine and good wines. We have beautiful gardens with a swimming pool, and the fabulous Torbay coastal footpath is nearby for the energetic. A brochure will be sent with pleasure.

Bed & Breakfast per night: single room from £24.00–£27.00; double room from £48.00–£54.00
Half board per person: £36.00–£39.00 daily; £224.00–£252.00 weekly
Lunch available: 1230–1400

Evening meal 1830 (last orders 1900)
Bedrooms: 2 single, 4 double, 2 twin, 2 triple, 2 family rooms
Bathrooms: 10 private, 1 private shower
Parking for 16

Open: February–December
Cards accepted: Access, Visa

293 ORESTONE MANOR HOTEL AND RESTAURANT   〰〰〰〰 HIGHLY COMMENDED
Rockhouse Lane, Maidencombe, Torquay, Devon TQ1 4SX Tel (01803) 328098 Fax (01803) 328336

The only official country-house hotel in the Torquay area is near the village of Maidencombe but only three miles from the Harbour-side. Set in two acres of its own sheltered gardens, overlooking the sea, but actually in the countryside, away from the hustle and bustle of the town and sea-front. We serve Anglo-French, award-winning cuisine in our non-smoking restaurant with a menu that changes daily – every night is GOURMET night.

Bed & Breakfast per night: single occupancy from £60.00–£78.00; double room from £100.00–£160.00
Half board per person: £75.00–£120.00 daily; £290.00–£525.00 weekly
Lunch available: Sunday lunch

Evening meal 1900 (last orders 2030)
Bedrooms: 11 double, 7 twin
Bathrooms: 18 en-suite
Parking for 30
Open: February–December

Cards accepted: Access, Visa, Diners, Amex

294 EASTCLIFF HOUSE

≋≋ HIGHLY COMMENDED

14 Marine Parade, Budleigh Salterton, Devon EX9 6NS Tel (01395) 445555

Eastcliff House is a large family house on the sea-front with large comfortable rooms. It is set in delightful gardens, and is on the South-West coastal path, with golf course and estuary bird-watching locally.

Bed & Breakfast per night: single occupancy from £25.00–£32.00; double room from £45.00–£50.00
Bedrooms: 2 twin

Bathrooms: 2 en-suite
Parking for 2

⌂10 🛏 🍴 🍷 🔒 🗡 📷 ✿

A la Ronde

THIS EXTRAORDINARY BUILDING, on the outskirts of Exmouth in Devon was the brainchild of a pair of energetic and creative cousins, Jane and Mary Parminter. Built on an octagonal plan, it has windows on each of its eight corners. Its steep conical roof was originally thatched and had a little cupola on the top surrounded by four chimneys and topped by a weather vane. In the 1880s one stunned visitor wrote of it that it 'would not be out of place in one of the South Sea islands', and indeed with its thatched roof and lime-washed walls the building did have something of the air of a tropical mud hut, though on a grander scale. Its model was, in fact, the octagonal basilica of San Vitale in Ravenna. The intrepid cousins had visited Ravenna on a ten year grand tour which they completed in 1795, and on their return determined to build themselves a house which would remind them of their travels and provide a home for their souvenirs.

More intriguing even than the building itself is the interior of A la Ronde (tel. 01395 265514). In the 18th century it was fashionable for ladies of leisure to craft elaborate decorations for their homes; at A la Ronde a vast range of these skills has been employed to prodigious – almost ludicrous – effect. The rooms, in particular the gallery and drawing room, are adorned with pictures and patterns created with feathers, shells, dried flowers, marbled paint, cut paper, sand, and even seaweed and straw.

When Mary Parminter died in 1849 she left clear instructions that A la Ronde and its contents should be preserved and that only unmarried kinswomen should inherit the property. These conditions were observed

National Trust Picture Library

for several generations, until changes in conveyancing law allowed a male relative finally to take over the house. Under the ownership of Rev Oswald Reichel in the 1890s major changes were made, including the replacement of the thatch with tiles, the addition of dormer windows, the demolition of an internal wall and the insertion of a gargantuan central heating system. Nevertheless, most of the cousins' extraordinary legacy has been preserved.

295 HOTEL RIVIERA ≋≋≋≋ DE LUXE

The Esplanade, Sidmouth, Devon EX10 8AY Tel (01395) 515201 Fax (01395) 577775

Splendidly positioned at the centre of Sidmouth's Esplanade over-looking Lyme Bay. With its mild climate and the beach just on the doorstep, the setting echoes the south of France and is the choice for the discerning visitor in search of relaxation and quieter pleasures. Behind the fine Regency façade lies an alluring blend of old-fashioned service and present-day comforts. Glorious sea views can be enjoyed from the recently re-designed and refurbished en-suite bedrooms, all of which are fully appointed. In the elegant bay-view dining room, guests are offered a fine choice of dishes from the extensive menus prepared by French and Swiss-trained chefs.

Bed & Breakfast per night: single room from £56.00–£78.00; double room from £98.00–£142.00
Half board per person: £56.00–£78.00 daily; £399.00–£483.00 weekly
Lunch available: 1200–1400

Evening meal 1900 (last orders 2100)
Bedrooms: 7 single, 6 double, 14 twin
Bathrooms: 27 en-suite
Parking for 23
Cards accepted: Access, Visa, Diners, Amex

296 BEACH END GUEST HOUSE ≋ HIGHLY COMMENDED

8 Trevelyan Road, Seaton, Devon EX12 2NL Tel (01297) 23388

We are situated at the mouth of the River Axe in unspoilt Seaton, from where you can enjoy unrivalled views over Axmouth Harbour and Seaton Bay. We offer you fine food and friendly, attentive service in our lovely Edwardian guesthouse. A warm welcome awaits you from Philip and Joan Millard.

Bed & Breakfast per night: double room from £32.00–£37.00
Half board per person: £24.95–£27.45 daily; £165.70–£183.20 weekly
Evening meal 1900 (last bookings 1500)

Bedrooms: 3 double, 1 twin, 1 family room
Bathrooms: 3 private, 1 public
Parking for 6
Open: February–October and Christmas

297 THE DOWER HOUSE HOTEL ≋≋≋≋ HIGHLY COMMENDED

Rousdon, Lyme Regis, Dorset DT7 3RB Tel (01297) 21047 Fax (01297) 24748

A beautiful, family-run, country-house hotel standing in its own lawned and wooded grounds which ensures safe easy parking. All rooms are en-suite and there is also an indoor heated swimming pool and sauna, central heating, colour television, radio, telephone, beverage tray, hairdryers, open fires, fine cuisine plus old fashioned courteous service. Enjoy the many nearby local walks, bracing coastal footpath walks and golf. Special Winter and Spring breaks.

Bed & Breakfast per night: single occupancy from £38.00–£45.00; double room from £66.00–£72.00
Half board per person: £42.00–£50.00 daily; £265.00–£300.00 weekly
Lunch available: 1200–1400

Evening meal 1900 (last orders 2100)
Bedrooms: 9
Bathrooms: 9 en-suite
Parking for 48
Cards accepted: Access, Visa, Diners, Amex

298 ALEXANDRA HOTEL

🍲🍲🍲🍲 HIGHLY COMMENDED

Pound Street, Lyme Regis, Dorset DT7 3HZ Tel (01297) 442010 Fax (01297) 443229

A former Georgian dower house standing in an acre of secluded peaceful gardens with panoramic views across Lyme Bay, the Alexandra has a plant-lined conservatory that looks out across the lawn to the sea. It also offers comfy sofas, fresh flowers in delightfully co-ordinated bedrooms and an elegant restaurant with award-winning food and wines.

Bed & Breakfast per night: single room from £30.00–£45.00; double room from £60.00–£104.00
Half board per person: £45.00–£60.00 daily; £90.00–£134.00 weekly
Lunch available: 1200–1400

Evening meal 1900 (last orders 2030)
Bedrooms: 2 single, 11 double, 6 twin, 7 triple
Bathrooms: 26 private
Parking for 17
Open: February–December

Cards accepted: Access, Visa, Diners, Amex, Switch/Delta

Lyme Regis Fossils

IN 1811 MARY ANNING was only 12 years old when she found the fossilised skeleton of a great, dolphin-like reptile in the cliffs of Lyme Regis. Remarkably, she had discovered the world's first ichthyosaur, and later, as a professional fossil collector, she also unearthed in the same area a plesiosaur (a seal-like creature with long neck and sharp teeth) and a dimorphodon (one of the earliest avian reptiles which could fly).

These impressive dinosaur skeletons are still occasionally found in the vicinity of Lyme Regis by professional fossil hunters. More common are ammonites (shell-like spirals, once part of a creature resembling a squid), which occur in a variety of sizes and colours. Some are formed out of fool's gold, iron pyrites, and are a beautiful burnished golden colour, while others are composed of calcite crystals and can be green, brown or sometimes white. Belemites are pencil-shaped fossils whose broken ends show fine radiating crystals and crinoids featuring feathery fronds attached to a five-sided stalk.

All the petrified remains found in this area were once creatures swimming in a warm, shallow ocean known as the Lias sea which, 190 million years ago (the Jurassic period), covered large areas of what is now Britain. In the area around Lyme Regis it seems as though the sea floor must have become very stagnant, allowing few living organisms to survive there. Those which lived in the open water above sank down into the sludge below when they died. Over time deposits of silt amassed on top of the dead creatures, hardening into limestone, and minerals such as iron pyrites and calcite filled and partially replaced the bones and shells,

preserving their structure. Eventually, movements in the earth's crust tilted the Jurassic rocks to the surface in a broad band stretching from Lyme Regis across the country to Whitby, where similar fossils are also found. The action of coastal erosion and mudflows continually exposes them and washes them out of the cliffs.

The Lyme Regis area has several premises where fossils can be bought or studied. The Philpot Museum in Lyme Regis (tel. 01305 252241) contains excellent examples of local fossils, while the Charmouth Heritage Coast Centre has plenty of information about the interesting geology of this coast; guided fossil tours are also available. If searching for specimens, do not climb the cliffs (they are crumbly and can be dangerous), avoid mudflows which may harbour quicksand, and don't get cut off by the incoming tide.

299 HENSLEIGH HOTEL

♨♨♨ HIGHLY COMMENDED

Lower Sea Lane, Charmouth, Bridport, Dorset DT6 6LW Tel (01297) 560830

A family-run hotel with a reputation for friendly service, comfort, hospitality and delicious food, complemented by a relaxing atmosphere which has made it a favourite with visitors to Charmouth. Situated just three hundred metres from the beach, in an area of outstanding beauty, with spectacular cliff walks and fossil hunting, we have ample car parking within the grounds.

Bed & Breakfast per night: single room from £22.00–£25.00; double room from £44.00–£50.00
Half board per person: £33.00–£36.00 daily; £214.00–£229.00 weekly
Evening meal 1830 (last orders 1945)

Bedrooms: 2 single, 4 double, 3 twin, 2 triple
Bathrooms: 11 en-suite
Parking for 30
Open: March–November
Cards accepted: Access, Visa

300 ROUNDHAM HOUSE HOTEL

♨♨♨ HIGHLY COMMENDED

Roundham Gardens, West Bay Road, Bridport, Dorset DT6 4BD Tel (01308) 422753 Fax (01308) 421145 Telex 417182 ENEL G ATN RO

Situated in an elevated location in an acre of cascading garden, with lovely views of the Dorset countryside and in an area of outstanding beauty, Roundham was built from local stone in 1903 and offers every modern amenity for the discerning guest looking for delicious home-cooked food, prepared from fresh local ingredients, and served with courtesy. Walking, riding, pony trekking and sea/fresh-water fishing all abound. An 18-hole golf club is just half-a-mile away, adjacent to the coastal path.

Bed & Breakfast per night: single room from £30.00–£39.50; double room from £48.00–£59.00
Half board per person: £38.00–£53.50 daily; £245.00–£273.00 weekly
Evening meal 1930 (last orders 2000)

Bedrooms: 1 single, 3 double, 2 twin, 2 triple
Bathrooms: 7 en-suite
Parking for 15
Open: February–October
Cards accepted: Access, Visa, Diners

301 HORNSBURY MILL HOTEL

♨♨♨ HIGHLY COMMENDED

Eleighwater, Chard, Somerset TA20 3AQ Tel (01460) 63317 Fax (01460) 68297

A working watermill set in a five-acre beauty spot with character en-suite bedrooms and a locally renowned restaurant and bar open to non-residents. Attractions include the lake with many breeds of duck, the curios & bygones museum and speciality cream teas. Hornsbury Mill is open all year and is conveniently situated on the borders of Dorset, Devon and Somerset between Chard and Ilminster. Please contact the owners, Frederick and Kathryn Orchard, for brochure and further details.

Bed & Breakfast per night: single occupancy from £32.50–£38.00; double room from £45.00–£55.00
Half board per person: £41.00–£54.00 daily; £252.00–£339.00 weekly
Lunch available: 1200–1400

Evening meal 1900 (last orders 2130)
Bedrooms: 5 double
Bathrooms: 5 private
Parking for 150
Cards accepted: Access, Visa, Amex

302 BROADVIEW

☗☗☗ DE LUXE

43 East Street, Crewkerne, Somerset TA18 7AG Tel (01460) 73424

An unusual Colonial c1926 residence set in an acre of feature gardens with many unusual plants. Carefully furnished en-suite rooms with easy chairs. Friendly informal atmosphere, extremely comfortable and relaxing, the colonial ambience being enhanced by our collection of porcelain, antiques and rugs. Enjoy the very best quality traditional English home cooking. Stay a while and explore National Trust gardens, houses, moors, quaint old villages, the Dorset coast and Hardy country – our list provides fifty varied places. No smoking.

Bed & Breakfast per night: single occupancy from £30.00–£35.00; double room £46.00
Evening meal 1830 (last bookings 1200), £12.00

Bedrooms: 1 double, 2 twin
Bathrooms: 2 en-suite, 1 private
Parking for 6

Cidermaking

SOMERSET IS FAMOUS for its 'scrumpy', its traditional cider made from apples with evocative names such as Kingston Black, Stoke Red, Yarlington Mill and Tremlett's Bitter. 'Scrumpy' is actually the nickname for any draught cider, but it has come to be associated with the strong, farmhouse brew which has been produced here for at least 700 years. At one time almost every farm had its own apple orchard and cider press, almost every village its cider house where the men gathered for a drink, a smoke and a chinwag.

In the past, when the cider apples were ready for harvest in the autumn, they were picked, packed into sacks and taken back to the cider house. An apple mill was used to break up the fruit into a kind of lumpy porridge called 'pomace', which was then shovelled into an apple press between layers of straw, and squeezed until every drop of juice had been extracted from the pulp or 'cheese'. The presses were turned either by hand or by horse power. The juice was then ladled into barrels and left to ferment, using yeast which occurred naturally in the apple skins, for a minimum of three or four weeks until it reached full dryness. It was then transferred into clean vessels and left to mature.

In Somerset there are a couple of cider farms which continue to brew cider on a commercial scale using traditional methods. The process has been brought up to date: for example, the pomace is now pumped rather than shovelled into the apple presses, which are hydraulically operated, and is spread out between layers of cloth rather than straw, but the basic procedure and end result are the same. At Perry's cider mills (tel. 01823 461233), at Dowlish Wake near Ilminster, the cider is pressed in a 16th-century thatched barn, while a new barn houses a museum of farm tools. Sheppy's, at Bradford-on-Tone (tel. 01460 52861), has a museum of rural life and provides guided tours around the cider-making operations. The best time to visit is the autumn.

A 1678 cider mill

Mary Evans Picture Library

303 YEW TREES GUEST HOUSE
HIGHLY COMMENDED

Silver Street, Misterton, Crewkerne, Somerset TA18 8NB   Tel (01460) 77192

This lovely house, created from two timber-beamed and stone-walled 17th-century cottages, on the border of Somerset and a short distance from the spectacular Dorset coast, is the ideal centre for exploring an area of many famous gardens and historic buildings: Montacute House, Forde Abbey, Parnham House and more. You will find comfortable bedrooms with pastel colours and pine furniture, a quiet secluded garden and delicious food. Good reductions for three or more days. A non-smoking house.

Bed & Breakfast per night: single room from
£16.00–£19.00; double room from £32.00–£38.00
Half board per person: £28.00–£31.00 daily;
£188.00–£204.00 weekly

Evening meal 1830 (last bookings 1600)
Bedrooms: 1 single, 1 double, 1 twin
Bathrooms: 2 public
Parking for 3

304 LITTLE BARWICK HOUSE
HIGHLY COMMENDED

Barwick, Yeovil, Somerset BA22 9TD   Tel (01935) 23902   Fax (01935) 20908

A listed Georgian dower house set in a delightful garden located in the corner of Barwick Park, a mile from Yeovil and five from Sherborne. Run as a restaurant with rooms by Christopher & Veronica Colley, whose home it is. Veronica's cooking has received widespread commendation and is featured by the leading hotel and restaurant guides. Ideally situated for a short break from London and within easy reach of National Trust properties and gardens. Come Winter Folly hunting. Telephone for our special breaks.

Bed & Breakfast per night: single occupancy from £48.00;
double room from £76.00
Half board per person: £51.00–£67.00 daily
Bedrooms: 2 double, 3 twin

Bathrooms: 5 en-suite
Parking for 20
Cards accepted: Access, Visa, Amex

305 HOLYWELL HOUSE
HIGHLY COMMENDED

Holywell, East Coker, Yeovil, Somerset BA22 9NQ   Tel (01935) 862612   Fax (01935) 863035

Delightful ham-stone house built in 1780, lovingly restored, tastefully decorated and furnished with many fine antiques. Our guests' every need seems to have been anticipated even to the hot water bottle for chilly nights! Jackie enjoys cosseting her guests, which is why she wins top awards. Standing in three acres of glorious grounds with a tennis court and a croquet lawn, Holywell House has literary connections with Thomas Hardy and T.S. Eliot. Recommended for country holidays.

Bed & Breakfast per night: single occupancy from
£30.00–£35.00; double room from £50.00–£60.00
Half board per person: £45.00–£50.00 daily
Evening meal 1900 (last orders 2030)

Bedrooms: 2 double, 1 family room
Bathrooms: 3 private
Parking for 15

306 RECTORY HOUSE
❦❦❦ HIGHLY COMMENDED
Fore Street, Evershot, Dorchester, Dorset DT2 0JW Tel (01935) 83273 Fax (01935) 83273

Rectory House is an 18th-century listed building of great charm in the quiet Dorset village of Evershot, offering the utmost comfort with well-sized bedrooms: two are located in the main house and the four other cottage-style rooms are in the converted stables. Each bedroom has its own en-suite bathroom, with fresh flowers and home-made shortbread adding a welcome touch. Delicious meals are served, including locally-made sausages and village-baked bread.

Bed & Breakfast per night: single occupancy from £30.00–£50.00; double room from £50.00–£60.00
Half board per person: £40.00–£60.00 daily;
£245.00–£270.00 weekly
Evening meal 1900

Bedrooms: 4 double, 2 twin
Bathrooms: 6 private
Parking for 8
Open: January–November
Cards accepted: Access, Visa

307 HUNTSBRIDGE FARM
❦❦ HIGHLY COMMENDED
Batcombe Road, Leigh, Sherborne, Dorset DT9 6JA Tel (01935) 872150

We are situated in open countryside in the beautiful part of Dorset that Thomas Hardy chose for his novel 'The Woodlanders'. We are ideally situated for walking or touring with golf, riding and fishing locally. Our two double and one twin en-suite bedrooms are tastefully furnished, all with tea/coffee facilities, colour television and alarm-radio. This is a lovely base for discovering all that Dorset has to offer, so why not come and relax far from the madding crowd! A non-smoking establishment.

Bed & Breakfast per night: single occupancy from £26.00;
double room from £36.00
Half board per person: £30.00–£36.00 daily
Evening meal 1830 by arrangement
Bedrooms: 2 double, 1 twin

Bathrooms: 3 en-suite
Parking for 5
Open: March–November
Cards accepted: Access, Visa

308 CHURCH FARM
❦❦ HIGHLY COMMENDED
Stockwood, Dorchester, Dorset DT2 0NG Tel (01935) 83221

Peacefully located beneath rolling hills, we are idyllically positioned for a relaxing break. Ours is a family farm where you are guaranteed a warm and friendly welcome. Discover, in the garden, one of England's smallest churches or enjoy one of many walks with breathtaking views. Try our delicious home-cooked food and then relax by an inglenook fireplace, where a log fire burns in winter. Perfect for touring: twelve miles from Dorchester, eight miles from Yeovil. We regret this is a non-smoking house.

Bed & Breakfast per night: single occupancy from £18.00–£25.00; double room from £36.00–£40.00
Half board per person: £30.00–£37.00 daily

Bedrooms: 2 double, 1 twin
Bathrooms: 3 en-suite
Parking for 3

309 YALBURY PARK

Frome Whitfield Farm, Frome Whitfield, Dorchester, Dorset DT2 7SE   Tel (01305) 250336

A charming new Purbeck stone farmhouse of interesting design, surrounded by an acre of picturesque gardens, offering peace and tranquillity with exceptional views over our meadowland and to the meandering River Frome. All our rooms are large and airy and furnished to the very highest standard for our guests' comfort. We are situated in the centre of Hardy's Wessex and an ideal base for visiting unspoilt Dorset, with Dorchester one mile and the sea seven miles away.

Bed & Breakfast per night: single occupancy from
£20.00–£22.00; double room from £40.00–£44.00
Bedrooms: 1 twin, 1 family room

Bathrooms: 2 private
Parking for 6
Open: February–December

☎3 ⌨ 🖵 ♣ 🍴 🎞 ♨ ∪ ♪ ✿
SP T

Hardy's Wessex

THE GREAT ENGLISH novelist and poet, Thomas Hardy, was born in 1840 in Higher Bockampton near Dorchester. His intimate knowledge of the Dorset countryside is reflected in his novels, which are set in half-real, half-fictional Wessex, a region which is brought to such vivid life in his books that it is hard to believe that it doesn't actually exist. Hardy's technique was to use the real names of some landscape features, such as Stonehenge, and combine them with fictional place names for towns and villages which he knew well. This device gave him the freedom to dispense with geographical accuracy, but enabled him to use his knowledge of real places to create vivid and realistic settings.

The large thatched cottage where Hardy was born is now owned by the National Trust and is open to the public. Literary associations are everywhere. The cottage itself provided the model for the home of the Dewy family in *Under the Greenwood Tree*, while the area of forestry rising up behind it was once wild open space, the inspiration for Egdon Heath in *Return of the Native*. Beyond is the fertile Frome Valley, in *Tess of the D'Urbevilles* the Valley of the Great Dairies where Tess spent happy days as a milkmaid.

From 1883 until his death in 1928 Hardy lived in Dorset's county town Dorchester. An architect by training, he designed his own home, Max Gate, on the edge of town, the garden and drawing room of which have recently been opened to the public (National Trust). Also, the writer's study there has been meticulously recreated at Dorchester's county museum. In Hardy's Wessex, Dorchester was Casterbridge, featured most vividly in *The Mayor of Casterbridge,* in which the King's Arms Hotel provides the setting for Henchard's banquet, while a large 18th-century house in South Street became Henchard's home.

Incidentally, Wessex was also the name Hardy gave his dog, a pugnacious little terrier whose grave may be seen in the garden at Max Gate...

Thomas Hardy in his Max Gate study, 1911

Mary Evans Picture Library

310 THE CHATSWORTH

🏵🏵🏵 HIGHLY COMMENDED

14 The Esplanade, Weymouth, Dorset DT4 8EB Tel (01305) 785012 Fax (01305) 766342

Overlooking the picturesque 17th-century Weymouth Harbour and the sweep of golden sands and Georgian Esplanade, all the bedrooms enjoy interesting views. Renowned for our quality food and memorable meals in our pleasant dining room, we combine only the freshest and most delicious of foods, with a choice of menu at every meal and a welcoming host's attention to care and service. The family-run Chatsworth Hotel is the ideal base to explore the unspoilt beautiful Dorset countryside and coastline.

Bed & Breakfast per night: single room from £19.50–£28.00; double room from £39.00–£56.00
Half board per person: £32.00–£43.00 daily; £214.00–£260.00 weekly

Evening meal 1800 (last orders 1900)
Bedrooms: 2 single, 2 double, 3 twin, 1 triple
Bathrooms: 8 en-suite
Cards accepted: Access, Visa, Amex

---

311 TOR FARM

🏵 HIGHLY COMMENDED

Nyland, Cheddar, Somerset BS27 3UD Tel (01934) 743710

Our working farm is situated on the beautiful Somerset levels, with open views from every window. The farmhouse is fully central-heated and has log fires on cold evenings in the guests' own lounge. En-suite and four-poster bedrooms available, some with private patios. Ideal base for visiting Bath, Wells, Glastonbury, Cheddar Gorge and the coast.

Bed & Breakfast per night: double room from £30.00–£43.00
Evening meal 1900 (last bookings 1800)
Bedrooms: 2 single, 4 double, 1 twin, 1 family room

Bathrooms: 5 en-suite, 2 public
Parking for 10
Cards accepted: Access, Visa

---

312 GLENCOT HOUSE

🏵🏵🏵🏵 HIGHLY COMMENDED

Glencot Lane, Wookey Hole, Wells, Somerset BA5 1BH Tel (01749) 677160 Fax (01749) 670210

Idyllically set in eighteen acres of gardens and parkland with river frontage, this elegantly furnished Victorian mansion offers high-class accommodation and excellent cuisine. Glencot has a homely atmosphere and friendly service. Facilities abound, with a small indoor pool, sauna, snooker, table-tennis, private fishing and more.

Bed & Breakfast per night: single room from £45.00–£48.00; double room from £60.00–£80.00
Half board per person: £45.00–£55.00 daily; £320.00–£350.00 weekly
Evening meal 1830 (last orders 2030)

Bedrooms: 2 single, 8 double, 2 twin
Bathrooms: 12 private
Parking for 21
Cards accepted: Access, Visa

313 THE PANTILES

HIGHLY COMMENDED

Bathway, Chewton Mendip, Bath, Avon BA3 4ND Tel (01761) 241519

A family home set in two acres of garden and paddock, offering three well-furnished bedrooms with views over the lovely Mendip countryside. Two en-suite bedrooms and one with private bathroom – all with colour television and hospitality trays. Ideal spot for touring the West Country beauty spots. No smoking.

Bed & Breakfast per night: single occupancy from £17.00–£21.00; double room from £32.00–£37.00
Bedrooms: 1 double, 2 twin

Bathrooms: 1 private, 2 private showers
Parking for 6

Wookey Hole

THE CAVES at Wookey Hole have a long history as a tourist attraction. As far back as the 15th century visitors came to peer into the dark caverns and subterranean passages, illuminating their progress with flickering candles. Today the route through the caves is paved, railed and lit by electricity, but it remains an exciting experience. Dramatic lighting reveals great fissures and crevices, a glassy green underground lake, huge pendulous stalactites and vast stacks of stalagmites – one particularly knobbly formation is known as the Witch of Wookey. The legend that a witch did once live in the caves was given credence in 1912 when excavations uncovered the skeleton of a woman buried deep in the cave floor, together with a dagger, a sacrificial knife and a round stalagmite like a witch's crystal.

The caves were carved out of the Mendip Hills by an underground river which still flows through them and emerges from Wookey Hole as the River Axe. Evidence of inhabitation by cave-dwellers has been found: weaving equipment, pottery, and perhaps even the remains of a human sacrifice suggest troglodytes were here as long ago as AD400. The name Wookey stems from the Old English word for an animal trap, *wocig.*

In 1973 Madame Tussaud's bought the caves and developed the site as a tourist complex with a number of attractions. The 19th-century paper mill here once employed as many as 200 people and produced some of the finest quality paper in the world: paper with exquisite watermarks and destined to be used as banknotes. The mill has now been re-opened and visitors can watch the remarkable transformation of cotton rags into high-quality, hand-made paper (tel. 01749 672243).

Other attractions include a collection of brightly painted fairground animals, merry-go-rounds and a steam-powered organ; a re-creation of Madame Tussaud's touring 'Cabinet of Curiosities' and an exhibit of working amusements from penny pier arcades.

314 MONKSHILL

⬦⬦ HIGHLY COMMENDED

Shaft Road, Monkton Combe, Bath, Avon BA2 7HL Tel (01225) 833028

Five minutes from the city centre of Bath, this delightful Edwardian house is set in its own beautiful gardens commanding views of a spectacular valley with the small medieval village of Monkton Combe at its base. Monkshill is renowned for its luxury accommodation with fine antiques, oil paintings and fireplaces in every spacious room. The individually-styled bedrooms are truly elegant with colourful flowing drapes, charming brass beds and fine views across the gardens and valley below.

Bed & Breakfast per night: single occupancy from £35.00–£45.00; double room from £45.00–£65.00
Bedrooms: 2 double, 1 twin

Bathrooms: 2 en-suite, 1 private shower
Parking for 10

---

315 THE OLD SCHOOL HOUSE

⬦⬦⬦ HIGHLY COMMENDED

Church Street, Bathford, Bath, Avon BA1 7RR Tel (01225) 859593 Fax (01225) 859590

Rodney & Sonia Stone are delighted to welcome guests to their picturesque Victorian schoolhouse in the peaceful conservation village of Bathford, overlooking the Avon Valley. A tranquil three-mile tow-path walk along the Kennet & Avon Canal leads into the city centre. Our four bedrooms are individually furnished and decorated – two at ground-floor and suitable for the less mobile. The pretty walled garden, antique furniture and winter log fires contribute to a charming country-house ambience. No Smoking.

Bed & Breakfast per night: single room from £40.00–£50.00; double room from £60.00–£65.00
Half board per person: £49.50–£52.00 daily; £325.00–£365.00 weekly
Evening meal 1900–2000 (last orders 1900)

Bedrooms: 3 double, 1 twin
Bathrooms: 4 en-suite, 1 private shower
Parking for 6
Cards accepted: Access, Visa

---

316 BLAIRGOWRIE HOUSE

⬦⬦ HIGHLY COMMENDED

55 Wellsway, Bath, Avon BA2 4RT Tel (01225) 332266

Situated on the A367 at Bear Flat and a twelve-minute walk to the city centre, you can experience the 'Tardis' effect of 'Blairgowrie' by simply stepping through the front door. Hidden by the external façade, guests are presented with extensively renovated and decorated rooms, each providing a high level of comfort, colour television, reading material, a hospitality tray and hairdryers. Plus each day starts with a delicious breakfast chosen from an extensive menu and designed for all tastes.

Bed & Breakfast per night: single occupancy from £32.00–£42.00; double room from £42.00–£52.00
Bedrooms: 2 double, 1 twin

Bathrooms: 2 en-suite, 1 private
Parking for 1

317 DORIAN HOUSE
⬥⬥ HIGHLY COMMENDED

One Upper Oldfield Park, Bath, Avon BA2 3JX Tel (01225) 426336 Fax (01225) 444699

There is always a warm welcome at this gracious Victorian house that has been lovingly restored and elegantly furnished to capture an aura of nostalgic luxury. The delightfully appointed bedrooms are all en-suite. Breakfast is selected from a generous and varied menu. The city centre, its historic attractions, restaurants and rail station is a gentle ten-minute stroll. Dorian House is the perfect centre for touring South Wales, the Cotswolds and the West Country. Parking available.

Bed & Breakfast per night: single room from £35.00–£48.00; double room from £48.00–£70.00
Bedrooms: 1 single, 3 double, 2 twin, 1 triple, 1 family room

Bathrooms: 8 private
Parking for 9
Cards accepted: Access, Visa, Diners, Amex

318 HAYDON HOUSE
⬥⬥ HIGHLY COMMENDED

9 Bloomfield Park, Bath, Avon BA2 2BY Tel (01225) 444919 or (01225) 427351 Fax (01225) 444919

Our elegant Edwardian townhouse reveals a true oasis of tranquillity, where high standards of hospitality prevail. The spacious reception rooms are tastefully furnished with antiques and the en-suite bedrooms are decorated to a very high standard, offering every comfort including a generous hospitality tray with complimentary sherry and home-made shortbread. Imaginative breakfasts are served and we present a secluded retreat from which you can readily enjoy all the pleasures of Georgian Bath. No smoking.

Bed & Breakfast per night: single occupancy from £40.00–£50.00; double room from £55.00–£70.00
Bedrooms: 3 double, 1 twin, 1 family room

Bathrooms: 5 en-suite
Parking for 5
Cards accepted: Access, Visa, Amex, Switch/Delta

319 LEIGHTON HOUSE
⬥⬥ HIGHLY COMMENDED

139 Wells Road, Bath, Avon BA2 3AL Tel (01225) 314769

Enjoy a haven of friendliness at Leighton House, a Victorian house set in award-winning gardens with views over the city. Ample private parking and a ten-minute walk from Bath's centre. The rooms are spacious, tastefully decorated and furnished to high standards with bedrooms offering every comfort and en-suite bathrooms. An excellent and wide choice of breakfasts including fresh fruit salad and scrambled eggs with smoked salmon — the hospitality is a delight to experience. Special breaks available.

Bed & Breakfast per night: single occupancy from £42.00–£45.00; double room from £58.00–£65.00
Bedrooms: 3 double, 3 twin, 2 triple

Bathrooms: 8 en-suite
Parking for 8
Cards accepted: Access, Visa

320 MEADOWLAND
DE LUXE
36 Bloomfield Park, Bath, Avon BA2 2BX Tel (01225) 311079

Set in its own quiet grounds offering the highest standards of en-suite accommodation, Meadowland has been elegantly furnished and decorated: the colour co-ordinated bedrooms have remote control television, hairdryers, trouser presses and a welcome tray. There is a comfortable lounge with a wide selection of books and magazines. Breakfast is served in our charming dining room where guests can choose from an imaginative menu. Lovely gardens and private parking surround our house. A peaceful retreat for the discerning traveller. No smoking.

Bed & Breakfast per night: single occupancy from £35.00–£40.00; double room from £48.00–£58.00
Bedrooms: 2 double, 1 twin

Bathrooms: 3 private
Parking for 6
Cards accepted: Access, Visa

321 SIENA HOTEL
HIGHLY COMMENDED
24/25 Pulteney Road, Bath, Avon BA2 4EZ Tel (01225) 425495 Fax (01225) 469029

An elegant Victorian hotel within a few minutes of a level walk to the Roman baths, city centre and all the local places of interest. In its garden setting and overlooking Bath's medieval abbey, the hotel offers an extensive range of facilities, quality accommodation, excellent home cuisine, licensed bar, gardens, a high standard of personal service and the advantage of a private car park. The friendly staff and a warm comfortable ambience create an ideal location for a memorable stay.

Bed & Breakfast per night: single room from £37.50–£47.50; double room from £55.00–£70.00
Half board per person: £40.00–£47.50 daily;
£250.00–£300.00 weekly
Evening meal 1900 (last orders 2100)

Bedrooms: 2 single, 6 double, 4 triple, 1 family room
Bathrooms: 13 private
Parking for 13
Cards accepted: Access, Visa

322 THE BATH TASBURGH HOTEL
HIGHLY COMMENDED
Warminster Road, Bath, Avon BA2 6SH Tel (01225) 425096 Fax (01225) 463842

This beautiful Victorian mansion stands in seven acres of lovely gardens and grounds with canal frontage and breath-taking views, creating a calm and peaceful setting conveniently near the centre of the magnificent Georgian city of Bath. There are ten tastefully furnished en-suite rooms with imaginative and pleasant colour schemes, combining Victorian elegance with all the comforts of a good hotel, and a fine sitting room and conservatory. Ample parking and many extras.

Bed & Breakfast per night: single room from £36.00–£50.00; double room from £58.00–£72.00
Bedrooms: 1 single, 6 double, 2 twin, 2 triple, 2 family rooms

Bathrooms: 10 en-suite, 1 private shower
Parking for 15
Cards accepted: Access, Visa, Diners, Amex

323 CRICKLADE HOTEL & COUNTRY CLUB 🌊🌊🌊🌊🌊 HIGHLY COMMENDED

Common Hill, Swindon, Wiltshire SN6 6HA Tel (01793) 750751 Fax (01793) 751767

This beautiful and dignified house is set in extensive grounds, offering a range of sporting activities including a golf course with an on-site golf professional. The luxurious lounge, warmed by open fires in winter, extends to a magnificent Victorian conservatory, and all the bedrooms are smartly furnished and fully equipped. The first-class restaurant offers a varied and interesting menu with an emphasis on fresh local produce and careful presentation. Regular live entertainment, dinner-dances and barbecues.

Bed & Breakfast per night: single room from
£70.00–£80.00; double room from £80.00–£95.00
Evening meal 1900 (last orders 2200)
Bedrooms: 8 single, 32 double, 6 twin

Bathrooms: 46 en-suite
Parking for 100
Cards accepted: Access, Visa, Amex, Switch/Delta

Fox Talbot and Lacock Abbey

A RATHER FAINT, blurred image of the oriel window of Lacock Abbey is remarkable for being one of the first photographs ever taken. The photographer was William Henry Fox Talbot and Lacock Abbey was his ancestral home. A series of experiments conducted by Fox Talbot here in the 1830s resulted in some of the world's earliest photographs, and provided the foundations for the development of modern photography. A museum about the photographer and his experiments is now housed in a barn near the entrance to the abbey.

The Talbot family had owned Lacock Abbey since the late 16th century. Before this it had belonged briefly to the Sharingtons. William Sharington acquired the mainly 15th-century abbey in 1540 after the religious foundation had been dissolved by Henry VIII, and he transformed it into an imposing dwelling . He razed the church to the ground and converted the domestic buildings to form his home, employing craftsmen familiar with the style of the Italian renaissance. His additions include an interesting octagonal tower overlooking the River Avon and some decorative twisted chimney stacks.

The Talbot family inherited Lacock Abbey through marriage, a marriage which, but for a quirk of fate, might not have taken place at all. Olive Sharington was desperate to marry her lover, John Talbot, but her father fiercely opposed the match. In despair, she leapt from the battlements of the abbey, but, miraculously, as she fell her petticoats billowed out around her, breaking her fall and saving her life. Her anxious lover, standing below, was almost killed when she landed unannounced on top of him. Upon Talbot's recovery, however, Olive's father, recognised his daughter's determination and withdrew his opposition to the marriage, for in his opinion 'since she had made such a leap she should e'en marrie him', as John Aubrey reported it. The couple were soon wed, thus ensuring the Talbot family's inheritance of Lacock Abbey. In 1944 the last descendant of the family, Matilda Talbot, ceded the property to the National Trust (tel. 01249 730459).

324 FENWICKS
♨♨ HIGHLY COMMENDED

Buccabank, Lower Goatacre, Lyneham, Calne, Wiltshire SN11 9HY Tel (01249) 760645

A delightful, secluded country home, idyllically set in two-and-a-half acres of beautiful gardens and meadowland on the outskirts of a hamlet. A relaxing haven from which to explore the many places of interest. The bedrooms are comfortably and charmingly furnished. Tea may be taken in the lovely garden in the summer. There is a large play area. The word 'cosy' describes a winter break. To quote: "An oasis in England"; "Just beautiful"; "So this is paradise"; "Superb!!"; "Outstanding". Non-smoking.

Bed & Breakfast per night: single room from
£27.00–£30.00; double room from £35.00–£39.00
Half board per person: £30.00–£32.50 daily;
£189.00–£268.00 weekly
Bedrooms: 1 twin, 1 triple, 1 single

Bathrooms: 2 en-suite, 1 private
Parking for 5
Cards accepted: Amex

325 BURFOOTS
♨♨ HIGHLY COMMENDED

The Close, Hilmarton, Calne, Wiltshire SN11 8TQ Tel (01249) 760492 Fax (01249) 760609

The accommodation at Burfoots is of an exceptionally high standard, with beautiful views of the rolling Wiltshire countryside from bedrooms luxuriously appointed with private facilities. The tastefully furnished dining room leads to the outdoor heated swimming pool and patio, complete with reclining chairs. Situated in some of England's most beautiful countryside, its idyllic rural setting belies the close proximity of the M4, allowing it to be easily reached by the motorway network.

Bed & Breakfast per night: single room from
£17.50–£20.00; double room from £35.00–£40.00
Half board per person: £24.50–£31.00 daily
Evening meal 1800 (last orders 1930)

Bedrooms: 1 single, 1 double, 1 twin
Bathrooms: 3 en-suite
Parking for 6

326 LAUREL COTTAGE GUEST HOUSE
♨♨ HIGHLY COMMENDED

Southend, Ogbourne St George, Marlborough, Wiltshire SN8 1SG Tel (01672) 841288

Situated in a fold of the Marlborough Downs, this picturesque 16th-century thatched cottage offers you a unique opportunity to savour a traditional English home. Lovingly and tastefully restored with modern facilities, including en-suite bedrooms, this is an experience that will live long in the memory. Full English breakfast is taken in the low beamed dining room around the family table – try the tempting smoked haddock, kippers or omelettes. We are a non-smoking establishment.

Bed & Breakfast per night: single occupancy from
£26.00–£34.00; double room from £33.00–£50.00
Bedrooms: 2 double, 2 twin

Bathrooms: 2 en-suite, 1 private shower
Parking for 5
Open: April–October

327 THE OLD VICARAGE

≋≋≋ HIGHLY COMMENDED

Burbage, Marlborough, Wiltshire SN8 3AG Tel (01672) 810495 Fax (01672) 810663

The Old Vicarage is a lovely brick and flint Victorian gothic house, between Hungerford and Marlborough. Beautifully decorated, furnished and centrally heated throughout, with log fires on cold days and many special extras in the three en-suite bedrooms. Come and share the comfort and welcome of our non-smoking home, relax in the peaceful gardens, explore the Kennet and Avon canal, Savernake Forest, the vale of Pewsey and the many other wonderful places to visit, such as Bath, Oxford and Salisbury.

Bed & Breakfast per night: single room from £35.00–£40.00; double room from £60.00–£80.00
Half board per person: £60.00–£65.00 daily
Bedrooms: 1 single, 1 double, 1 twin

Bathrooms: 3 en-suite
Parking for 10
Cards accepted: Access, Visa

---

328 BECKFORD ARMS

≋≋≋ HIGHLY COMMENDED

Fonthill Gifford, Tisbury, Salisbury, Wiltshire SP3 6PX Tel (01747) 870385 Fax (01747) 851496

The 18th-century Beckford Arms stands in an area of outstanding beauty. Stylishly refurbished to a high standard, the inn offers traditional comfort and value for the discerning traveller or tourist. It is an ideal base to explore Salisbury, Shaftesbury and the surrounding area: Stonehenge, Longleat and Stourhead are all within a leisurely drive through leafy lanes. Noted for fine food, real ales, traditional hospitality, log fires and splendid gardens, the Beckford Arms is truly somewhere special.

Bed & Breakfast per night: single room from £29.50–£29.50; double room from £49.50–£54.50
Half board per person: £35.75–£38.25 daily;
£192.50–£192.50 weekly
Lunch available: 1200–1400

Evening meal 1900 (last orders 2200)
Bedrooms: 2 single, 4 double, 1 twin
Bathrooms: 5 en-suite, 2 private
Parking for 42
Cards accepted: Access, Visa, Amex

KEY TO SYMBOLS

For ease of use, the key to symbols appears on the back of the cover flap and can be folded out while consulting individual entries. The symbols which appear at the end of each entry are designed to enable you to see at-a-glance what's on offer, and whether any particular requirements you have can be met. Most of the symbols are clear, simple icons and few require any further explanation, but the following points may be useful:

ALCOHOLIC DRINKS: Alcoholic drinks are available at all types of accommodation listed in the guide unless the symbol ⊍ (unlicensed) appears. However, even in licensed premises there may be some restrictions on the serving of drinks, such as being available to diners only.

SMOKING: Many establishments offer facilities for non-smokers, indicated by the symbol ⧸. These may include no-smoking bedrooms and parts of communal rooms set aside for non-smokers. Some establishments prefer not to accommodate smokers at all, and if this is the case it will be made clear in the establishment description in the guide entry.

PETS: The symbol ✕ is used to show that dogs are not accepted in any circumstances. Some establishments will accept pets, but we advise you to check this at the time of booking and to enquire as to whether any additional charge will be made to accommodate them.

South and South East England

Oxford

ONDON IS THE MAGNET for this region – but with roads and railways radiating out from its central hub it doesn't take too long to discover, only a few miles out, hidden areas of unspoilt countryside. Journey further south and west to the huge tracts of the New Forest, almost unchanged since the end of the last Ice Age, to eastern Dorset, where the scenic Purbeck ridge meets a dramatic coastline, or to the remote Berkshire Downs, populated as much by racehorses from the Lambourn stables as by people, and the pull of London seems weak indeed.

Nevertheless, it goes without saying that London has all that the greatest capital city should offer: its museums, galleries, theatres, shops, restaurants and hotels are amongst the best in the world. The West End is buzzing and lively, while smart residential districts – Chelsea, Knightsbridge, Kensington and Hampstead – are all graceful elegance. The great parks and gardens – Hyde Park, Green Park, Hampstead Heath – bring a refreshing greenness to the heart of the city.

Lulworth Cove

Kent has always been an important county in England's history. Here it was that the Romans landed, here is the centre of the Anglican faith, here England's closest point to the Continent. A long history and continued prosperity have given rise to glorious architecture, spanning almost the whole of the second millennium. Canterbury scores high on any list of historic English cities, while country houses and castles such as Knole, Chartwell, Penshurst Place, Leeds Castle and Hever Castle give Kent top billing on this score, too. But Kent's architectural glory is not solely in its grand buildings: villages such as Penshurst and Chiddingstone and towns such as Tunbridge Wells and Tenterden exhibit a startling array of vernacular architecture, especially of Tudor half-timbered houses.

Thomas Hardy's Cottage

The White Cliffs of Dover mark the extreme eastern end of the North Downs, while another famous south-coast landmark, Beachy Head, signals the abrupt halt of the South Downs. Between these two chalk ridges lies the fertile Weald, once heavily wooded, but now largely given over to agriculture. Nevertheless, Surrey, with which Kent and East Sussex share the Weald, remains the most wooded county in England.

East and West Sussex are rich not just in landscape terms – the South Downs with their smooth, bald roundness are magnificent – but also in historic towns (Chichester, Lewes and Arundel) and in coastal resorts. Here there is a long list to choose from – Hastings, Eastbourne, Brighton, Bognor Regis and many others, enjoying some of the highest sunshine figures of anywhere in the country.

Sharing both the sunny climate and the chalk downland scenery is the Isle of Wight. The pace of life on the island is markedly slower than on the mainland and much of the island's economy centres on leisure. The island is perfect walking territory: quiet lanes with few cars, a marvellous coast, fine views in every direction, and myriad paths are all a walker could wish for. Views due west stretch to the Isle of Purbeck on Dorset's eastern flank. Here, more wonderful coastal scenery such as Lulworth Cove is backed by the limestone ridge of the Purbeck Hills and picturesque sleepy villages, together forming a thoroughly pleasing landscape.

Eastbourne

Hampshire is the home of two fine angling rivers, the Test and the Itchen, as well as England's former capital, Winchester, yet another rewarding city with magnificent ecclesiastical architecture (including the longest medieval cathedral in Europe). In the south-western corner is the New Forest, once the hunting preserve of the monarchy, now a huge expanse of heath and woodland offering leisure opportunities aplenty. The south-eastern corner of the county meets the South Downs in some style; Butser Hill, near Petersfield, is their highest point at 888ft. Further north the Hampshire Downs merge into the Berkshire Downs in an upland area which almost – but not quite – reaches 1,000ft. The region's highest point, Walbury Hill (974ft), just over into Berkshire, commands extensive views in all directions, so it is not too surprising to find a hillfort bang on the top. Hillforts, indeed, are a common feature and just a few miles into Oxfordshire is the White Horse of Uffington, one of the most impressive of our early ancestors' chalk carvings, next to a large hillfort.

Arundel Castle

Most of these forts are in close proximity to the Ridgeway, an ancient track which leads along the tops of the Berkshire Downs and into the Chilterns. Still in use today, the Ridgeway offers a rewarding walk to those prepared to tackle its 80-odd miles, though there's no necessity to walk its entirety! Up in the north-western corner of this region the character of the landscape changes to the warm golden colours of the Cotswolds. Oxfordshire is the home of some most perfect English towns – Burford and Chipping Norton for example – and one of the most perfect of English cities, Oxford, where spires and academics dream. Running through the county for much of its course is the Thames, and prosperous riverside towns such as Windsor, Henley and Marlow make most attractive detours.

Henley-on-Thames

One of the advantages of the region's proximity to London is the density of sumptuous country houses. England's nobility looked favourably upon the Home Counties for their rural estates since they were close enough to the capital to participate regularly both in the affairs of parliament and the events of the social calendar. Buckinghamshire has its fair share of such houses, as well as a trio of remarkable Rothschild properties (Ascott, Mentmore and the extravagant Waddesdon Manor, all open to the public).

161

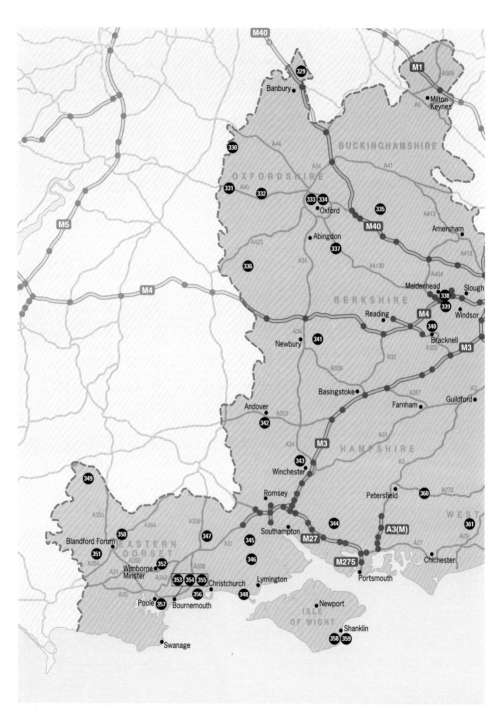

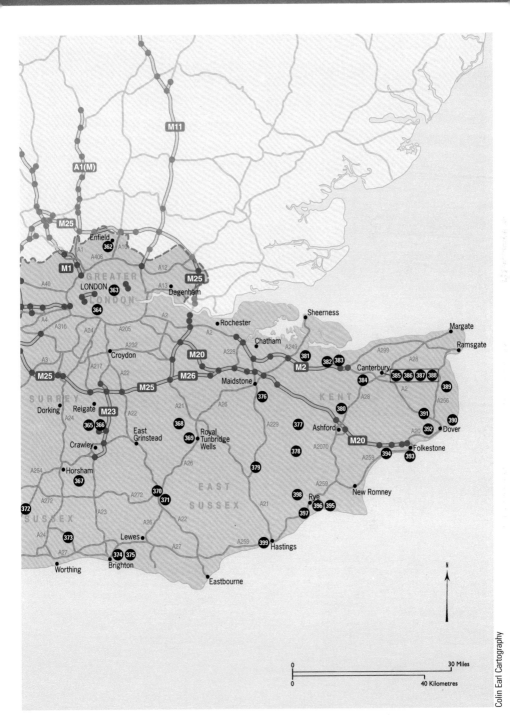

329 THE OLD MANOR

Listed HIGHLY COMMENDED

Cropredy, Banbury, Oxfordshire OX17 1PS Tel (01295) 750235 Fax (01295) 758479

Our lovely former manor house is set in two acres of garden bordering the Oxford canal. The double room, with its canopied bed, has an en-suite shower and the pretty twin room has a private bathroom. Both rooms have television, tea/coffee-making facilities, plus many other little touches of luxury. A traditional English breakfast is served in the 16th-century dining room. A private motor museum and rare-breed farm animals add to the special atmosphere.

Bed & Breakfast per night: single occupancy from £25.00–£28.00; double room from £44.00–£48.00
Bedrooms: 1 double, 1 twin

Bathrooms: 2 private
Parking for 20
Cards accepted: Access, Visa, Amex

---

330 THE MILL HOUSE HOTEL & RESTAURANT

HIGHLY COMMENDED

Kingham, Oxfordshire OX7 6UH Tel (01608) 658188 Fax (01608) 658492

Situated in the heart of the beautiful Cotswolds, in our own seven-acre grounds. Bordered by a trout stream, the hotel sits well back from a minor road, ensuring complete peace and relaxation whilst within easy travelling distance of Oxford, Stratford and Cheltenham. The award-winning restaurant has menus that change daily and an excellent choice of one hundred and eighty wines.

Bed & Breakfast per night: single occupancy from £40.00–£45.00; double room from £80.00–£90.00
Half board per person: £49.95–£66.00 daily; £346.00–£378.00 weekly
Lunch available: 1230–1400

Evening meal 1900 (last orders 2130)
Bedrooms: 11 double, 11 twin, 1 triple
Bathrooms: 23 en-suite
Parking for 60
Cards accepted: Access, Visa, Diners, Amex, Switch/Delta

---

331 THE BIRD IN HAND

HIGHLY COMMENDED

Whiteoak Green, Burford, Witney, Oxfordshire OX8 5XP Tel (01993) 868321 or (01993) 868811 Fax (01993) 868702

This delightful residential inn is surrounded by open fields and is one mile north of Hailey, on the B4022 between Witney and Charlbury. The inn rambles through five stone-walled rooms, one with a huge inglenook wood fireplace where meals can be chosen from an imaginative menu of home-cooked food and the freshest fish. Sixteen spacious and comfortable rooms are in a separate u-shaped building that surrounds a very peaceful courtyard, with two ground-floor rooms for the disabled.

Bed & Breakfast per night: single occupancy from £42.00–£47.50; double room from £49.00–£55.00
Evening meal 1900 (last orders 2200)
Bedrooms: 10 double, 4 twin, 2 family rooms

Bathrooms: 16 private
Parking for 100
Cards accepted: Access, Visa

332 NORTH LEIGH GUEST HOUSE

苍苍 HIGHLY COMMENDED

28 Common Road, North Leigh, Witney, Oxfordshire OX8 6RA Tel (01993) 881622

Near the centre of a friendly village, North Leigh Guest House is a warm and welcoming family home. A spacious drive, providing ample parking, leads directly to the self-contained guest suite's own entrance. The bedrooms are cheerful, cosy and spotlessly clean, looking out over a relaxing country view. Rooms are available for use all day and guests are welcome to use the conservatory and the large, peaceful garden. Uncommonly good food is a speciality.

Bed & Breakfast per night: single occupancy from £25.00–£28.00; double room from £38.00
Half board per person: £29.50 daily
Evening meal 1900 (last bookings 1900)

Bedrooms: 1 twin, 1 triple
Bathrooms: 2 en-suite
Parking for 5

---

333 THE OLD PARSONAGE HOTEL

苍苍苍苍苍 HIGHLY COMMENDED

1 Banbury Road, Oxford, Oxfordshire OX2 6NN Tel (01865) 310210 Fax (01865) 311262

In a central city location with its own car park, this 17th-century building was completely refurbished in 1991 and now features thirty individually designed bedrooms of varying sizes, all with fine marble bathrooms, mini-bar, mini-safe, hairdryers and satellite television. The popular Parsonage Bar is the hotel's only dining area and is open from 0700 to midnight; imaginative cooking in an informal setting has meant that it has also become a fashionable meeting place for local Oxford personalities.

Bed & Breakfast per night: single occupancy from £100.00–£180.00; double room from £140.00–£190.00
Lunch available: 1200–1500
Evening meal 1800 (last orders 2300)

Bedrooms: 18 double, 8 twin, 4 triple
Bathrooms: 30 en-suite
Parking for 15
Cards accepted: Access, Visa, Diners, Amex, Switch/Delta

---

334 RECTORY FARM

苍苍 HIGHLY COMMENDED

Northmoor, Oxford, Oxfordshire OX8 1SX Tel (01865) 300207

Come and enjoy peace and tranquillity in our beautiful 16th-century farmhouse (a non-smoking house) which is situated in the centre of the quiet village of Northmoor (ten miles west of Oxford). Both our rooms have en-suite facilities and hospitality trays. There is a large sitting/dining room, exclusively for our guests' use, with a wood-burning stove and television. The village pub is within walking distance and there are other excellent eating places locally. A warm welcome awaits you and personal service is guaranteed.

Bed & Breakfast per night: single occcupancy from £30.00; double room from £37.00–£40.00
Bedrooms: 1 double, 1 twin

Bathrooms: 2 en-suite
Parking for 2
Open: February–December

335 BELFRY HOTEL

♛♛♛♛ HIGHLY COMMENDED

Milton Common, Thame, Oxfordshire OX9 2JW Tel (01844) 279381 Fax (01844) 279624

A privately-owned and extended seventy seven bedroom mock Tudor-style hotel. Situated on the A40 near Junctions 7 & 8/M40, this hotel is an ideal location for touring the Thames, the Chilterns, Oxford and the Cotswolds. One hour from London and Birmingham, with Heathrow a forty five minute drive away.

Bed & Breakfast per night: single room from £74.00;
double room from £92.50
Lunch available: 1230–1400
Evening meal 1930 (last orders 2130)
Bedrooms: 11 single, 36 double, 30 twin

Bathrooms: 77 private
Parking for 200
Cards accepted: Access, Visa, Diners, Amex,
Switch/Delta

336 SHOTOVER HOUSE

♛♛ HIGHLY COMMENDED

Uffington, Oxfordshire SN7 7RH Tel (01367) 820351

Many original paintings adorn the walls of this warm and welcoming home with views of the famous Uffington White Horse. Three romantically-styled bedrooms with private or en-suite bathrooms enjoy crisp white cotton bedlinen, fluffy white towels, tea/coffee making facilities and colour television. Breakfasts include home-baked bread, freshly squeezed orange juice, home-made preserves and eggs from the hens in the garden. A non-smoking home.

Bed & Breakfast per night: single room from £25.00;
double room from £50.00
Half board per person: £35.00–£40.00 daily;
£210.00–£240.00 weekly
Evening meal 1900

Bedrooms: 1 single, 1 double, 1 twin
Bathrooms: 2 en-suite, 1 private
Parking for 3
Cards accepted: Access, Visa

337 WHITE HART HOTEL

♛♛♛♛ HIGHLY COMMENDED

High Street, Dorchester on Thames, Oxfordshire OX10 7HN Tel (01865) 340074 Fax (01865) 341082

An ancient coaching inn in the beautiful Thames Valley, with nineteen bedrooms and fine dining. Oxford, Blenheim, Henley and the Cotswolds are all convenient. Heathrow, London, Stratford-upon-Avon, Cheltenham and Stonehenge are a mere hour away. We combine old-style, relaxed, quality service with modern-day facilities. An ideal location for touring, golf, culture, walking – or just relaxing in good friendly company with fine food and friendly hospitality.

Bed & Breakfast per night: single room £55.00; double
room from £80.00–£120.00
Evening meal 1900 (last orders 2145)
Bedrooms: 1 single, 12 double, 5 twin

Bathrooms: 18 private
Parking for 24
Cards accepted: Access, Visa, Diners, Amex

338 MONKEY ISLAND HOTEL

🌊🌊🌊🌊 HIGHLY COMMENDED

Bray, Maidenhead, Berkshire SL6 2EE Tel (01628) 23400 Fax (01628) 784732

Situated close to Windsor on its own island amidst the Thames with many species of wildlife, our hotel is the perfect retreat for that special weekend away. Our Pavilion Restaurant has magnificent upstream river views and offers innovative cuisine along with friendly attentive service. Each of our en-suite bedrooms has river or garden views. Enjoy a unique and beautiful environment away from the mainland and you may find it difficult to leave!

Bed & Breakfast per night: single room from £80.00; double room from £95.00
Evening meal 1930 (last orders 2145)
Bedrooms: 2 single, 8 double, 13 twin, 2 suites

Bathrooms: 25 en-suite
Parking for 100
Cards accepted: Access, Visa, Diners, Amex

Swan Upping

IN THE MIDDLE AGES swan was considered a delicacy fit only for a king. Richard I, who is believed to have introduced the breed into Britain in the 12th century, accorded them royal protection, and the penalties for anyone killing a swan – or even taking an egg – were severe. Ownership was by special licence, and these were obtainable only by a few privileged landowners or City guilds. A special 'swanmark' notched into the swans' beaks indicated ownership; any swan on open water without a mark was automatically royal property.

This is still the case today, but the custom of marking swans has largely died out. Only the Vintners and the Dyers Livery Companies continue the practice and, since the time of Elizabeth I, have carried out an elaborate procedure to enforce their ancient rights. On the

Monday of the third week of July the swan markers of the two livery companies, together with the Royal Keeper of Swans, don special uniforms and set off from Sunbury in a procession of rowing skiffs to 'up' the swans from the Thames. The birds are counted and their beaks examined to establish ownership. Two nicks on the beak mark the property of the Vintners; a bird with only one nick belongs to the Dyers. Depending on their parentage, the new cygnets are allotted either to one of the livery companies or to the Queen. If they are of mixed parentage, as they often are, complicated rules come into play. The journey ends at Pangbourne, usually after four days.

The artist, Stanley Spencer, born at Cookham on the River Thames in 1891, recorded this ceremony in one of his most famous paintings, *Swan Upping*, now in the Tate Gallery, London. Others of his paintings, however, are on view at the Stanley Spencer Gallery, King's Hall, Cookham-on-Thames.

339 MOOR FARM

〰〰 HIGHLY COMMENDED

Ascot Road, Holyport, Maidenhead, Berkshire SL6 2HY Tel (01628) 33761 Fax (01628) 33761

Guests can stay in the seven-hundred-year-old manor for bed & breakfast or in Four-Key, Highly Commended self-catering courtyard cottages. House guests have exclusive use of a wing with a sitting room, dining room and bedrooms with private bathrooms furnished with antiques. The cottages were converted from barns and stables and are furnished in antique pine. Good pubs are within walking distance. Close to Junction 8 & 9/M4, Maidenhead's main line station is one-and-a-half miles and Windsor is four miles. Easy access from London.

Bed & Breakfast per night: double room from £38.00–£45.00
Bedrooms: 1 double, 2 twin
Bathrooms: 3 private
Parking for 4

Self-catering cottages from £200.00–£380.00 per week

340 COPPID BEECH HOTEL

〰〰〰〰〰 DE LUXE

John Nike Way, Bracknell, Berkshire RG12 8TF Tel (01344) 303333 Fax (01344) 301200

A luxury alpine-style hotel with two-hundred-and-five bedrooms including nineteen suites, five minutes from Junction 10/M4 and close to Ascot, Windsor and Henley. A fine dining restaurant, Bier Keller, Brasserie, Night Club and health & fitness club. Dry-skiing and ice skating are also available on site. Golf, hot air ballooning, Thames boat trips, horse riding and fly-fishing can also be arranged. Twenty four-hour room service and ample free car parking. Baby minding facilities.

Bed & Breakfast per night: single room from £60.00–£105.00; double room from £70.00–£125.00
Half board per person: £57.50–£135.00 daily
Lunch available: 1200–1430 (not open Saturday lunch time)
Evening meal 1800 (last orders 2200)

Bedrooms: 44 single, 33 double, 100 twin, 6 triple, 22 family rooms
Bathrooms: 205 private
Parking for 350
Cards accepted: Access, Visa, Diners, Amex, Switch/Delta

341 REGENCY PARK HOTEL

〰〰〰〰〰 HIGHLY COMMENDED

Bowling Green Road, Thatcham, Newbury, Berkshire RG13 3RP Tel (01635) 871555 Fax (01635) 871571

In the heart of Berkshire countryside, with five acres of landscaped gardens, the Regency Park is a tranquil oasis from the stress and pressure of modern life. A warm welcome awaits you from the staff who have many commendations for courtesy and care. Large comfortable bedrooms are a feature, some with their own balcony. Terraces Restaurant has an enviable reputation for the finest of fresh food, winning many accolades. Fountains Cocktail Bar and the south-facing lounge complete the picture.

Bed & Breakfast per night: single room from £50.00–£94.00; double room from £60.00–£108.00
Half board per person: £68.50–£112.50 daily
Evening meal 1830 (last orders 2230)

Bedrooms: 5 single, 30 double, 14 twin, 1 triple
Bathrooms: 50 en-suite
Parking for 125
Cards accepted: Access, Visa, Diners, Amex

342 MALT COTTAGE

Upper Clatford, Andover, Hampshire SP11 7QL Tel (01264) 323469 Fax (01264) 334100

A warm welcome will await you at our two-hundred-and-fifty year old converted malting barn, situated in an attractive Hampshire village containing many thatched cottages. A feature of the property is the idyllic six-acre garden, with a lake and chalk stream. The garden is part formal and part natural water-meadows.

Bed & Breakfast per night: single room from £25.00;
double room from £36.00–£43.00
Half board per person: £30.50–£34.00 daily
Evening meal 1800

Bedrooms: 1 single, 1 double, 1 twin
Bathrooms: 3 private
Parking for 5

Sandham Memorial Chapel

THE SANDHAM MEMORIAL CHAPEL is an austere little red-brick building. It was specially built, not for its exterior, but to house an extraordinary series of wall-paintings by the English artist, Stanley Spencer, and was actually designed by the artist himself. Spencer conceived the idea of a series of murals some years after serving in World War I. His plans were seen by Mr and Mrs Behrend, a couple from Burghclere, Berkshire, who arranged for the chapel to be built, afterwards dedicating it to the memory of Mrs Behrend's brother, Lieutenant HW Sandham, who had died in 1919 from illness contracted while serving in Macedoni.

During World War I Spencer served in the army medical corps, and the murals in the Sandham memorial chapel at Burghclere are a remarkable record of the war – not the great campaigns or the famous generals, but the everyday humdrum events in the lives of the typical British soldier. They show soldiers cleaning floors, filling tea-urns, making beds, sorting the laundry, getting dressed and a whole variety of other daily chores, both on the front and in the army hospitals. But Spencer imbues mundane objects with exaggerated proportion and stylised perspective, so that the scenes take on the aura of both importance and horror. Tea-urns are glistening cylinders, tent guy-ropes writhe manically, and mosquito nets resemble eerie shrouds. As they grapple with these ordinary/extraordinary objects, the soldiers seem locked in a great endeavour, and what shines through it all is their human companionship. The chapel is dominated by a great

Resurrection scene on the wall behind the altar, showing soldiers rising up from their graves and handing in their crosses to a white clothed figure, just as soldiers hand in their rifles when the battle has ended. The white clothed figure might be Jesus (Spencer described him as the 'one who is') but he is quite small and almost disappears into the middle distance of the painting. The men themselves dominate the scene; they are what matter. To Spencer, their joint sacrifice and struggle could alone make sense of the ghastly carnage of war.

Details of the Sandham Memorial Chapel can be obtained on tel.0163 527 292.

Sir Stanley Spencer CBE RA

Beca Megibbon

343 EAST VIEW
 ≋≋ HIGHLY COMMENDED

16 Clifton Hill, Winchester, Hampshire SO22 5BL Tel (01962) 862986

A comfortable and elegant Victorian townhouse in a quiet elevated position with views over the city and to the South Downs beyond. A few minutes walk from the city centre and railway station, East View is secluded in a landscaped garden with off-street parking. In summer, breakfast is served in the conservatory, and elegant sitting and dining rooms are there to enjoy. Each bedroom has private or en-suite bathroom, colour television, tea/coffee making facilities and more. No smoking.

Bed & Breakfast per night: single occupancy from £30.00–£35.00; double room from £40.00–£45.00
Bedrooms: 1 double, 2 twin

Bathrooms: 2 en-suite, 1 private
Parking for 3
Cards accepted: Access, Visa

344 MONTROSE
≋≋ HIGHLY COMMENDED

Solomons Lane, Shirrell Heath, Southampton, Hampshire SO32 2HU Tel (01329) 833345

A delightful Victorian country house situated in the lovely Meon Valley area, but convenient for continental ferries and visiting the towns of Winchester, Portsmouth and Southampton. An attractive decor and surroundings offer every comfort and a warm welcome. Attention to detail with personal and courteous service ensures that your stay will be a pleasant one. This is a non-smoking establishment.

Bed & Breakfast per night: single occupancy from £22.00–£27.00; double room from £40.00–£45.00
Bedrooms: 2 double, 1 twin

Bathrooms: 1 en-suite, 1 public
Parking for 6

345 PARKHILL HOTEL
≋≋≋≋ HIGHLY COMMENDED

Beaulieu Road, Lyndhurst, Hampshire SO43 7FZ Tel (01703) 282944 Fax (01703) 283268

Graciously Georgian, Parkhill has a romantic setting in a superb elevated position amid beautiful grounds complete with great trees, stone statues, picturesque lake, secluded swimming pool, putting green and croquet lawn. All around is the peace, profusion and sylvan beauty of the New Forest. Delightful bedrooms conform to the highest standard and beautiful public rooms, with roaring log fires throughout the cooler months, open out onto terraces and lawns. The spacious dining room offers a cuisine to delight.

Bed & Breakfast per night: single room from £45.00–£63.00; double room from £90.00–£126.00
Half board per person: £70.50–£86.50 daily; £357.00–£546.00 weekly
Evening meal 1900 (last orders 2130)

Bedrooms: 1 single, 12 double, 5 twin, 2 triple
Bathrooms: 20 private
Parking for 60
Cards accepted: Access, Visa, Diners, Amex

346 WHITLEY RIDGE COUNTRY HOUSE HOTEL ☗☗☗☗ HIGHLY COMMENDED

Beaulieu Road, Brockenhurst, Hampshire SO42 7QL Tel (01590) 622354 Fax (01590) 622856

A small secluded Georgian country house in beautiful grounds with views overlooking open fields where ponies graze. We pride ourselves on a high standard of cuisine and this quality also reflects in the same care that we show in our rooms and the courtesy we provide in our service. Log fires burn in cooler months. Special two-night breaks available.

Bed & Breakfast per night: single room from
£48.00–£58.00; double room from £82.00–£90.00
Half board per person: £44.00–£58.00 daily;
£287.00–£301.00 weekly
Lunch available: 1200–1400 (Sunday only)

Evening meal 1900 (last orders 2030)
Bedrooms: 2 single, 8 double, 3 twin
Bathrooms: 13 en-suite
Parking for 24
Cards accepted: Access, Visa, Diners, Amex, Switch/Delta

347 PLANTATION COTTAGE ☗☗ HIGHLY COMMENDED

Mockbeggar, Ringwood, Hampshire BH24 3NL Tel (01425) 477443

A charming two hundred year-old Grade II listed cottage in three acres of gardens and paddocks in the New Forest between Ringwood and Fordingbridge. Plantation Cottage is in Mockbeggar, a peaceful hamlet with a post office/store and within easy reach of the major towns of Bournemouth, Poole and Salisbury. There are plenty of good pubs and restaurants in the area and it is ideal for walking, riding at stables close by, and exploring the beautiful New Forest. Sorry no smoking.

Bed & Breakfast per night: single occupancy from
£25.00–£30.00; double room from £39.00–£45.00
Bedrooms: 2 double, 1 twin

Bathrooms: 3 en-suite
Parking for 6

348 SOUTH LAWN HOTEL ☗☗☗☗ HIGHLY COMMENDED

Lymington Road, Milford-on-Sea, Lymington, Hampshire SO41 0RF Tel (01590) 643911 Fax (01590) 644820

A delightful country house hotel in peaceful surroundings where comfort and good food predominate. Owner/chef Ernst Barten supervises excellent cuisine in an award-winning restaurant complemented by an interesting well-stocked wine cellar. Spacious comfortable lounges and en-suite bedrooms with colour television, telephone and trouser press. Nearby facilities include wind-surfing and sailing from Keyhaven, golf at Brockenhurst and Barton-on-Sea, the beach at Milford and walking or riding in the beautiful New Forest.

Bed & Breakfast per night: single occupancy from
£47.50–£52.50; double room from £84.00–£95.00
Half board per person: £49.25–£63.50 daily;
£375.55–£411.15 weekly
Lunch available: 1230–1345 Sunday Only

Evening meal 1900 (last orders 2030)
Bedrooms: 6 double, 18 twin
Bathrooms: 24 en-suite
Parking for 50
Cards accepted: Access, Visa

349 STOCK HILL COUNTRY HOUSE HOTEL　　🦢🦢🦢🦢 DE LUXE

Stock Hill, Gillingham, Dorset SP8 5NR　Tel (01747) 823626　Fax (01747) 825628

Holiday visitors will appreciate and value the flair, personality and quality found in this hotel. All aspects of this amazing country house mark it out for excellence from the exemplary housekeeping to the generous international cuisine.

Half board per person: £90.00–£110.00 daily
Lunch available: 1230–1345
Evening meal 1930 (last orders 2045)
Bedrooms: 2 single, 3 double, 3 twin

Bathrooms: 8 private
Parking for 40
Cards accepted: Access, Visa, Diners, Amex

350 FAIRFIELD HOUSE COUNTRY HOTEL　　🦢🦢🦢 HIGHLY COMMENDED

Church Road, Pimperne, Blandford Forum, Dorset DT11 8UB　Tel (01258) 456756　Fax (01258) 480053

A distinctive Grade II listed Georgian manor with a delightful licensed à la carte restaurant, fine wine list and home cooking at its best. Within one and a half acres of gardens in a peaceful village setting. The en-suite bedrooms are tastefully furnished, retaining much antiquity whilst offering modern facilities. A family-suite and ground floor disability suite are available. Easy access to the coast and the historical heritage of Dorset, golf, horse riding, clay shooting and stables are available. Large car park.

Bed & Breakfast per night: single room from £42.50–£45.00; double room from £64.00–£70.00
Half board per person: £56.00–£58.50 daily
Evening meal 1900 (last orders 2100)

Bedrooms: 1 single, 2 double, 2 twin, 1 family room
Bathrooms: 6 private, 1 private shower
Parking for 20
Cards accepted: Access, Visa, Diners, Amex

351 RESTHARROW　　🦢🦢 HIGHLY COMMENDED

North Street, Winterborne Stickland, Blandford Forum, Dorset DT11 0NH　Tel (01258) 880936 or Mobile 0850 285645

Restharrow is in the pretty village of Winterborne Stickland near the head of the Winterborne valley, and in an area of outstanding natural beauty. The house offers every comfort and Julia & Jeff will do all they can to make you feel at home and enjoy your holiday. Your hosts cater for individual requirements and use home produce wherever possible. Explore the county from Restharrow, deep in the heart of Dorset. No smoking.

Bed & Breakfast per night: single occupancy from £22.00–£28.00; double room from £32.00–£38.00
Bedrooms: 2 double

Bathrooms: 1 en-suite, 1 private
Parking for 3

352 BEECHLEAS HOTEL

🛏🛏🛏 HIGHLY COMMENDED

17 Poole Road, Wimborne Minster, Dorset BH21 1QA Tel (01202) 841684

A delightful Georgian Grade II listed town-house hotel situated a five-minute walk from the centre of Wimborne Minster. Beautifully restored with nine tastefully furnished en-suite bedrooms of quality and an award-winning restaurant. Many National Trust properties are within easy reach including Kingston Lacey, Corfe Castle and Badbury Rings. Walking, fishing, sailing, shopping, sandy beaches, the New Forest, Purbeck Hills, Poole and Bournemouth are all within a twenty minute drive.

Bed & Breakfast per night: single occupancy from £61.50–£81.50; double occupancy from £80.00–£100.00. Half board single occupancy: £80.00–£100.00 daily; £504.00–£630.00 weekly. Half board double occupancy: £117.00–£137.00 daily; £737.00–£863.00 weekly

Evening meal 1930 (last orders 2100)
Bedrooms: 7 double, 2 twin
Bathrooms: 9 en-suite
Parking for 9
Open: February–December

Cards accepted: Access, Visa, Amex

353 SOUTHLANDS HOTEL

🛏🛏🛏 HIGHLY COMMENDED

11 Crabton Close Road, Boscombe Manor, Bournemouth, Dorset BH5 1HN Tel (01202) 394887

Southlands is a family-run hotel situated in a tree-lined area, a few minutes' walk from the sea, main shopping centre, and nearby tennis and bowls. All the rooms are furnished to a high standard and every care is taken to ensure your holiday is an enjoyable one. Fresh home-cooked food is served in our spacious dining room and there is a comfortable lounge and cosy bar for the residents of the hotel.

Bed & Breakfast per night: single occupancy from £16.00–£18.00; double room from £30.00–£36.00. Half board per person: £20.00–£23.00 daily; £140.00–£152.00 weekly. Evening meal 1800

Bedrooms: 8 double, 1 twin
Bathrooms: 8 en-suite
Parking for 9
Open: May–October

354 HINTON FIRS

🛏🛏🛏🛏 HIGHLY COMMENDED

Manor Road, East Cliff, Bournemouth, Dorset BH1 3HB Tel (01202) 555409 or 0500 655450 (free) Fax (01202) 299607

Family-run and acclaimed by many for its warm and friendly atmosphere. Set in the heart of East Cliff amongst pines and rhododendrons, four south-facing lounges overlook a sheltered suntrap garden and outdoor pool. Take a dip in the pool, followed by a leisurely stroll down to the beach to feel the sand between your toes and the breeze in your hair. Mention 'Somewhere Special' when booking and claim a FREE bottle of wine.

Bed & Breakfast per night: single room from £25.50–£41.50; double room from £51.00–£78.00. Half board per person: £33.50–£49.50 daily; £234.50–£320.00 weekly. Lunch available: 1230–1400 Bar Lunch

Evening meal 1900 (last orders 2030)
Bedrooms: 12 single, 14 double, 14 twin, 12 triple
Bathrooms: 48 en-suite, 4 en-suite showers
Parking for 40
Cards accepted: Access, Visa, Switch/Delta

355 NORFOLK ROYALE HOTEL 🛁🛁🛁🛁🛁 HIGHLY COMMENDED

Richmond Hill, Bournemouth, Dorset BH2 6EN Tel (01202) 551521 Fax (01202) 299729

This luxuriously restored Edwardian hotel, situated within a minute's walk from theatres, shops, gardens and golden beaches, provides the perfect blend of friendly and efficient service to ensure a relaxing short break. The Orangery Restaurant offers international cuisine and a fine wine list. The individually-designed bedrooms, studios and suites and the dome-covered pool set in the lovely garden, make this the perfect location for that special occasion.

Bed & Breakfast per night: single room from £65.00–£100.00; double room from £90.00–£140.00
Half board per person: £65.00–£80.00 daily; £390.00–£490.00 weekly
Evening meal 1900 (last orders 2300)

Bedrooms: 9 single, 46 double, 32 twin, 8 triple
Bathrooms: 95 private
Parking for 88
Cards accepted: Access, Visa, Diners, Amex

---

356 WILLOWDENE HOTEL 🛁🛁 HIGHLY COMMENDED

43 Grand Avenue, Southbourne, Bournemouth, Dorset BH6 3SY Tel (01202) 425370

Situated three hundred yards from nine miles of sandy beach, with delightful walks and panoramic views over Poole Bay, Isle of Wight Needles and Purbeck Hills. Central for many places of interest along the coast and New Forest, Grand Avenue is an attractive road, lined with trees and shrubs, quiet yet close to shops. Our small six-bedroom hotel is furnished to a superior standard and we are proud of the appreciation shown by our many regular guests. We guarantee you a friendly and quiet stay. Willowdene is a non-smoking establishment.

Bed & Breakfast per night: single occupancy from £17.00–£18.00; double room from £32.00–£36.00
Bedrooms: 3 double, 1 twin, 1 triple

Bathrooms: 4 en-suite, 1 public
Parking for 6
Open: March–October

---

357 MANSION HOUSE HOTEL 🛁🛁🛁🛁 HIGHLY COMMENDED

11 Thames Street, Poole, Dorset BH15 1JN Tel (01202) 685666 Fax (01202) 665709

A beautiful Georgian house in the old town of Poole, just off the busy quay. Each room is individually decorated, creating every comfort for a home away from home. Our restaurant Benjamin's has won many awards and has an excellent local reputation for modern English cooking. Beautiful beaches, the New Forest and Hardy country are all within minutes of the Mansion House.

Bed & Breakfast per night: single room from £50.00–£75.00; double room from £80.00–£110.00
Half board per person: £60.00–£80.00 daily; £450.00–£480.00 weekly
Lunch available: 1230–1400

Evening meal 1930 (last orders 2130)
Bedrooms: 9 single, 13 double, 6 twin
Bathrooms: 28 private
Parking for 40
Cards accepted: Access, Visa, Diners, Amex

358 CHINE COURT HOTEL

🏆🏆🏆 HIGHLY COMMENDED

Popham Road, Shanklin, Isle of Wight PO37 6RG Tel (01983) 862732 Fax (01983) 862732

Welcome to Chine Court. A truly elegant Victorian residence, lavishly furnished and decorated throughout. Standing in large grounds, it commands magnificent sea views from its elevated cliff-top position. Beautifully appointed public rooms including a large luxurious bar lounge, dry lounges and an elegant Victorian dining room offering a sumptuous five-course dinner with a full choice of traditional and continental dishes. For our guests' exclusive use, there is a large outdoor heated swimming pool, sauna, solarium, hairdressing salon.

Bed & Breakfast per night: single room from £21.00–£28.00; double room from £40.00–£54.00
Half board per person: £28.00–£37.00 daily; £190.00–£250.00 weekly
Evening meal 1830 (last orders 1915)

Bedrooms: 3 single, 8 double, 6 twin, 5 triple, 4 family rooms
Bathrooms: 25 en-suite, 1 private shower
Parking for 24
Open: April–October

Wight Wine

DESPITE THE POPULAR misconception that English winemaking is still in its infancy, viniculture in England has a very long history. The Romans brought vines with them and, by the time of the Domesday Book, there were at least 40 vineyards in the south of England, many attached to monasteries. The Dissolution of the monasteries, however, signalled the end of the industry when the vineyards were ploughed up.

English winemaking is now experiencing something of a renaissance and one of the most successful

wine-growing regions is the Isle of Wight. Surprisingly, despite its southerly position, and although there were monasteries on the island in the Middle Ages, there is no history of winemaking here – the first vineyard to be established was at Cranmore, near Yarmouth, in 1967. A year later another, Adgestone, near Brading, began producing wine, and now produces some of the best of the English wines on the market. Its '91 vintage is used as the Government's hospitality wine and, as such, was selected to accompany the Royal banquet at the Guildhall to celebrate the 50th anniversary of the D-day landings.

Isle of Wight wines are (naturally!) white. Red wine is very difficult to make successfully anywhere in England, as red grape varieties need a lot of sun to ripen. In a country renowned for its high rainfall (the bane of winemakers everywhere), the Isle of Wight, with its mild climate, offers a better chance than most parts of England for the grapes ripening in time for harvest. The grapes used are generally German varieties, specially developed to sweeten despite the cooler temperatures of northerly latitudes.

Although wine from the Isle of Wight is available in some specialist wine shops, the best way to taste it is to buy it direct from the vineyard. At Adgestone and most Wight vineyards visitors are welcome to wander round, watch the activities of the winemaking year (harvesting takes place in late autumn) and, of course, taste and buy the wine. Barton Manor (tel. 01983 293923) and Morton Manor (tel. 01983 406168) cater more for tourists and have more to offer throughout the year.

359 THE BONDI HOTEL

🛏🛏🛏 HIGHLY COMMENDED

Clarence Road, Shanklin, Isle of Wight PO37 7BH Tel (01983) 862507 Fax (01983) 862326

Take a short trip across the Solent and discover the Island and our charming hotel. Set in pleasant gardens, a short walk from the beach, town and station. The ideal place for an affordable relaxing stay, if you appreciate care and attention, traditional British food at its best and an informal atmosphere. Ferry-inclusive short breaks and walking holidays arranged. We are open all year, including Christmas, and look forward to welcoming you.

Bed & Breakfast per night: single room from £18.00–£25.00; double room from £36.00–£50.00
Half board per person: £26.00–£33.00 daily; £170.00–£190.00 weekly
Evening meal 1830

Bedrooms: 1 single, 5 double, 2 twin, 1 family room
Bathrooms: 9 en-suite, 1 public
Parking for 4
Cards accepted: Access, Visa, Diners, Amex

Petworth and Turner

PETWORTH HOUSE, with its long, many-windowed facade, is as imposing as any country house in England. The present 17th-century building stands on the site of an earlier house which, for most of the Middle Ages, was home to the Percy family, Earls of Northumberland. In 1682 the 10th Earl's only child, Elizabeth, married Charles Seymour, 6th Duke of Somerset. The new owner used his wife's fortune to remodel her ancestral home in the French Baroque style, all but demolishing the original building. He employed some of the foremost craftsmen of the day: the 'carved room' contains fine Grinling Gibbons carving. In the mid-18th-century, the grounds were landscaped by the famous landscape architect 'Capability' Brown.

Petworth houses (tel. 01789 42207) the remarkable art collection amassed by the Egremont family (The Earldom of Egremont was conferred on the family in 1749). It contains works by Titian, Van Dyck, Lely, Reynolds, Gainsborough and Blake. Paintings hang on every available area of wall-space. Amongst them are

many by JMW Turner, who came to the attention of Lord Egremont in about 1802 and was patronised by him for many years. Between 1827–31 Turner spent long periods at Petworth and was even given his own studio in a room above the chapel.

The majority of Turner paintings displayed are early works commissioned and acquired by the 2nd Earl long before the main period of association with the family. They depict a variety of English landscapes: Cockermouth Castle, the Forest of Bere, the Thames at Eton, for example, some of which had special relevance for the Egremont family. Most are executed in the manner of the great classical landscape artist, Claude, whom Turner greatly admired, but even at this early date there are signs of the later development of his distinctive, impressionistic style and his preoccupation with the effects of light and colour. By the time he painted the four specially commissioned panels in the dining room his style had moved on. Light has become the main subject of the paintings, and the shapes of deer, trees or ships are subservient to the misty effects of the sun upon the landscape.

Left: ornate limewood carvings Above: the 700-acre deer park at Petworth

National Trust Picture Library

360 SOUTHDOWN'S COUNTRY HOTEL AND RESTAURANT   HIGHLY COMMENDED
Trotton, Rogate, West Sussex GU31 5JN Tel (01730) 821521 Fax (01730) 821790

A Victorian country hotel set in peaceful and relaxing surroundings at the foot of the South Down hills. The hotel has full leisure facilities and the air-conditioned country restaurant offers the finest of English cooking and excellent wines. An ideal base for visiting Chichester and Goodwood or the antique shops of Midhurst and Petworth, with Arundel Castle only a few miles away.

Bed & Breakfast per night: single occupancy from £59.00–£69.00; double room from £79.00–£109.00
Half board per person: £49.50–£63.50 daily
Lunch available: 1230–1400
Evening meal 1900 (last orders 2130)

Bedrooms: 10 double, 9 twin, 1 triple
Bathrooms: 20 en-suite
Parking for 70
Cards accepted: Access, Visa, Diners, Amex

361 WHITE HORSE INN   HIGHLY COMMENDED
The Street, Sutton, Pulborough, West Sussex RH20 1PS Tel (01798) 869221 Fax (01798) 869291

Sutton is a picture-postcard village tucked away at the foot of the South Downs. Great sensitivity has been used to bring our charming Georgian inn up to the standards expected by the discerning traveller, whilst retaining its essential character. The bedrooms are elegantly furnished, each with its own spacious bathroom. The food has a strong emphasis on traditional country cooking, enhanced by a selection of other well-chosen dishes. Log fires in the winter!

Bed & Breakfast per night: single occupancy from £48.00–£48.00; double room from £58.00–£58.00
Half board per person: £41.00–£60.00 daily; £206.00–£290.00 weekly
Lunch available: 1200–1400

Evening meal 1900 (last orders 2140)
Bedrooms: 4 double, 2 twin
Bathrooms: 6 private
Parking for 10
Cards accepted: Access, Visa

362 OAK LODGE HOTEL   HIGHLY COMMENDED
80 Village Road, Bush Hill Park, Enfield, Middlesex EN1 2EU Tel (0181) 360 7082

Exclusive country-style hotel with exquisite restaurant overlooking evergreen gardens. With good central London access, it is just forty-five minutes from four of London's airports. With its warm ambience and charm, Oak Lodge has a reputation for being the Director's choice and at weekends, a family favourite for wedding guests and honeymooners. The university town of Cambridge, the cathedral and Roman amphitheatre of St. Albans' and the old fishing port of Leigh-on-Sea are all within an hour's drive.

Bed & Breakfast per night: single room from £45.00–£65.00; double room from £55.00–£80.00
Half board per person: £62.50–£80.00 daily; £437.50–£525.00 weekly
Evening meal 1930 (last orders 2130)

Bedrooms: 1 single, 1 double, 2 twin
Bathrooms: 4 en-suite, 1 private
Parking for 4
Cards accepted: Access, Visa, Diners, Amex

363 BLOOMS HOTEL
7 Montague Street, London WC1B 5BP Tel (0171) 323 1717 Fax (0171) 636 6498

⚜⚜⚜⚜ HIGHLY COMMENDED

Blooms Hotel is an elegant 18th-century house with a walled garden covered with seasonal flowers and ideal for afternoon tea or a moon-lit dinner. With twenty seven bedrooms, it is conveniently located next to the British Museum and a five-minute walk from the theatre district and Oxford Street for shopping. The restaurant is open weekdays and serves traditional English food; there is also twenty four-hour room service.

Bed & Breakfast per night: single room from £95.00–£105.00; double room from £135.00–£145.00. Half board per person: £120.00–£130.00 daily; £840.00–£910.00 weekly
Evening meal 1700 (last orders 2359)

Bedrooms: 5 single, 9 double, 12 twin, 2 triple
Bathrooms: 28 private
Cards accepted: Access, Visa, Diners, Amex, Switch/Delta

Castles of the Weald

THE WEALD (from the Saxon word for forest) is that fertile area of Kent and East Sussex – both agriculturally and historically – which lies between the twin ridges of chalk upland, the North and South Downs. The wealth of the area, together with its strategic location, close to court in London, potential invasion from the Continent and the ecclesiastical headquarters of Canterbury, gave rise to a diversity of impressive buildings, several of which were fortified.

Leeds Castle, east of Maidstone, is a fairy-tale castle. This beautiful building, in part 14th century, sits on two islands in a moat formed by the River Len. The building on the smaller island, the Gloriette, is the older of the two parts of the castle, which are linked by a two-storey stone bridge, known, rather grandly, as the *Pons Gloriettae*.

Scotney Castle (NT 0171 222 9251), near Lamberhurst, is also set off by a fine moat, this time formed by the River Bewl. Scotney (dating from the 14th century) is now only a shell, its dilapidation hastened in the early 19th century due to its deliberate destruction by the owner, Edward Hussey. His motive was an attempt to create the perfect landscape garden for which a ruin was *de rigueur*. His planting of azaleas, rhododendrons and various trees is now the main reason to visit (spring and autumn are best).

Although a 13th-century fortified manor-house in origin, Hever Castle clearly bears the stamp of an American millionaire, William Waldorf Astor, who bought the castle in 1905. He employed talented Edwardian craftsmen to create a marvellous imitation Tudor impression both within and without.

Bodiam Castle (NT) in East Sussex, is a robust 14th-century edifice complete with moat. Built to guard a crossing of the River Rother, it is the fortified medieval castle of any child's imagination, with huge round towers at its four corners and massive walls six feet six inches thick. The castle was saved from demolition in the early 19th century by Mad Jack Fuller, a notable local eccentric.

The Weald is full of many magnificent houses and castles, including Knole (NT), Chartwell (NT), Penshurst Place, Finchcocks, Bateman's (NT), Ightham Mote (NT), Down House and Quebec House (NT) to name but eight.

The beautiful Leeds Castle, bathed in the amber light of a summer sunset

364 FIVE SUMNER PLACE HOTEL   Listed HIGHLY COMMENDED
5 Sumner Place, South Kensington, London SW7 3EE   Tel (0171) 584 7586   Fax (0171) 823 9962

BTA Award-Winner: 'Best Small Hotel'
This delightful hotel is situated in South Kensington, the most fashionable area of London. The hotel itself has been sympathetically restored to recreate the ambience and style of a bygone era. Family-owned and run, it offers excellent service and personal attention. All rooms are luxuriously appointed and come with private en-suite facilities, telephone, colour television, trouser press and full buffet breakfast.

Bed & Breakfast per night: single room from £62.00–£72.00; double room from £85.00–£116.00
Bedrooms: 3 single, 10 double

Bathrooms: 13 private, 13 private showers
Cards accepted: Access, Visa, Amex

365 CRUTCHFIELD FARM   HIGHLY COMMENDED
Hookwood, Horley, Surrey RH6 OHT   Tel (01293) 863110   Fax (01293) 863233

Crutchfield Farm is a beautiful Grade II listed 15th-century farmhouse with many massive exposed oak beams and inglenook fireplaces. The comfortable residents' lounge and lovely bedrooms are tastefully furnished and all have colour television and tea/coffee making facilities. Set in ten acres of beautiful grounds with a swimming pool, tennis court and a lake; an ideal base from which to explore London and the South East. Gatwick is three miles away. Parking and transport to airport available.

Bed & Breakfast per night: single occupancy from £30.00; double room from £40.00–£50.00
Bedrooms: 1 double, 2 twin

Bathrooms: 1 en-suite, 1 public
Parking for 10

366 THE LAWN GUEST HOUSE   HIGHLY COMMENDED
30 Massetts Road, Horley, Surrey RH6 7DE   Tel (01293) 775751   Fax (01293) 821803

A warm welcome is assured at this elegant Victorian house just one-and-a-half miles from Gatwick Airport. With a town centre location, we are within walking distance of pubs, shops and the main-line railway station for London and the south coast. Close by, is a 14th-century church beside a 9th-century pub and restaurant. All the rooms have tea/coffee facilities, central heating, colour television, and comfortable chairs. En-suite and standard rooms are available. No smoking throughout.

Bed & Breakfast per night: double room from £35.00–£42.00
Bedrooms: 1 double, 4 twin, 1 triple, 1 family room

Bathrooms: 3 private, 2 public
Parking for 10
Cards accepted: Access, Visa, Diners, Amex

367 SOUTH LODGE HOTEL

HIGHLY COMMENDED

Brighton Road, Lower Beeding, Horsham, West Sussex RH13 6PS Tel (01403) 891711 Fax (01403) 891253

A Victorian country house hotel set in ninety three acres of wooded parkland in the heart of the Sussex countryside with thirty nine individually furnished bedrooms, some overlooking the South Downs, and an excellent restaurant presenting exquisitely beautiful dishes with a complementary extensive wine list. Leisure pursuits include clay-pigeon shooting, archery, fishing, croquet, tennis, putting, petanque and Mannings Heath Golf Club. Ideally situated for the varied local attractions; an hour from London; twenty minutes from Gatwick; an easy drive to M23/25.

Bed & Breakfast per night: single room from £90.00–£255.00; double room from £110.00–£255.00
Half board per person: £85.00–£127.50 daily
Lunch available: 1230–1400 Mon–Sat 1230–1500 Sun
Evening meal 1930 (last orders 2200)

Bedrooms: 2 single, 28 double, 9 twin
Bathrooms: 39 private
Parking for 120
Cards accepted: Access, Visa, Diners, Amex

368 SWALE COTTAGE

Listed HIGHLY COMMENDED

Old Swaylands Lane, Off Poundsbridge Lane, Penshurst, Tonbridge, Kent TN11 8AH Tel (01892) 870738

Nestled in a hilly wooded river valley close to medieval Penshurst Place and four miles from Tunbridge Wells, this charming Grade II award-winning country home has a unique artistic atmosphere. Cynthia Dakin invites you to enjoy her watercolour and pastel paintings and artwork. Antiques, canopy beds, en-suite rooms, fresh flowers and candle-lit breakfasts envelope you in a mood of gracious tranquillity. Explore walks, stately homes and gardens, inns, restaurants and go antiquing. London is only forty minutes by train. Totally non-smoking.

Bed & Breakfast per night: single occupancy from £35.00–£38.00; double room from £50.00–£58.00
Bedrooms: 2 double, 1 twin

Bathrooms: 2 en-suite, 1 private
Parking for 7

369 ASHTON LODGE

Listed HIGHLY COMMENDED

69 London Road, Royal Tunbridge Wells, Kent TN1 1DX Tel (01892) 532948

A Grade II listed former coaching house overlooking the common and within easy reach of the town centre and the Pantiles. There are two luxury en-suite bedrooms with colour television and beverage tray. Ideally situated for touring many National Trust properties and other historic buildings, gardens and parks. Children over twelve, pets and non-smokers welcomed.

Bed & Breakfast per night: single occupancy from £30.00–£35.00; double room from £45.00–£50.00

Bedrooms: 2 double
Bathrooms: 2 en-suite
Parking for 4

370 SOUTH PADDOCK

≝≝ HIGHLY COMMENDED

Maresfield Park, Uckfield, East Sussex TN22 2HA Tel (01825) 762335

A comfortable country house, beautifully furnished with an atmosphere of warmth and elegance. All rooms face south, overlooking three-and-a-half acres of mature gardens, landscaped for attractive colouring throughout the year. A peaceful setting for relaxing on the terrace beside the fishpond and fountain or in spacious drawing rooms with log fires. Centrally located, forty-one miles from London and within easy reach of Gatwick, the Channel Ports, Glyndebourne, Nymans, Sissinghurst and Chartwell. Good restaurants locally.

Bed & Breakfast per night: single occupancy from £32.00–£36.00; double room from £50.00–£53.00
Bedrooms: 1 double, 2 twin

Bathrooms: 1 private, 1 public
Parking for 6

371 HOOKE HALL

≝≝≝ HIGHLY COMMENDED

250 High Street, Uckfield, East Sussex TN22 1EN Tel (01825) 761578 Fax (01825) 768025

Hooke Hall is an elegant Queen Anne townhouse, that has been fully restored by its owners whose home it also is, to give a blend of comfort with informality. All the rooms are individually decorated to very high standards. In the panelled study, guests can relax by the open fire before dining at La Scaletta, well-known for its high-quality Italian regional food.

Bed & Breakfast per night: single occupancy £40.00–£60.00; double room £70.00–£115.00
Half board per person: £55.00–£80.00 daily
Lunch available: 1200–1400
Evening meal 1930 (last orders 2100)

Bedrooms: 5 double, 4 twin
Bathrooms: 9 private
Parking for 7
Cards accepted: Access, Visa, Amex

372 CHEQUERS HOTEL

≝≝≝≝ HIGHLY COMMENDED

Church Place, Pulborough, West Sussex RH20 1AD Tel (01798) 872486 Fax (01798) 872715

Situated in the heart of the local conservation area and facing out over the Arun Valley towards the South Downs, we pride ourselves upon being the quintessential small English country hotel. Built in 1548 and carefully extended and refurbished, we offer luxury en-suite bedrooms, fine food in our award-winning restaurant, a Conservatory coffee shop, and ample parking. Straight outside is our nine acre meadow for walks for you and your dog.

Bed & Breakfast per night: single room from £47.50–£52.50; double room from £72.00–£82.00
Half board per person: £43.50–£48.50 daily; £290.00–£325.00 weekly
Lunch available: 1200–1400

Evening meal 1930 (last orders 2045)
Bedrooms: 1 single, 5 double, 2 twin, 3 triple
Bathrooms: 11 private
Parking for 16
Cards accepted: Access, Visa, Diners, Amex

373 THE OLD TOLLGATE RESTAURANT AND HOTEL   〰〰〰 HIGHLY COMMENDED

The Street, Bramber, Steyning, West Sussex BN44 3WE Tel (01903) 879494 Fax (01903) 813399

In a lovely old Sussex village nestling at the foot of the South Downs, standing on the original Tollhouse site, a perfect blending of the old with the new. The carvery-style restaurant, a well-known and popular eating spot, offers a magnificent hors d'oeuvres display followed by a vast selection of roasts, pies and casseroles, with delicious sweets and cheeses to add the final touch. Luxuriously appointed bedrooms, including two four-posters with jacuzzi baths, and two suites.

Bed & Breakfast per night: single occupancy from £57.50–£77.50; double room from £63.00–£83.00
Half board per person: £48.75–£94.45 daily
Lunch available: 1200–1345
Evening meal 1900 (last orders 2130)

Bedrooms: 18 double, 11 twin, 2 triple
Bathrooms: 31 en-suite
Parking for 60
Cards accepted: Access, Visa, Diners, Amex, Switch/Delta

The Bloomsbury Group in Sussex

PUSH OPEN THE DOOR of the church of St Michael and All Angels in the pretty Sussex village of Berwick, near Eastbourne, and a surprise awaits. The church is mainly 12th-century, but the walls inside are covered with an astonishing display of modern painting, in complete contrast to the building's ancient exterior.

The murals were commissioned in the early years of World War II, following bomb damage to the church. They depict biblical events – a *Nativity*, a *Christ in Glory*, a *Victory of Calvary* – but their setting is the Sussex countryside, and biblical characters rub shoulders with real figures – a group of local shepherds and the parson of the church.

The paintings were carried out by Duncan Grant, Vanessa Bell and her son Quentin Bell who lived near by at Charleston Farmhouse in Firle. They were members of the Bloomsbury Group, an eccentric affiliation of writers and artists bound together by friendship and a shared interest in the arts.

Duncan Grant was Vanessa Bell's lover and lived at Charleston with Vanessa and her husband Clive Bell. The comfortable farmhouse became a gathering place for others in the group, and before long was transformed in accordance with their artistic ideals. Walls, fireplaces and furniture are painted with abstract patterns and naturalistic designs, while remaining surfaces are crowded with their own textiles, ceramics, and other *objets d'arts*.

Not far away, at Rodmell, is Monk's House (NT 0171 222 9251), once the home of Vanessa Bell's sister, the novelist Virginia Woolf. She and her husband bought this small weather-boarded farmhouse in the main street in 1919, and spent much time here – Virginia wrote in the garden lodge while Leonard worked in the garden. It was from Monk's House that Virginia walked away one March day in 1941 suffering from severe depression and waded into the River Ouse, her pockets weighed down with stones. Leonard lived here until his death in 1969. The house, occasionally open to the public, contains both furniture and canvases painted by Vanessa Bell.

Opening times may be obtained from Eastbourne's Tourist Information Centre (tel: 01323 411400).

Left: *Virginia Woolfe* by Steven Tomalin
Below: the studio at Charleston Farmhouse

374 ADELAIDE HOTEL   ≋≋≋ HIGHLY COMMENDED
51 Regency Square, Brighton, East Sussex BN1 2FF Tel (01273) 205286 Fax (01273) 220904

This elegant Regency townhouse hotel centrally situated in Brighton's premier seafront square offers, among its hallmarks, a warm welcome, friendly service and delicious food. All the bedrooms are en-suite and include the extras that guarantee a relaxing and comfortable stay. Brighton's extensive and diverse shopping, many restaurants, theatre, etc., are all within easy walking distance, and parking is available in the square. An ideal centre from which to explore the Sussex hinterland.

Bed & Breakfast per night: single room from £38.00–£60.00; double room from £55.00–£75.00
Evening meal 1830 (last orders 2030)
Bedrooms: 3 single, 7 double, 1 twin, 1 triple

Bathrooms: 12 en-suite, 1 public
Cards accepted: Access, Visa, Diners, Amex, Switch/Delta

375 ASCOTT HOUSE HOTEL   ≋≋≋ HIGHLY COMMENDED
21 New Steine, Marine Parade, Brighton, East Sussex BN2 1PD Tel (01273) 688085 Fax (01273) 623733

Located in one of the most convenient central positions in Brighton, this Grade II listed building is situated in a sea-front garden-square close to the Palace Pier, Royal Pavilion, Theatre Royal, famous Lanes and the Brighton conference centre. Whether your visit is for business or pleasure, enjoy a delicious individually-prepared English breakfast served in the elegant dining room. This excellent well-established licensed hotel offers all the home comforts in a relaxed and welcoming atmosphere.

Bed & Breakfast per night: single room from £22.00–£36.00; double room from £42.00–£70.00
Evening meal 1830 (last orders 1930)

Bedrooms: 4 single, 6 triple, 2 family rooms
Bathrooms: 9 private, 2 private showers, 1 public
Cards accepted: Access, Visa, Diners, Amex

376 TANYARD   ≋≋≋ HIGHLY COMMENDED
Wierton Hill, Boughton Monchelsea, Maidstone, Kent ME17 4JT Tel (01622) 744705 Fax (01622) 741998

Tanyard is a medieval country house hotel perched on a ridge with far-reaching views across the weald of Kent. All six bedrooms have en-suite facilities and are furnished with antiques combined with modern comforts. The top-floor suite, which is heavily beamed, has a spa bath and is particularly popular. The non-smoking restaurant seats thirty and is in the oldest part of the building, dating from 1350. The modern English food uses all fresh local produce.

Bed & Breakfast per night: single room from £50.00–£70.00; double room from £80.00–£110.00
Half board per person: £65.00–£95.00 daily;
£455.00–£665.00 weekly
Lunch available: 1200–1345

Evening meal 1900 (last orders 2100)
Bedrooms: 1 single, 3 double, 2 twin
Bathrooms: 6 en-suite
Parking for 20
Cards accepted: Access, Visa, Diners, Amex

377 MUNKS FARM
Listed HIGHLY COMMENDED

Smarden, Ashford, Kent TN27 8PN Tel (01233) 770265

A beautiful listed Grade II restored oak-beamed and timbered farmhouse in landscaped gardens surrounded by countryside, halfway between the lovely villages of Headcorn and Smarden in the heart of Kent, and perfectly situated for Leeds and Sissinghurst castles. Comfortable and attractive bedrooms with colour television and private or en-suite bathrooms. Guests may use the charming drawing room with a fine inglenook fireplace and enjoy the outdoor solar-heated swimming pool. Traditional breakfasts served in dining hall. No smoking.

Bed & Breakfast per night: single room from £27.00–£30.00; double room from £44.00–£50.00
Bedrooms: 2 twin

Bathrooms: 2 private
Parking for 3

378 LITTLE SILVER COUNTRY HOTEL
HIGHLY COMMENDED

Ashford Road, St Michaels, Tenterden, Kent TN30 6SP Tel (01233) 850321 Fax (01233) 850647

Little Silver Country Hotel is set in its own landscaped gardens. The restaurant provides an intimate, tranquil atmosphere where local produce is enjoyed, pre-dinner drinks and after-dinner coffee are offered in the beamed, log-fired sitting room. Breakfast is enjoyed in a Victorian conservatory overlooking the waterfall rockery. Luxury bedrooms, tastefully and individually designed, some with four-posters and jacuzzi baths, others with brass-beds. Facilities for disabled. Personal attention, care to detail, warmth and friendliness create a truly unique experience.

Bed & Breakfast per night: single occupancy from £60.00–£80.00; double room from £80.00–£100.00
Lunch available: pre booked groups only
Evening meal 1830 (last orders 2200)

Bedrooms: 5 double, 3 twin, 2 family rooms
Bathrooms: 10 private
Parking for 50
Cards accepted: Access, Visa

379 CONGHURST FARM
HIGHLY COMMENDED

Conghurst Lane, Hawkhurst, Cranbrook, Kent TN18 4RW Tel (01580) 753331

Conghurst is situated in a totally unspoilt corner of Kent, in an area of outstanding natural beauty. Though secluded, it is within comfortable distance of many of the fine houses, gardens and places of historical interest that Kent and Sussex have to offer. By prior arrangement, evening meals are freshly cooked using the best local produce. Our aim is to give you a relaxed, peaceful holiday or short break in our fine Georgian farmhouse. This is a non-smoking house.

Bed & Breakfast per night: single occupancy from £27.50; double room from £40.00–£45.00
Half board per person: £31.50–£34.00 daily; £203.00–£220.50 weekly
Evening meal 1900 (last bookings 1100)

Bedrooms: 1 double, 2 twin
Bathrooms: 1 en-suite, 2 private
Parking for 8
Open: March–November

380 EASTWELL MANOR HOTEL

🍴🍴🍴🍴🍴 DE LUXE

Eastwell Park, Boughton Lees, Ashford, Kent TN25 4HR Tel (01233) 635751 Fax (01233) 635530

Eastwell Manor dates back to 1069 and lies within sixty-two acres of tranquil gardens and grounds amidst a three thousand acre estate. Today, lovingly restored, it is one of England's finest country house hotels with an award-winning restaurant. Oak-panelled dining room, lounges, open log fires and individually furnished bedrooms complete the atmosphere of a splendid country house where fine cuisine and attentive service make for a memorable stay.

Bed & Breakfast per night: single occupancy from £100.00–£250.00; double room from £120.00–£270.00
Half board per person: £125.00 daily
Lunch available: 1230–1400
Evening meal 1930 (last orders 2130)

Bedrooms: 10 double, 13 twin
Bathrooms: 23 private
Parking for 112
Cards accepted: Access, Visa, Diners, Amex

Gertrude Jekyll Gardens

National Trust Picture Library

TODAY'S GARDENS of flower-filled borders and secluded lawns were largely inspired by the Victorian gardener, Gertrude Jekyll. Jekyll, who lived most of her life near Godalming in Surrey, was a close friend of the architect Edwin Lutyens (he referred to her affectionately as Aunt Bumps). With him she established a productive working relationship and created gardens for many of his buildings. Two very different examples are the impressive gardens of Hestercombe in Somerset, considered the best surviving example of the Lutyens/Jekyll partnership, and the tiny walled enclosure at Lindisfarne Castle (converted into a private house by Lutyens) uncharacteristically quite separate from the castle.

Unlike the formal and landscape creations of the past, Jekyll gardens were not designed to be great set pieces, best appreciated from a particular vantage point, usually the house. They were designed to be walked in, sat in and looked at from all angles and at different times of year. They were meticulously planned, usually in a series of separate but interlinking sections, and plants were placed to complement one another and provide interest throughout the year. The overall effect was designed to look luxuriant, even wild – and indeed wild and woodland gardens were often incorporated.

Jekyll advised Lutyens on the design of the wonderful garden at Great Dixter in Northiam, East Sussex (tel. 01797 253160). Her ideas are revealed here in the pattern of separate interlinked 'rooms' and in the spectacular borders. Nymans, at Handcross in West Sussex (tel. 01444 400321), is not strictly a Jekyll garden, but its creators, Ludwig Messel and his son, Leonard, knew her well, and were clearly influenced by her. The famous herbaceous borders have been planted in typical Jekyll style with each plant carefully positioned for maximum effect. Nymans (NT) is open all summer, but many Jekyll gardens are privately owned and only open under the National Gardens Scheme (tel. 0483 63093). Hascombe Court, near Godalming, epitomises the Jekyll style, with its contrasts between different levels, and between formal borders and woodland walks. Another garden, at the Manor House, Upton Grey, Hampshire, has only recently been restored to its full glory. This has the only surviving example of a Jekyll wild garden.

Above: the Rose Garden at Nymans

381 HEMPSTEAD HOUSE
≋≋≋ HIGHLY COMMENDED

London Road, Bapchild, Sittingbourne, Kent ME9 9PP Tel (01795) 428020

Exclusive private Victorian country-house hotel, set in three acres of beautifully-landscaped gardens. We extend exceptional warmth and hospitality to all our guests, offering luxurious en-suite accommodation and excellent surroundings. You can spend a memorable evening in our licensed dining room and relax in our spacious drawing rooms and conservatory. In the daytime, wander around our peaceful grounds or relax by our outdoor heated swimming pool.

Bed & Breakfast per night: single occupancy from £50.00–£55.00; double room from £62.00
Half board per person: £46.00–£70.00 daily; £258.00–£392.00 weekly
Evening meal 1800 (last orders 2100)

Bedrooms: 5 double, 1 twin, 1 triple, 1 family room
Bathrooms: 7 en-suite
Parking for 12
Cards accepted: Access, Visa, Diners, Amex, Switch/Delta

Hops and hop-pickers

WHEREVER HOPS WILL GROW, you'll find oast houses: in Herefordshire, in Hampshire, in Sussex, and in Suffolk, but, above all, in Kent. These elegant buildings, characterised by their conical roofs leading towards jaunty white cowls, are synonymous with the Garden of England – though in the 18th century they were more commonly square than round. Their purpose is simple: to kiln dry the hop flowers in order to prepare that constituent of bitter which gives it its bitter-ness. The cultivation of hop plants ('bines') in fields ('hop gardens') has declined from earlier this century – lager needs few hops and dwarf bines are now more common so fewer plants are trained (or 'twiddled') up strings – but is still quite widespread. Hops are now dried in large modern buildings, so the traditional oast lives on largely as the local variant of the barn conversion, its round rooms taxing the ingenuity of interior designers.

The end of August finds the female hop flower ready for picking, and every year until mechanisation in the 1950s and 1960s, thousands would descend upon the Kentish countryside to do just that. Many would come down from London on especially-built railway-lines. For almost all, it was a gruelling working 'holiday', in which meagre London wages were supplemented by meagre Kentish wages. Whole families spanning three or four generations were known to turn up, complete with furniture, on certain hop farms.

The particular skills of the hop farmers and hop pickers are celebrated at the working Whitbread Hop Farm at Beltring near Tonbridge (tel: 01622 872068).

An elegant Kentish oast house

382 THE GRANARY   Listed HIGHLY COMMENDED
Plumford Lane, Ospringe, Faversham, Kent ME13 0DS   Tel & Fax (01795) 538416 or Mobile 0860 817713

Set deep in apple-orchard country, The Granary – recently part of a working farm – has been tastefully and beautifully converted to provide an interesting and spacious home. All rooms are delightfully furnished to a very high standard, whilst retaining a certain rustic charm. The guests' own lounge, with balcony, overlooks the surrounding countryside. Well situated for local pubs specialising in excellent food. Ideal location for touring historic Kent. Alan & Annette assure you a warm welcome. Sorry, we are a non-smoking household.

Bed & Breakfast per night: single occupancy from £25.00–£30.00; double room from £32.00–£38.00
Bedrooms: 1 double, 1 twin, 1 triple

Bathrooms: 2 en-suite, 1 private
Parking for 8

---

383 PRESTON LEA   👑👑 HIGHLY COMMENDED
Canterbury Road, Faversham, Kent ME13 8XA   Tel (01795) 535266   Fax (01795) 533388

This beautiful spacious house, built a century ago, was designed by a French architect and has many unique and interesting features including two turrets, an oak-panelled hall, staircase, dining room and guest drawing room. Situated in lovely secluded gardens but by the A2, it is convenient for Canterbury, all the Channel ports, the M2 to London and beautiful countryside. Each bedroom is individually designed and all are large and sunny. A warm welcome is assured by caring hosts.

Bed & Breakfast per night: double room from £45.00–£60.00
Bedrooms: 2 double, 1 twin

Bathrooms: 2 en-suite, 1 private
Parking for 11

---

384 THE WILLOWS   👑 HIGHLY COMMENDED
Howfield Lane, Chartham Hatch, Canterbury, Kent CT4 7HG   Tel (01227) 738442

Dr. and Mrs Gough welcome you to The Willows. Let us spoil you in the comfort of our home, furnished with family antiques, where you can relax in a peaceful atmosphere. We are situated in a quiet country lane, just two miles from Canterbury Cathedral and only twenty minutes from Dover and the channel ports. Traditional English breakfast is served in the conservatory, overlooking a garden for enthusiasts. Ample parking space is available. No smoking.

Bed & Breakfast per night: single occupancy from £28.00; double room from £40.00
Evening meal by prior booking 1900 (last orders 2000)

Bedrooms: 1 double, 1 twin
Bathrooms: 1 private shower
Parking for 8

385 CLARE-ELLEN GUEST HOUSE
🛏🛏 HIGHLY COMMENDED

9 Victoria Road, Wincheap, Canterbury, Kent CT1 3SG Tel (01227) 760205 Fax (01227) 784482

A warm welcome and bed & breakfast in style. Large elegant quiet en-suite rooms, all with colour television, clock/radio, hairdryer and tea/coffee making facilities. Ironing centre and trouser press for our guests' convenience. Cosy residents' lounge. Full English breakfast. Vegetarian and special diets catered for upon request. Six-minute walk to city centre/cathedral. Five minutes to British Rail Canterbury East station. Private car park and garage available. Contact Mrs. L. Williams.

Bed & Breakfast per night: single room from £20.00–£24.00; double room from £40.00–£46.00
Bedrooms: 1 single, 2 double, 1 twin, 1 family room

Bathrooms: 4 en-suite, 2 public
Parking for 9
Cards accepted: Access, Visa, Switch/Delta

386 MAGNOLIA HOUSE
🛏🛏 HIGHLY COMMENDED

36 St Dunstans Terrace, Canterbury, Kent CT2 8AX Tel (01227) 765121 Fax (01227) 765121

Come and enjoy a home away from home in a quiet location within a short walk of the Westgate Towers and the city centre. From your arrival to departure you are special, and Ann and John are here to make your visit to their historic city memorable. A welcome tray, a cosy lounge with local information, beautiful co-ordinated en-suite bedrooms, delicious breakfasts and a peaceful walled garden to relax in after a busy day's sightseeing, all combine to make your visit unforgettable!

Bed & Breakfast per night: single room from £36.00–£45.00; double room from £50.00–£80.00
Half board per person: £40.00–£55.00 daily
Bedrooms: 1 single, 4 double, 2 twin

Bathrooms: 7 private
Parking for 4
Cards accepted: Access, Visa, Amex

387 ORIEL LODGE
🛏🛏 HIGHLY COMMENDED

3 Queens Avenue, Canterbury, Kent CT2 8AY Tel (01227) 462845

On a tree-lined residential road, a five-minute walk from the city centre through Westgate Gardens, Oriel Lodge is a detached Edwardian house that carefully retains the tranquil character of the arts-and-crafts period. The attractive lounge area with a log fire, well-furnished bedrooms with up-to-date facilities and high standards of cleanliness contribute to a restful stay in the hospitable atmosphere of a family home. Private parking and gardens. Smoking in lounge area; non-smoking bedrooms.

Bed & Breakfast per night: single room from £19.00–£24.00; double room from £33.00–£54.00
Bedrooms: 1 single, 3 double, 1 twin, 1 triple

Bathrooms: 2 en-suite, 2 public
Parking for 6

388 THANINGTON HOTEL
☰☰ HIGHLY COMMENDED

140 Wincheap, Canterbury, Kent CT1 3RY Tel (01227) 453227 Fax (01227) 453225

Only minutes from Canterbury Cathedral and the city centre, Thanington Hotel offers superior bed & breakfast accommodation. Together with a quiet, relaxed and friendly atmosphere, you will enjoy the comfort and facilities offered with the ten pretty en-suite bedrooms, indoor heated swimming pool, snooker room, bar, the delightful walled garden, private parking and, of course, the delicious English breakfast served in our elegant dining room. Each evening sample the international cuisine of Canterbury's excellent restaurants.

Bed & Breakfast per night: single occupancy from £39.00–£48.00; double room from £56.00–£63.00
Bedrooms: 5 double, 3 twin, 2 family rooms

Bathrooms: 10 en-suite
Parking for 12
Cards accepted: Access, Visa, Diners, Amex

389 FINGLESHAM GRANGE
☰☰ HIGHLY COMMENDED

Finglesham, Deal, Kent CT14 0NQ Tel (01304) 611314

Far from the madding crowd yet within easy distance of the channel ports and championship golf courses, this listed building stands in four and a half acres of secluded garden and woodland. The house is spacious and elegant and all the bedrooms have private facilities. An open fire welcomes visitors during winter months and there is also a snooker room. A beamed 15th-century pub in the nearby village of Finglesham always has a friendly atmosphere and serves excellent meals.

Bed & Breakfast per night: single occupancy from £22.50–£27.50; double room from £45.00
Bedrooms: 1 double, 2 twin

Bathrooms: 3 private
Parking for 5

390 WALLETTS COURT HOTEL AND RESTAURANT
☰☰☰☰ HIGHLY COMMENDED

Westcliffe, St-Margarets-at-Cliffe, Dover, Kent CT15 6EW Tel (01304) 852424 Fax (01304) 853430

A restored 17th-century manor and barns in a rural setting, with inglenook fireplaces and ideal for history enthusiasts. Only three miles from Dover, we feature Saturday evening gourmet dinners at only £20-£25 with non-residents welcome; open as a restaurant Monday to Saturday for dinner only.

Bed & Breakfast per night: single occupancy from £40.00–£60.00; double room from £50.00–£70.00
Evening meal 1900 (last orders 2100)
Bedrooms: 6 double, 2 twin, 2 triple

Bathrooms: 10 en-suite
Parking for 10
Cards accepted: Access, Visa

391 COLDRED COURT FARM
Church Road, Coldred, Dover, Kent CT15 5AQ Tel (01304) 830816

♛♛♛ HIGHLY COMMENDED

Built in 1620, Coldred Court stands in seven acres of meadow within the Ringwouk and Bailey of an Anglo-Saxon hill fort and in the secluded village of Coldred. We are ideally situated for trips to the continent, only ten minutes from Dover and fifteen minutes from the historic city of Canterbury. We have plenty of private parking. Traditional farmhouse cooking, home-made bread and preserves. All rooms have en-suite bathrooms and tea/coffee making facilities.

Bed & Breakfast per night: single occupancy from £25.00–£32.00; double room from £38.00–£45.00
Half board per person: £31.00–£44.00 daily; £200.00–£270.00 weekly

Evening meal 1800 (last orders 2030)
Bedrooms: 2 double, 1 twin
Bathrooms: 3 private
Parking for 13

392 THE OLD VICARAGE
Chilverton Elms, Hougham, Dover, Kent CT15 7AS Tel (01304) 210668 or (01304) 225117 Fax (01304) 225118

♛♛ HIGHLY COMMENDED

Guests are welcomed in a warm and relaxed style at our Victorian country house, elegantly furnished with lovely antiques and pictures. Situated in the peaceful Elms Vale valley with outstanding views, yet only minutes from Dover. The Vicarage provides everything for your stay to the highest standards and in spacious comfort. Large informal gardens – log fires in winter – secure parking – dinner is available by arrangement.

Bed & Breakfast per night: double room from £40.00–£45.00; single occupancy £30.00–£35.00
Half board per person: £35.00–£50.00 daily; £210.00–£300.00 weekly

Evening meal 1930
Bedrooms: 2 double , 1 twin, 1 family room
· Bathrooms: 1 en-suite, 2 private
Parking for 10

393 HARBOURSIDE
14 Wear Bay Road, Folkestone, Kent CT19 6AT Tel (01303) 256528 Fax (01303) 241299

♛♛ HIGHLY COMMENDED

Superb location with panoramic views across the sea and harbour for boats to France. Licensed and fully geared for your personal care and comfort. Our simple aim is to give you exceptional value for your money so that, like so many of our guests, you will be eager to tell your friends about our qualities and your experience. A luxury sauna; public telephone; no evening meal. Strictly no smoking.

Bed & Breakfast per night: single room from £25.00–£40.00; double room from £40.00–£60.00
Bedrooms: 1 single, 4 double, 2 twin

Bathrooms: 6 en-suite, 1 en-suite shower
Cards accepted: Amex

394 THE HYTHE IMPERIAL HOTEL
👑👑👑👑👑 HIGHLY COMMENDED

Princes Parade, Hythe, Kent CT21 6AE Tel (01303) 267441 Fax (01303) 264610

An impressive sea-front resort hotel set within fifty acres in the historic Cinque port of Hythe. All the rooms enjoy sea or garden views with executive, four-poster, half-tester or jacuzzi rooms and suites available. Conference facilities available for up to two hundred, as well as superb leisure facilities, including 9-hole golf course, indoor swimming pool, luxurious spa bath, steam room, sauna, gym, sunbed, tennis, croquet, karting, beauty salon and hairdressing.

Bed & Breakfast per night (inc VAT and service): single room from £85.00–£95.00; double room from £105.00–£145.00
Half board per person (inc VAT and service): £62.00–£104.00 daily; £372.00–£456.00 weekly
Lunch available: 1230–1400

Evening meal 1900 (last orders 2130)
Bedrooms: 13 single, 33 double, 40 twin, 14 triple
Bathrooms: 100 en-suite
Parking for 160
Cards accepted: Access, Visa, Diners, Amex, Switch/Delta

395 PLAYDEN COTTAGE GUESTHOUSE
👑👑👑 HIGHLY COMMENDED

Military Road, Rye, East Sussex TN31 7NY Tel (01797) 222234

On the old Saxon shore, less than a mile from Rye town and on what was once a busy fishing harbour, there is now only a pretty cottage with lovely gardens, a pond and an ancient right of way. The sea has long receded and, sheltered by its own informal gardens, Playden Cottage looks over the River Rother and across the sheep-studded Romney Marsh. It offers comfort, peace, a care for detail – and a very warm welcome.

Bed & Breakfast per night: single occupancy from £37.50–£50.00; double room from £50.00–£60.00
Half board per person: £35.00–£40.00 daily;
£227.50–£259.00 weekly
Evening meal 1800 (last orders 2030)

Bedrooms: 1 double, 2 twin
Bathrooms: 3 en-suite
Parking for 7
Cards accepted: Access, Visa

396 GREEN HEDGES
👑👑 HIGHLY COMMENDED

Hillyfields, Rye Hill, Rye, East Sussex TN31 7NH Tel (01797) 222185

A country house with large gardens and a heated outdoor swimming pool. Dining includes full English and an imaginative vegetarian menu using seasonal organic home-grown produce. Private parking and close to town. Totally non-smoking.

Bed & Breakfast per night: double room from £46.00–£56.00
Bedrooms: 2 double, 1 twin

Bathrooms: 1 public, 3 en-suite showers
Parking for 7
Cards accepted: Access, Visa

397 THE COUNTRY HOUSE AT WINCHELSEA   🏆🏆🏆 HIGHLY COMMENDED
Hastings Road, Winchelsea, East Sussex TN36 4AD Tel (01797) 226669

Glorious views reach out from the old walled garden and sweet-scented wistaria cascades from the barn roof in spring. All the joys of the English countryside surround this traditional Sussex farmhouse. You will experience its welcoming atmosphere the moment you step into the spacious hall – and this is only the beginning of what we hope will be your special place. You may wine, dine and stay a while in this truly delightful home. Special rates for two or more nights.

Bed & Breakfast per night: single occupancy from £45.00–£53.00; double room from £56.00–£68.00
Half board per person: £44.50–£50.50 daily
Evening meal 1930 (last orders 2030)

Bedrooms: 2 double, 1 twin
Bathrooms: 3 en-suite
Parking for 8
Cards accepted: Access, Visa, Amex

398 FLACKLEY ASH HOTEL & RESTAURANT   🏆🏆🏆🏆 HIGHLY COMMENDED
London Road, Peasmarsh, Rye, East Sussex TN31 6YH Tel (01797) 230651 Fax (01797) 230510 Telex 957210 RLTG

A Georgian country house hotel set in beautiful gardens with croquet and putting lawns, an indoor swimming pool, a leisure centre with gym, saunas, whirlpool spa and flotation tank, and a hairdressing salon. Warm, friendly atmosphere, fine wines and good food. Well situated to visit the castles and gardens of East Sussex and Kent and the ancient Cinque port of Rye. Golf, birdwatching, country or seaside walks, potteries and steam trains are some of the attractions in the area.

Bed & Breakfast per night: single occupancy from £69.00–£85.00; double room from £98.00–£114.00
Half board per person: £59.50–£65.00 daily;
£280.00–£360.00 weekly
Lunch available: 1230–1345

Evening meal 1900 (last orders 2130)
Bedrooms: 20 double, 10 twin, 1 triple, 1 family room
Bathrooms: 32 en-suite
Parking for 60
Cards accepted: Access, Visa, Diners, Amex

399 TOWER HOUSE   🏆🏆🏆 HIGHLY COMMENDED
28 Tower Road West, St Leonards-on-Sea, Hastings, East Sussex TN38 0RG Tel (01424) 427217 or (01424) 423771

Enjoy the friendly atmosphere of our family-run hotel. The Tower has the ambience of a country house, yet it is situated in the heart of St. Leonards, close to all amenities. All meals are freshly prepared and varied, with a vegetarian menu available. A separate licensed bar and sun lounge has Sky television. The en-suite bedrooms are decorated to the highest standards, some with half-tester and French beds, all with tea/coffee making facilities, television, hairdryers, radios and toiletries.

Bed & Breakfast per night: single room from £25.00–£30.00; double room from £42.00–£47.50
Half board per person: £35.50–£40.00 daily;
£201.00–£255.00 weekly

Evening meal 1800 (last orders 1900)
Bedrooms: 1 single, 6 double, 3 twin
Bathrooms: 9 private, 1 private shower, 1 public
Cards accepted: Access, Visa, Diners, Amex

SYMBOLS

For ease of use, the key to symbols appears on the back of the cover flap and can be folded out while consulting individual entries. The symbols which appear at the end of each entry are designed to enable you to see at-a-glance what's on offer, and whether any particular requirements you have can be met. Most of the symbols are clear, simple icons and few require any further explanation, but the following points may be useful:

ALCOHOLIC DRINKS

Alcoholic drinks are available at all types of accommodation listed in the guide unless the symbol ⊎ (unlicensed) appears. However, even in licensed premises there may be some restrictions on the serving of drinks, such as being available to diners only. You may wish to check this in advance.

SMOKING

Many establishments offer facilities for non-smokers, indicated by the symbol ⌿. These may include no-smoking bedrooms and parts of communal rooms set aside for non-smokers. Some establishments prefer not to accommodate smokers at all, and if this is the case it will be made clear in the establishment description in the guide entry.

PETS

The symbol ⚞ is used to show that dogs are not accepted in any circumstances. Some establishments will accept pets, but we advise you to check this at the time of booking and to enquire as to whether any additional charge will be made to accommodate them.

BOOKING CHECKLIST

When enquiring about accommodation remember to state your requirements clearly and precisely. It may be necessary or helpful to discuss some or all of the following points:

- Your intended arrival and departure dates.
- The type of accommodation you require. For example, a twin-bedded room, a private bath and WC, whether the room has a view or not.
- The terms you require, such as room only; bed & breakfast; bed, breakfast and evening meal (half board); bed, breakfast, lunch and evening meal (full board).
- If you have any children travelling with you, say how old they are and state their accommodation requirements, such as a cot, and whether they will share your room.
- Any particular requirements, such as a special diet or a ground-floor room.
- If you think you are likely to arrive late in the evening, mention

this when you book. Similarly, if you are delayed on your journey a telephone call to inform the management may well help avoid any problems on your arrival.

- If you are asked for a deposit or the number of your credit card, find out what the proprietor's policy is if, for whatever reason, you can't turn up as planned – see below.
- Exactly how the establishment's charges are levied – see below.

Misunderstandings can easily occur over the telephone, so it is advisable to confirm in writing all bookings, together with special requirements. Please mention that you learnt of the establishment through *Somewhere Special*. Remember to include your name and address, and please enclose a stamped, addressed envelope – or an international reply coupon if writing from outside Britain. Please note that the English Tourist Board does not make reservations; you should address your enquiry directly to the establishment.

PRICES

The prices given throughout this publication will serve as a general guide, but you should always check them at the time of booking. The following information may prove useful when determining how much a trip may cost:

- Prices were supplied during the early winter of 1994, and changes may have occurred since publication.
- Prices include VAT where applicable.
- You should check whether or not a service charge is included in the published price.
- Prices for double rooms assume occupancy by two people; you will need to check whether there is a single person supplement.
- Half board means the price for the room, breakfast and evening meal per person per day or per person per week.
- A full English breakfast is not always included in the quoted price; you may be given a continental breakfast unless you are prepared to pay more.
- Establishments with at least four bedrooms or eight beds are obliged to display in the reception area or at the entrance overnight accommodation charges.
- Reduced prices may apply for children; check exactly how these reductions are calculated, including the maximum age for the child.
- Prices are often much cheaper for off-peak holidays; check to see whether special off-season packages are available.

DEPOSITS AND ADVANCE PAYMENTS

For reservations made weeks or months ahead a deposit is usually payable which will be deducted from the total bill at the end of your stay.

Some establishments, particularly the larger hotels in big towns, now require payment for the room upon arrival if a prior reservation has not been made. Regrettably this practice has become necessary because of the number of guests who have left without settling their bills. If you are asked to pay in advance, it is sensible to see your room before payment is made to ensure that it meets your requirements.

If you book by telephone and are asked for your credit card number, you should note that the proprietor may charge your credit card account even if you subsequently cancel the booking. Ask the owner what his or her usual practice is.

CREDIT/CHARGE CARDS

Any credit/charge cards that are accepted by the establishment are indicated at the end of the written description. The abbreviations used in this guide are:

Access – Access/Eurocard/Mastercard
Visa – Visa/Barclaycard
Diners – Diners
Amex – American Express
Switch/Delta – Direct debit card

If you intend to pay by either credit or charge card you are advised to confirm this at the time of booking. Please note that when paying by credit card, you may sometimes be charged a higher rate for your accommodation in order to cover the percentage paid by the proprietor to the credit card company. Again find this out in advance.

When making a booking, you may be asked for your credit card number as 'confirmation'. The proprietor may then charge your credit card account if you have to cancel the booking, but if this is the policy, it must be made clear to you at the time of booking.

CANCELLATIONS

When you accept offered accommodation, even over the telephone, you are entering into a legally binding contract with the proprietor. This means that if you cancel a reservation or fail to take up all or part of the accommodation booked, the proprietor may be entitled to compensation if the accommodation cannot be re-let for all or a good part of the booked period. If you have paid a deposit, you will probably forfeit this, and further payment may be asked for.

However, no such claim can be made by the proprietor until after the booked period, during which time every effort should be made to re-let the accommodation. It is therefore in your interests to advise the management immediately if you have to cancel or curtail a booking. Travel or holiday insurance, available quite cheaply from travel agents, and some hotels, will safeguard you if you have to cancel or curtail your stay.

SERVICE CHARGES AND TIPPING

Some establishments levy a service charge automatically, and, if so, must state this clearly in the offer of accommodation at the time of booking. If the offer is accepted by you, the service charge becomes part of the contract. If service is included in your bill, there is no need for you to give tips to the staff unless some particular or exceptional service has been rendered. In the case of meals, the usual tip is 10% of the total bill.

TELEPHONE CALL CHARGES

There is no restriction on the charges that can be made by hotels for telephone calls made from their premises. Unit charges are frequently considerably higher than telephone companies' standard charges in order to defray the costs of providing the service. It is a condition of being awarded a national Crown rating that the telephone unit charges are displayed alongside the telephone. However, it may not always be clear how these compare with the standard unit charge. Before using a hotel telephone, particularly for long-distance calls, you should enquire how much extra you will be paying per unit.

SECURITY OF VALUABLES

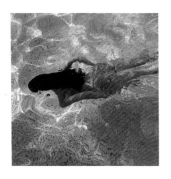

It is advisable to deposit any valuables for safe-keeping with the management of the establishment in which you are staying. If the management accept custody of your property they become wholly liable for its loss or damage. They can however restrict their liability for items brought on to the premises and not placed in their special custody to the minimum amounts imposed by the Hotel Proprietors Act, 1956. These are the sum of £50 in respect of one article and a total of £100 in the case of one guest. In order to restrict their liability the management must display a notice in the form required by the Act in a prominent position in the reception area or main entrance of the premises. Without this notice, the proprietor is liable for the full value of the loss or damage to any property (other than a motor car or its contents) of a guest who has booked overnight accommodation.

FEEDBACK

Let us know about your holiday. We welcome suggestions about how the guide itself may be improved.

Most establishments welcome feedback. Please let the proprietor know if you particularly enjoyed your stay. We sincerely hope that you have no cause for complaint, but should you be dissatisfied or have any problems, make your complaint to the management at the time of the incident so that immediate action may be taken.

The English Tourist Board, Jarrold Publishing and Celsius cannot guarantee the accuracy of the information in this guide and accept no responsibility for any error or misrepresentation. All liability for any

loss, disappointment or damage caused by reliance upon the information contained in this guide, or in the event of bankruptcy or liquidation or cessation of trade of any company, individual or firm mentioned, is hereby excluded. All establishments listed are bound by the Trades Description Acts of 1968 and 1972 when describing and offering accommodation and facilities, but we strongly recommend that prices and other details should be confirmed at the time of booking.

Details listed were believed correct at time of going to press. It is advisable to telephone in advance to check the details have not altered and to discuss any specific requirements.

CODE OF CONDUCT

All establishments appearing in this guide have agreed to observe the following Code of Conduct:

1   To ensure high standards of courtesy and cleanliness; catering and service appropriate to the type of establishment.

2   To describe fairly to all visitors and prospective visitors the amenities, facilities and services provided by the establishment, whether by advertisement, brochure, word of mouth or any other means. To allow visitors to see accommodation, if requested, before booking.

3   To make clear to visitors exactly what is included in all prices quoted for accommodation, meals and refreshments, including service charges, taxes and other surcharges. details of charges, if any, for heating or for additional services or facilities available should also be made clear.

4   To adhere to, and not to exceed, prices current at time of occupation for accommodation or other services.

5   To advise visitors at the time of booking, and subsequently, of any change, if the accommodation offered is in an unconnected annex, or similar, or by boarding out, and to indicate the location of such accommodation and any difference in comfort and amenities from accommodation in the main establishment.

6   To give each visitor, on request, details of payments due and a receipt if required.

7   To deal promptly and courteously with all enquiries, requests, reservations, correspondence and complaints from visitors.

8   To allow an English Tourist Board representative reasonable access to the establishment, on request, to confirm that the Code of Conduct is being observed.

Index

Entries are cross referred to the maps within each regional introduction

Entries are cross referred to the maps within each regional introduction

Index